# BRUTE

# BRUTE

## The Life of Victor Krulak, U.S. Marine

## Robert Coram

Little, Brown and Company
New York  Boston  London

Little, Brown and Company
Hachette Book Group
237 Park Avenue, New York, NY 10017
www.hachettebookgroup.com

First Edition: November 2010

Little, Brown and Company is a division of Hachette Book Group, Inc.
The Little, Brown name and logo are trademarks of Hachette Book Group, Inc.

Library of Congress Cataloging-in-Publication Data
Coram, Robert.
  Brute : the life of Victor Krulak, U.S. Marine / Robert Coram. — 1st ed.
    p. cm.
  Includes bibliographical references and index.
  ISBN 978-0-316-75846-8
  1. Krulak, Victor H.  2. Generals—United States—Biography.  3. United States.
Marine Corps.—Officers—Biography.  4. United States—History, Military—
20th century.  I. Title.
  E745.K78C67 2010
  355.0092—dc22
  [B]                                                          2010006985

10  9  8  7  6  5  4  3  2

RRD-IN

Printed in the United States of America

*This book is dedicated to the Sarge.*

# Contents

# BRUTE

# Introduction

THE story of every Marine must begin at Belleau Wood.

Lieutenant General Victor Harold Krulak was not present—he was five years old at the time—but neither he nor any other Marine can be understood without appreciation of this battle, which took place thirty-nine miles east of Paris in the early summer of 1918. The battle was a turning point not just for World War I, but for American military history. The modern Marine Corps was born at Belleau Wood, and the motivation for every accomplishment of every Marine since then has been to build upon what happened in this dark copse surrounded by a sea of wheat punctuated with bloodred poppies.

The U.S. Army would never forgive the Marines for what happened at Belleau Wood. George C. Marshall and Douglas MacArthur were Army officers in France in 1918, and they seethed with anger toward the Marines. Both men would become generals and achieve great prominence in World War II, and their resentment toward the Marine Corps would color American military history up through Korea and even to Vietnam and beyond.

As one of the most important Marines in the bitter interservice squabbles after World War II, Victor Krulak was instrumental in saving the Marine Corps from extinction, and in so doing he exacerbated Army animosity toward the Marines. Even today, the Army as an institution remains jealous of the warrior spirit of the Marine Corps.

And it all goes back to Belleau Wood.

THE Great War opened in 1914 and involved eleven of the most powerful empires on earth. On the western front, early battles ranged over hundreds of miles before the industrialized misery of trench warfare set in, and for about three years the war was more or less static. The Belgians, British, and French manned a dank and squalid system of trenches that stretched from the North Sea to the Swiss border. During quiet times on the ninety-mile segment of the British front, more than a thousand soldiers a day perished: "wastage," staff members called it. It was a bloodbath that, according to Paul Fussell in *The Great War and Modern Memory*, "domesticates the fantastic and normalizes the unspeakable." The horrors of trench warfare cast a pall over much of the world—frozen mud, poison gas, stacked corpses, all for the sake of a few feet here, a few feet there—and it seemed the carnage would go on forever.

America read of all this, sniffed, and remained aloof. Those were European empires at war, and a pacifist mood characterized America. Indeed, there was a certain sense of moral superiority in being an ocean removed from the madness in Europe.

On May 7, 1915, a German U-boat sank the British liner *Lusitania*, killing 1,198 passengers, 128 of whom were Americans. President Woodrow Wilson sent Germany a letter of protest, but he would not be drawn into war. In fact, he was reelected in 1916 on the slogan "He Kept Us Out of War." It would have been hard to get into it, regardless; while European armies counted their troops by the millions, the U.S. Army had 133,000 men in uniform, the Navy had 67,000, and the Marine Corps had 15,000. Few countries were ever so ill prepared for conflict.

In January 1917 came the intercepted Zimmerman Note, in which Germany asked Mexico to join an alliance against the United States, and Wilson could no longer afford to be neutral. In April, he asked Congress for a declaration of war against Germany.

The Army wanted to build up and train a force of at least half a million men before sending them to Europe, but the staggering French and British wanted the Americans *now*. So Wilson ordered a symbolic force, a single Army division of about 20,000 soldiers that would be known as the American Expeditionary Force (AEF), to France. It was under the command of General John "Black Jack" Pershing, fresh from a fruitless yearlong chase of Pancho Villa down in Mexico. Pershing was a bland and colorless commander whose greatest attribute was obstinacy.

The Marines had been the first American military unit to fight in both the Philippines and Cuba during the Spanish-American War. They had previously fought in China, Nicaragua, Panama, the Dominican Republic, Mexico, and Haiti — whenever America needed a small amphibious force to send ashore. Coming from ships, the Marines were not considered an army of invasion, merely a seagoing police force to protect American interests. But when the Marines were not needed, there were ongoing efforts to abolish them or to absorb them into the Army. In 1829, 1831, 1834, 1866, 1908, and 1909, the Navy, the Army, and several presidents tried to get rid of the Marines. It seemed that the hardest fighting the Marines ever did was fighting for the privilege of defending their country.

Pershing did not like the Marines and was offended by their "First to Fight" motto. This thing in Europe, he decided, would be an all-Army affair. But if the Marines were not part of the fighting, they almost certainly would be disbanded.

The Commandant of the Marine Corps went over General Pershing's head to the secretary of war, who sent two Marine regiments to France. They formed the 4th Brigade of Marines, fewer than 8,000 men.

Pershing thought the fighting would be over in a short while. He scorned the stasis of trench warfare and believed that Americans would break the war wide open. His soldiers began training with experienced French and British officers, getting ready to go into the line sometime after the first of the year. All the while, the Army scorned the Marines. One general referred to them in official correspondence as "adventurers, illiterates, and drunkards."

Pershing sent most of the Marines to rear areas, where they built warehouses and barracks, unloaded ships, helped dredge harbors, strung telephone lines, patrolled icy docks, and pulled drunken soldiers from bars. Far from the front, the Marines drilled and practiced their marksmanship. A fundamental tenet of the Marine Corps is that every Marine is a rifleman, and these Marines were only months away from proving that they ranked among the best in the world.

Marines were not alone in being prevented from doing their jobs by the stoic and bureaucratic Pershing. His headquarters at Chaumont would not allow American war correspondents near the front, and Pershing ordered that when American forces went into battle, correspondents could not identify by name any of the Army regiments, could not say which state the soldiers were from, and could not distinguish between regular troops and National Guard troops, or between infantry and artillery. They could report only that "units" or "elements" of the Army were in combat. Little did he know it, but Pershing had condemned the Army to anonymity.

Several stories exist as to how correspondents were able to use the word "Marines" in their dispatches. The most logical is that correspondents argued that since they could use the word "Army," they should be able to write of "Marines." Censors agreed, overlooking the fact that there was only one brigade of Marines in

France and that simply saying "Marines" was the same as using a unit designation.

In a very short time, Pershing's decisions would explode in ways he never anticipated and would forever regret.

FIELD Marshal Paul von Hindenburg, a jovial little fat man with a big mustache, and his deputy, General Erich Ludendorff, an unsmiling model of Teutonic efficiency, thought it would take America at least a year to raise and train enough troops to become a factor in the war. Hindenburg proposed to end the war before the Yanks gained strength. Come spring of 1918, the Germans would launch an offensive on the western front that would cut off and destroy the British and at the same time take Paris. Although the city held no particular strategic value, its symbolic importance was such that if it fell, French soldiers would almost certainly lay down their arms.

By late winter, Ludendorff had moved numerous divisions from Russia—where because of the fall of the czar and Russia's withdrawal from the war, they no longer were needed—and added them to the western front. Very soon he would have 194 divisions—about 3.6 million soldiers—to throw against the French, British, and AEF.

Ludendorff knew that the fate of Germany depended on the outcome of the spring offensive. But while Ludendorff plotted strategy and moved great armies, the Allies squabbled like schoolboys. The French commander in chief, Henri Pétain, was incompetent, pessimistic, and arrogant. The British senior officer, Sir Douglas Haig, in addition to being even less competent than Pétain, was provincial, inflexible, and devoid of imagination, and he had the smugness of one who believed his every step was guided by divine providence. Haig was the paradigm for what Paul Fussell calls the "unredeemable defectiveness" of generals.

What Pétain and Haig had in common was their utter contempt

for the AEF's military ability. The French and British, they declared, were *the* experts on trench warfare — and could point to 2.6 million dead to prove that expertise. America, on the other hand, was not a world power and had never fought an overseas war on this scale. Not only were the Yanks unproven, but they also lacked sufficient training, and they knew little about trench warfare, artillery and machine guns, and snipers. Therefore, the European commanders insisted, the Americans must "amalgamate"—that is, go into battle as small replacement units under French or British officers. They absolutely could not fight as a separate force, nor could they be given their own sector of the line.

Pershing was adamant that his troops would not fight under foreign officers. Either they would fight in strength and have their own section of the line, or he would not commit them, or the hundreds of thousands on the way to France, to battle. "I will not parcel out American boys," he was quoted as saying.

Throughout the fall and winter of 1917, the Allied high command was a microcosm of the war: opposing sides across a line, with little or no advance in either direction.

At 4 a.m. on March 21, 1918, Ludendorff launched his attack. Led by elite *sturmtruppen*, fast-moving riflemen and machine gunners trained to punch through enemy defenses and hold the rear areas as they waited for reserves, Germany struck at the Somme, launching what some historians consider the most horrific battle of the war. The attack almost destroyed the British Fifth Army, which was pushed back forty miles and suffered 300,000 casualties. Haig issued his famous "Backs to the Wall" order of the day, in which he decreed that his troops would hold every position and would fight to the last man.

Although the German army made great advances, the momentum slowed before Ludendorff could break through and romp on toward Paris. He attacked again, made more advances, and again lost momentum. Germany, nevertheless, had seized more territory than had either side in the past three years.

Desperate, Pétain and Haig beseeched Pershing for American replacements. Pershing was implacable: we go in as the AEF, or we don't go at all.

In late April, a young American intelligence analyst prepared a report saying the Germans were consolidating their forces for a major attack and the attack would come within thirty days. Pétain and Haig scoffed: the Americans had not been here long enough to develop reliable intelligence sources. Besides, surely the Germans were as tired as the British and French, their supply lines were overextended, and they had suffered heavy casualties.

About midnight on May 27, the Germans attacked. They advanced twelve miles the first day and were approaching the French city of Château-Thierry. The most important part of Château-Thierry was located north of the Marne River, another part on an island, and a third part south of the river. By June 1, Ludendorff's forces had taken the part of town located north of the Marne, which meant the German salient was only thirty-nine miles from Paris.

The French destroyed the bridge leading to the part of Château-Thierry located on the island, and the German army was temporarily checked. But long-range German artillery was dropping shells onto the streets of Paris, causing French soldiers to retreat, throw up their hands, and exclaim, *"La guerre est fini!"* In the past few days, the Germans had taken 65,000 prisoners.

Haig and Pétain blamed the disaster in large part on the failure of the Americans to join the war. They went over Pershing's head to President Wilson and told him that the war might be lost unless American troops entered the fray. When Wilson refused to interfere, the Allies agreed to let the Americans fight in force and to have their own section of the line. Pétain, as angry as he was desperate, put his finger on a map, pressed so hard that his finger-nail made a groove in the surface, and asked if Pershing could send AEF forces *there*, to the area northwest of Château-Thierry.

THE late spring of 1918 was one of those historical moments when gigantic forces collide and afterward the world is never the same. The air was redolent with the knowledge that years of trench war-fare were coming to a head, that a great and decisive battle was looming, and that more than the fate of France was at stake—the fate of the Western world was about to be decided. Americans were going into battle against the unstoppable German army, and everywhere people asked, with as much hope as curiosity, "Can these Americans fight?"

For their part, American war correspondents were ecstatic that the AEF was moving into the line. Most American journalists attached themselves to Army units, but Floyd Gibbons, a flam-boyant correspondent for the *Chicago Tribune*, decided that he would go over the top with the Marines. Many Marines had worn out their distinctive green uniforms and now were wearing the same khaki uniforms as the Army. But Marine officers also wore the Marine Corps insignia—the eagle, globe, and anchor—on their helmets and collars. By now the Marines accounted for less than one percent of the AEF and were described by an Army historian as "that little raft of sea soldiers in an ocean of Army." But they were a proud and cocky bunch, and Gibbons liked that.

For twenty-four hours, the Marines rode in trucks called cami-ons on dusty roads leading to the front lines. Along the way, they met retreating Frenchmen whose eyes were sunken and whose bodies were stooped, men worn-out by war. The Marines, most of them too young to grow beards, were laughing, joking, ogling young women in every village, singing American songs, radiating American energy, and showing the weary and dispirited French the meaning of "joie de vivre." They were about to face the foe, and they were happy.

As they approached the front, a retreating French major told a Marine captain that the French lines had been overrun and the Marines should turn back. When the captain pretended that he did not understand, the French officer took a pad from his tunic and wrote an order for the Marines to retreat. The captain read the note, looked at the French officer, and said, "Retreat, hell! We just got here."

It was happenstance, mere coincidence, an ironic decision by the gods of war, that the Army was deployed south of the Paris–Metz road and the Marines were ordered to a place north of the road, to a place in the line between and slightly north of the villages of Lucy-le-Bocage and Bouresches. They would occupy the Bois de Belleau, or "Belleau Wood," a bosky patch of woods about one and a half miles long and half a mile wide that French intelligence said was "lightly held."

Pilots of German aircraft and personnel in observation balloons saw the hustle and bustle behind the Allied lines and knew replacements were arriving. Those new troops were identified as Americans. French, British, or Americans—what did it matter?

Because his advance had again stalled, Ludendorff, in a move that was a precursor of the blitzkrieg tactics of World War II, wheeled and moved the point of his advance to another position: through Belleau Wood. Once the attack resumed, there would be nothing between the Germans and Paris.

Nothing but the U.S. Marines.

The Marines had no aircraft, no observation balloons, and very little artillery support. But they had their rifles, and that was enough.

On June 6, the Germans marched out of Belleau Wood. Their perfect formation, coal-scuttle helmets, and rifles at the ready gave them an air of terrible efficiency. Their eyes were on the Americans some 800 yards away. At the time, opposing forces in open areas usually engaged at 400 yards, so it would be a few moments before they were close enough to fire.

The Marines gave a few clicks of elevation to their rifle sights, waited a moment, and began firing. Almost every shot dropped a German. Hitting a target from 700 yards was not difficult for a Marine. At 600 yards, 500 yards, or 400 yards, it was downright easy.

The Germans were astonished. This was their first indication that they were up against a new kind of opponent. The effectiveness of the rifle fire broke up the German attack.

Now it was time for the Marines to do what they had come to France to do: attack. Now it was their turn to march across the wheat field. The most chilling of military orders was given: *Fix bayonets!* This meant hand-to-hand combat with no quarter asked. It would be a fight to the death.

The Marines marched in line abreast across the open field, their officers waving walking canes to emphasize their orders. Maxim machine guns with interlocking fields of fire began stuttering at five hundred rounds per minute — *taka-taka-taka-taka* — and Marines fell as if cut down by a scythe. Hugging the ground provided no safety, as some Maxims had been sighted to fire almost at ground level. The first Marine attack in World War I was faltering. Then rose Gunnery Sergeant Dan Daly, rifle high in the air, and he thundered, *"Come on, you sons of bitches! Do you want to live forever?"*

Daly charged through the wheat, into the dark hell of Belleau Wood and the deadly chatter of the Maxims. The Marines followed, shouting, screaming, intent only on their orders: "Occupy Belleau Wood."

The Marines suffered 1,087 casualties on June 6, 1918, more than in any other day in the preceding 143 years of Marine Corps history. When captains fell, they were replaced by lieutenants. When lieutenants fell, they were replaced by sergeants. When sergeants fell, they were replaced by corporals. And when corporals fell, they were replaced by privates. In the stubble of the wheat and the crushed poppies, the Marines, as poet Rupert Brooke wrote of an earlier battle, "poured out the red / Sweet wine of youth."

Ludendorff knew that if the Americans were victorious during their first battle, the engagement not only would have a great impact on the Allies' morale, but it would also hasten the introduction of more American troops into the war. To the Germans, Belleau Wood was the pivot point of the war. The Allies knew this and were determined to win no matter the cost. National wills were locked in mortal combat, and whoever won, the victory would assume mythic significance.

Five times the Germans counterattacked, and five times the Marines held. For the next nineteen days, the Marines had little sleep, food, or water. They did not take off their shoes or wash their faces, and their only rest was a quick nap on bare ground. Inch by inch and foot by foot and yard by yard, they advanced through Belleau Wood. They charged machine-gun nests. They endured artillery bombardments that splintered trees, blasted away the thick undergrowth, and left nothing unbroken except their spirit. The Germans fired shells containing mustard gas, and the poison was so thick it dripped from the trees and lingered in the low places. Death was everywhere, but the Marines had only one goal in mind: "Occupy Belleau Wood." A letter taken from a German body said, "The Americans are savages. They kill everything that moves."

The German army, until then considered the greatest on earth, was stopped and then pushed back. After the Marines advanced more than two miles, the Germans threw in two more divisions. But the Marines dug no trenches; they advanced or they died.

Floyd Gibbons was in the thick of the battle until his left eye and part of his face was shot away. After surgery, and wearing an eye patch, he returned to America as the most famous World War I correspondent.

His June 6 story ran under a superheated banner headline:

> U.S. MARINES SMASH HUNS
> GAIN GLORY IN BRISK FIGHT ON THE MARNE
> CAPTURE MACHINE GUNS, KILL BOCHES, TAKE PRISONERS

The next day, there was another piece from Gibbons, topped with a headline that read:

> MARINES WIN HOT BATTLE
> SWEEP ENEMY FROM HEIGHTS NEAR THIERRY

The usually reserved *New York Times* got into the act with this ecstatic headline:

> OUR MARINES ATTACK,
> GAIN MILE AT VEUILLY,
> RESUME DRIVE AT NIGHT,
> FOE LOSING HEAVILY

There were some reports of unnamed Army units, but they were virtually ignored. Americans knew only of "Our Marines," whom, so it was reported, the Germans called teufelhunden— "devil dogs." Back home, those reading the newspapers could be forgiven if they thought there was nothing on the western front but U.S. Marines and dead Germans.

Pershing realized his mistake and forbade correspondents to mention Marines in future dispatches. But it was too late. America had begun its love affair with the U.S. Marines.

On June 26, Marine major Maurice Shearer sent a message: "Belleau Woods now U.S. Marine Corps entirely," and the question "Can these Americans fight?" was answered. The Marines, along with the 2nd Army Division, so damaged the German army that after Belleau Wood, five opposing German divisions were declared by their commanding officer to be "unfit for further combat."

In 1918, Belleau Wood would be the closest the German army got to Paris.

On June 30, the French high command, over the objections of Pershing, sent out word that in all official papers Bois de Belleau henceforth would be known as Bois de la Brigade de Marine.

On July 4, a few dozen Marines were pulled out of the line to go to Paris and be part of a parade honoring the Americans. That small group of Marines evoked a far greater response from the French than did larger Army units. It did not matter when Pershing truthfully spoke of the contribution his soldiers had made; to the French, it was the Marines who had saved the City of Light. Two regiments, the 5th and 6th Marines, were awarded the Croix de Guerre, and today they still wear a braided green and red rope called a fourragère on their left shoulders, a quiet announcement that their professional antecedents fought at Belleau Wood.

On July 10, President Wilson reported to the U.S. Senate that the Marines had "turned the tide of battle" and that Belleau Wood had "begun the rout that was to save Europe and the World."

After Belleau Wood, the Marines counted their dead and hoped for rest. Then they saw the camions and knew they were going into battle again. History records that the Marines were the spearhead of the next great battle, the victorious Soissons campaign. In the weeks afterward, the Allies gathered their strength and on August 8 broke through and began to collapse the German army. Now the British no longer had their backs to the wall. Now the French no longer were in retreat. One writer described the western front as a great rubber band that had been stretched to its limit and now snapped back toward Germany. With the example of the U.S. Marines before them, the Allies, their blood high, had seized the initiative. The German army was in retreat. Both the end of the war and the outcome were obvious. In November, the armistice was signed.

By then the Marine brigade had taken about 4,000 casualties, some 55 percent of its original strength and the largest number of casualties suffered by any American brigade in World War I. The Marines had captured 12,000 German soldiers—almost one-fifth of the total number captured by the AEF—but the Germans had captured only twenty-five Marines. The explanation is simple: Marines don't surrender. They win or they die.

Before June 1918, few people had ever heard of the U.S. Marines. Now people the world over knew about them.

For the Marines, other wars and other great battles lay ahead: Guadalcanal and Iwo Jima in World War II, the Pusan Perimeter and Chosin Reservoir in Korea, Hue City and Khe Sanh in Vietnam, Anbar Province and Fallujah in Iraq, and Helmand Province in Afghanistan. But Belleau Wood is still the most significant battle ever fought by the United States Marine Corps.

Many of the Marines who died at Belleau Wood were later taken home for reburial, but more than three hundred are buried there in the Aisne-Marne American Cemetery, an out-of-the way piece of France that is forever American. After the war, however, the Army-dominated American Battle Monuments Commission would not allow the Marine Corps emblem to be placed in the cemetery, nor would the Army allow a statue of a Marine or a marker to be erected to acknowledge this place as the Bois de la Brigade de Marine.

Nevertheless, those who fought at Belleau Wood were men around whom the Marine Corps placed a special aura. Among them were Holland M. Smith, Lemuel C. Shepherd, and Gerald

Introduction

C. Thomas. Remember these names, because not only would these men become the senior leadership of the Marine Corps in World War II, but they would have an enormous impact on the career of the man who is the subject of this book. He would read of their experience in France, and he would remember.

And America would remember the Marines. In dark times ahead, when America needed rough men whose hearts were filled with the spirit of attack, the Marines would be the first ones called upon. After Belleau Wood, the Marines were no longer a small, shipborne gendarmerie. They had entered the world of massed firepower, and in future wars they would demonstrate that they could respond with more trained and equipped combat troops quicker than any other branch of the U.S. military. Not only would their boots be the first on the ground in America's future wars, but the word "Marine" would become synonymous with the word "victory." If the Marines could win at Belleau Wood, it was now expected that they could win anywhere.

Of course, the Army simmered with anger over all this. The Army had fought alongside the Marines, and Pershing saw the Marines as grandstanding publicity hounds. In 1956, Army general Matthew B. Ridgway, a hero of the Korean conflict, looked back on Belleau Wood as "one of many prime examples of men's lives being thrown away against objectives which were not worth the cost."

But in truth, Belleau Wood belongs in the pantheon of great military battles, alongside Cannae, where Hannibal defeated the Romans; Gaugamela, where Alexander the Great defeated the Persians; and Agincourt, where Henry V defeated the French. In all these battles, relatively small military units were called upon to do the impossible against vastly superior forces. The fact that they were victorious is the reason those battles are still remembered.

In 1997, the Commandant of the Marine Corps went to Belleau Wood to videotape a message to all Marines upon the occasion of the 222nd birthday of the Marine Corps. He ended a powerful and emotional address by putting the events of June 1918 in perspective: "Belleau Wood is a great river that runs through the heart of every Marine."

Now we can begin the story of Victor Krulak.

# 1

## Once Upon a Time

HE was never a promising young man.

From a selfish and headstrong boy who lied, falsified documents, and was guilty of moral turpitude, he grew to become the most important officer in the history of the United States Marine Corps, a man of dazzling intellect and extraordinary vision who was at the center of or deeply involved in some of the most important issues facing America during the tumultuous middle years of the twentieth century. He became a man whose contributions to his country are almost impossible to measure.

In America we believe that a person's early years are crucial to the understanding of that person's life, and we have common, even trite, expressions to bolster that belief: "The child is father of the man," "As the twig is bent, so grows the tree," and "The apple does not fall far from the tree." In one sense, the life of Victor Harold Krulak is a stark refutation of this belief. Krulak's icy intellect, unbending will, and extraordinary self-control enabled him to turn his back on his childhood—even on some family members—and create a life far removed from his early years.

Krulak changed, hid, or denied almost everything of importance about his childhood, and for good reason. If the great secret of his childhood—a secret not known to his wife and three sons—had been revealed, he may not have been admitted to the U.S. Naval Academy. Had he not minimized another part of his youth, he either would have been driven from the Marine Corps or would have advanced no further in rank than captain or major. He became an important historical figure only because he kept a secret and because he never looked back. "My father steered by the stars, not by the wake," said one of his sons.

Krulak wrote three books, numerous magazine articles, dozens of speeches, and hundreds of letters. Yet those close to him over the years say that rarely did he make even tangential reference to his parents, his childhood, and his personal beliefs. They remember only that he was assertive and controlling and that he had a pile-driving personality—attributes that indicate an attempt to hide the inner man.

Krulak's bravery in four wars—the second Sino-Japanese War, World War II, the Korean War, and the Vietnam War—are well documented, as are his contributions to the Marine Corps, to the U.S. military, and to America. But the glory was never enough. Krulak was driven by a dark wind and all his life was a fabulist who craved recognition, concocted stories, and added untrue events to his highly decorated career.

Many will find it difficult to sympathize with Krulak's duplicity—with the fact that even as a boy, he displayed such a marked lack of character. But the thirty-four-year arc of Krulak's military life is a model of rectitude, discipline, and duty. Nothing more demonstrates this than when, at the pinnacle of his career, when the two things he wanted most—a fourth star and to become Commandant of the Marine Corps—were within reach, he risked everything by confronting a U.S. president. For that act of great moral courage, a vengeful commander in chief would deny Krulak his dream.

The story of Victor Krulak is a quintessential American story. And like many American stories, it begins elsewhere, among the Jews of Russia.

As America entered the twentieth century, more than two million Jews flooded its ports, made their way through the confusing and often humiliating immigration procedures, and dispersed into the marrow of this still-raw country. That first generation of Jews helped fill out and make whole their adopted country.

Many of those Jews were from Russia and had experienced the pogroms, the large-scale anti-Semitic riots ordered by Czar Alexander III. They heard that the area around Denver, a town in the state of Colorado, would welcome them. By 1900, this western town was home to some 7,000 Jews, one of the largest Jewish populations in America. The Denver Jews were educated professionals from Germany and central Europe, who were fighting to become accepted by the "Sacred 36," the families who ruled Denver's social life. They were embarrassed by the poor and uneducated Jews coming out of Russia—a rowdy, raucous, and darker-skinned Yiddish-speaking group, many of whom would become peddlers or clerks. In many ways, Russian Jews faced more discrimination from fellow Jews than they did from the Christian business community in Denver. The president of Denver's Temple Emanuel even sent a warning to Russian Jews to stay away from the city. Nevertheless, they came—8,167 by 1910.

Many of these Russian Jews were *catootniks*, a twist on the Yiddish word *catooteh*, which means "quarrel" and was a euphemism for "consumption," as tuberculosis was then called. Indigent, they came to Denver in hopes that the dry mountain air would alleviate their symptoms.

The story of Jews in the West is largely unknown, overshadowed by that of those who settled in the East and Midwest. But Jews helped build western states and were active in politics almost from the beginning. In 1876, the year Colorado became a state, a road builder and railroad man named Otto Mears—a "Hebrew," as the Denver newspapers referred to prominent Jews—carried the electoral votes to Washington that elected Rutherford B. Hayes president. Colorado's Simon Guggenheim was elected to the U.S. Senate in 1906. Idaho had a Jewish governor in 1915, Utah in 1916. By contrast, it was not until 1948 that Herbert Lehman of New York became the first Jewish U.S. senator from the East, and not until 1974 that Abraham Beame became the first Jewish mayor of New York.

On July 24, 1889, Meyer Krulak, a Russian Jew from Boslov (Bugoslav), a town on the fertile steppes east of the Carpathian Mountains and some sixty-three miles southeast of Kiev, arrived in Philadelphia aboard the SS *Pennland*. Two of Krulak's brothers were already in America, Samuel in Philadelphia and Harold in Denver.

Little is known of the Krulak family in the next few years, except that Samuel and most of his family moved to Cleveland. Also, about a year after Meyer arrived, on September 17, 1890, the SS *Belgenland* arrived in Philadelphia carrying four of his children—Milke, thirteen; Rochel, eleven; Moschku, nine; and Jochled, seven. Upon landing in Philadelphia, Moschku (a Yiddish nickname for the Hebrew Moshe) became Morris. Though only nine years old, Morris had taken—or had been forced to take— the first step toward creating a new life.

Morris first shows up in the Denver city directory in 1908 as a jewelry store clerk; his age is given as nineteen rather than twenty-seven. He would later fill out documents describing himself as a slender man with brown eyes and black hair. The 1910 U.S. census shows him living in a boardinghouse and working as a clerk in a pawnshop. It lists his nationality as Russian and his native language as Yiddish.

It was probably through the pawnshop that Morris met Bessie Zalinsky, the daughter of Herman and Jennie Zalinsky, both Russian Jews from Brest Litovsk who had immigrated to Denver in 1888. Herman, who later changed the family name to Zall, owned a jewelry store. Bessie and Morris were married on November 27, 1910. She was sixteen.

These details, gleaned from ships' manifests, immigration records, census records, city directories, draft registrations, and other documents, are important because in a few more years Morris and Bessie would construct a fable about their origins. Their only child would elaborate on the fable, continuing even after he became a general officer in the U.S. Marine Corps.

Morris and Bessie—who would soon prefer "Bess"—were living with her parents when Morris filed a declaration of intention to become a U.S. citizen on September 28, 1911. On the application, he said that he had entered the United States through the port of New York in 1898. Given that he was only nine years old and in the company of older siblings when he actually arrived, in 1890, he should be given the benefit of the doubt in misrepresenting both the year and the place of his entry. Nevertheless, considering the smoke screen he would create over the next several decades to obscure his origins, it gives one pause.

Morris and Bess had been married a little more than two years when, on January 7, 1913, their son, Victor Harold Krulak, was born. In 1915, Victor's parents were involved in an auto accident that only bruised Morris but caused Bess severe abdominal injuries. The resulting surgery rendered her incapable of having any more children. Disconsolate, Morris and Bess showered their love and attention on Victor. They were determined that all the opportunities of America would be available to their only child.

In 1917, Morris registered for the draft. His registration form identifies him as a native of Russia. By then he and his family had moved out of the Zall house and into their own apartment. Morris, his age now listed as twenty-eight, was proprietor of his own pawnshop.

But by the fall of 1917, Morris was no longer a pawnbroker and, in fact, did not provide an occupation for the city directory. In the 1918 and 1919 city directories, his occupation is listed as watchmaker. No employer is given, so it is likely he was working for the Zall family.

In September 1919, Victor entered the first grade at Gilpin Elementary School, a block away from the Zall home. He left the school on October 24 and ten days later was enrolled at Cheyenne Central School in Cheyenne, Wyoming.

HERE we must pause to gain perspective. Morris left a relatively sophisticated city of more than 225,000 inhabitants—a city where his wife's family was prosperous and becoming well-known—to move some hundred miles north to a rough-and-ready cow town of 13,829. The Jewish population in Cheyenne was so small that the single synagogue had trouble keeping a rabbi. There would have to have been some sort of serious precipitating incident to justify Morris's withdrawing his son from school less than two months after he began the first grade and moving the family to another state, especially given that Morris was a thoughtful and deliberate man. Samuel Zall, Bess's brother, moved to Cheyenne at the same time.

These were years of rampant anti-Semitism in America. A man named Leo Frank was lynched near Atlanta. Membership in the Ku Klux Klan reached four million. Henry Ford would soon take over the *Dearborn Independent*, make it the second-largest paper in America, and fill it with such virulent anti-Semitic articles that it would eventually be shut down by legal action.

But national events rarely inform personal actions. Whatever Morris's reason for uprooting his family, it is almost certain it was immediate and personal. He may have wanted to start a new life in Cheyenne. He may have wanted to break away from his in-laws and go into business for himself. Surviving family members do not know. When Victor Krulak was ninety-five, he said that the sole reason his father left Denver was "to make my life a success." He would not elaborate.

The West is the part of America that gave us our origin myth, and few places better represented that myth—the chance to create a new life—than Cheyenne, Wyoming. When the Krulaks arrived, they found a town on the make.

Cheyenne was created by the Union Pacific Railroad and was a major stop on the first transcontinental route. It would be a refueling stop for pilots flying mail from the East to San Francisco. There had once been an opera, and people boasted that the town had "culture." But steam locomotives would fade away and long-distance aircraft would mean that planes could overfly Cheyenne, and eventually the town would return to its cowboy heritage.

In 1919, Cheyenne still had more horses than cars, and horse manure dotted the main street. The town thrived on its history of cowboys and Indians and the Johnson County range war, fought between cattlemen and farmers. Tom Horn, the legendary detective-assassin, had been hanged only a few decades earlier, and people still talked of him. During Frontier Days, a weeklong celebration at the end of July, cowboys raced horses up and down the main street.

James Montgomery Flagg, the artist who created the World War I recruitment poster of Uncle Sam leaning forward and saying, "I Want You," went through Cheyenne a few years later and reported that the town was shabby and dusty and that all the citizens talked about was Frontier Days. He said local post cards featured just one subject: "a horse giving an imitation of interpretative dancing."

If Cheyenne was a town on the make, Morris Krulak was a man on the make, for himself and his son. In the 1920 census, he no longer identified himself as a Russian Jew. Instead, he now said that he had been born in Pennsylvania, and that is what he told his son. Perhaps because his "official" birthplace was now Pennsylvania, he allowed his citizenship application to lapse. He never became a U.S. citizen.

Victor knew that his parents were Jewish, but they never spoke Yiddish in their home or elsewhere. "I never heard my father use a foreign word," Krulak said. "He always spoke simple King's English." Bess Krulak, however, sprinkled her conversation with Yiddish words, and it is difficult to imagine that her son never heard his parents use the language.

Nevertheless, Morris was a secular Jew, and his desire for assimilation was so strong that Victor never received any religious instruction, never attended synagogue, and, as far as can be determined, never had a bar mitzvah. In this way, Morris paved the way for his son later to minimize his Jewish background. "It is not who you were or where you were from, but it is what you do that is important," he told Victor. "If you study and if you succeed, it will not matter what you were."

Victor later said that when he moved to Cheyenne, he began attending St. Mark's Episcopal Church, the only Episcopal church in town. He may have attended—although his three sons doubt it—but he never became a member. On his admission form for the Naval Academy, however, he wrote that he was "Jewish," showing that he still self-identified as a Jew. When he said, "I grew up Episcopalian," he was telling the story he wanted to be true.

Morris became manager of the Hub Shoe & Clothing Store, a dry goods store at 210 West Lincoln Highway, a short block from the imposing Union Pacific train station and across the street from the Atlas Hotel and the Atlas Theatre. The train station, hotel, and theater were the epicenter of Cheyenne's business, political, and social life. Senator Francis Warren, the political muscle of Wyoming, had a mansion around the corner, and when he was home, he walked the streets visiting local businesses. Cheyenne remained a small town — everyone knew everyone — and it was the seat of Senator Warren's national political power. Morris met the distinguished senator and was also on good terms with Vincent Carter, the state's sole congressman.

John (Jochled) Krulak, Morris's younger brother, who served as an enlisted man in the U.S. Army, flitted in and out of Cheyenne during these years and may have lived with Morris and Bess for a while. The Cheyenne school census of 1923 and 1924 shows Victor living with "J," which would have been his uncle John, a mystifying entry. In later years, when Victor spoke of his uncle, it would be with scorn.

A few doors down from the Hub, Bess's brother Samuel, who was three years older than Morris, worked as a jeweler. Despite what Victor would later say, the Krulaks were open about being Jewish, about Samuel being Bess's brother, and about most of their close friends being Jewish. But those people, too, were secular Jews.

Not long after moving to Cheyenne, Morris told his son, "Nobody ever learned a bad habit from a horse." He went out to nearby Fort D. A. Russell, until a few years earlier the largest Army cavalry post in America, and bought a horse for Victor. (The gentle old animal was retired and came at a good price.) Named Jim, the horse stood at sixteen hands, so tall that Victor had to climb up on a fence to mount him. He rode bareback until he was a skilled horseman, then Morris bought him a pony named Beauty, a spirited animal who threw Victor countless times. One year his Christmas present was a small western saddle. Learning to ride a horse, a common skill in Cheyenne, would later stand Krulak in great stead.

School census records in Cheyenne present strong but inconclusive evidence that Victor spent at least part of the seventh grade in Coronado, California. If he did go to California, records indicate that Morris and Bess did not. Why Victor went, whom he stayed with, and why the stay was so short are not known. All his life, Krulak talked about how important Coronado was to him in his youth, but he never disclosed precisely how he ended up there.

In 1928, when Victor was a freshman at Cheyenne High School, he became a member of the two-person debate team. The next year, he joined the Dramatic Club, the newspaper staff, and the Boys' Pep Club. In retrospect, these four activities foreshadowed crucial aspects of a career in which he would become a feared advocate with a pronounced flair for the dramatic.

As a sophomore, Victor stood a little over five feet tall and weighed about 110 pounds, a size that indicates he would have had a tough time in the cowboy culture of Cheyenne. But photographs in *The Lariat*, the school yearbook, show him standing, feet apart, with a self-confident, even cocky, expression on his face. Genetics had given him a small, slight body but, almost in compensation, an outsize intellect, a dominating personality, and far more self-confidence than reposes in most boys.

Victor took part in no athletics at Cheyenne High School, and surprisingly, given his career, he did not join the Reserve Officers' Training Corps (ROTC). The latter is significant for two reasons. First, pictures of the Cheyenne High ROTC unit indicate that almost every boy at the school joined. Second, Victor was about to apply for a nomination to the U.S. Naval Academy, and the ROTC training would have been of considerable benefit to him. Perhaps he did not join ROTC because of his involvement in so many other school activities. Or perhaps it was because of a budding cerebral bent. "I was thinking about things that boys that age don't usually think about," he later said.

When Victor was a freshman in high school, Morris asked Senator Warren to nominate his son as a candidate to the U.S. Military Academy. Warren would have been happy to accommodate Morris's request, but his nominations to West Point were filled. However, landlocked Wyoming lads had little interest in the Navy, and there was an opening at the Naval Academy for the class entering the next summer. In a December 15, 1928, letter, the senator offered Victor the chance to take the entrance exams in April 1929. Victor was one of the senator's last military academy nominations, as Warren died in November 1929.

THE Naval Academy would be a pivot point in Victor Krulak's life. Thus it is important to understand why he wanted to go there and how he got there. The why is the more important question. Why would a short, scrawny boy from Wyoming want to enter the harsh physical world of the Naval Academy? Why would a boy from a Jewish family want to enter a place then infamous for its anti-Semitism and overt racism? Why would a boy with a Jewish background want to leave the relatively tolerant environs of the West and move to a part of America where hotels and restaurants bore signs saying "Christians Only" and "No Dogs or Jews"? Why would Morris want his only son to go to a service academy when Russian Jews, because of the pogroms, generally loathed the military?

The answers are complex. First, Morris Krulak did not have the money to send his son to college. Second, he knew that graduates of a U.S. military academy were afforded automatic entry into the boardrooms and drawing rooms of America. Being a military officer was a shortcut to the American dream. What better way for a Jew to show his allegiance to America than by joining the military and fighting for his country? It would be a matter of immense pride in the Jewish community back in Denver that a second-generation Jewish boy was accepted at the Naval

Academy. Victor's cousin Ronnie Zall, Samuel's son, would later say, "That was a big deal. He was the hero of the family. We were all proud of him."

Victor later gave researchers various reasons for why he wanted to go to the Academy, one of which was that while he was in Coronado, the sight of warships in the bay had excited his interest in the Navy. He also said that his uncle John had awakened his interest in the military. And he had still another reason, this one probably true: "I had a friend whose father was in the military, and that influenced me." The friend was Doris Macklin, daughter of Major Walter F. Macklin, an Army physician stationed at Fort Russell. Doris was in the Dramatic Club with Victor, and she was more than a friend.

Sometimes Krulak said that his father wanted him to go to Harvard and become a lawyer, while his mother wanted him to go there and become a doctor. There may have been conversations along these lines, but given that Morris was a clerk in a clothing store, he probably couldn't afford the tuition to Harvard. In addition, Jews were far from welcome at Harvard. The truth is that had it not been for his appointment to the Naval Academy, Victor Krulak may not have received a college education. Krulak recalled, "I was the apple of my mother's and father's eye. They spoiled me." Beyond that, and noting that every Christmas his mother made little sugar cookies called kiffles for him, he had little to say about his parents. "My childhood was too boring for me to remember much about my parents," he declared. In 2007, when Krulak was shown the family genealogy going back to Russia, he was amazed—particularly that Morris had never become a U.S. citizen. "I thought my father came from Philadelphia. I must study this for several days before I can discuss it," he said.

A few days later, Krulak said more. His choice of words was revealing in that when he talked about his parents, he could not force himself to utter the words "Jew," "Jewish," or "Yiddish."

"My father never talked of his spirituality. It was always about hard work. My father was a very serious man. He was very quiet about his background, about everything, almost silent. I learned from him that life is serious, that sometimes you have only one chance. My father always talked of my future."

He paused and added, "I would hope that this book not dwell on my father's spirituality, but rather his lessons of hard work."

If he and his father never discussed their religion, what of importance did they discuss?

"He told me, 'You will be short, and you will be bald. But you don't have to be fat.'"

There was but one addition: "He told me the way to get along with a new acquaintance is to express genuine interest in the day-to-day affairs of the other person."

And that is all Victor Krulak would say about his parents.

On March 23, 1929, when he was sixteen, and only a few weeks before he was to take the entrance examinations for the Naval Academy, Victor assumed the name Donald V. Merrell and boarded a train for Boulder, Colorado. Accompanying him was Doris Macklin, age fifteen, who assumed the name Virginia D. King. The young couple went to the county clerk in Boulder, affirmed that they were twenty-one and eighteen, respectively, and obtained a marriage license. Then they went before a justice of the peace in Longmont, Colorado, and were married. Nine days later, the marriage was annulled, and Doris resumed her maiden name. (The annulment is not surprising. Because Victor and Doris had married under assumed names, the marriage was invalid. Immediately after the annulment, Major Macklin obtained an emergency transfer to Schofield Barracks in Hawaii. Three years later, he was ordered to Fort McPherson in Atlanta, where Doris met and married an Army lieutenant.) Given that the Naval Academy does not accept students who are married or who have been married, Morris Krulak was no doubt outraged that his son would jeopardize his opportunity to attend Annapolis. Everything Morris had planned for his son was now at risk.

When I asked Krulak why he married at sixteen, he threw his arms wide and said, "Goddamned if I know." The most likely explanation is that Doris was pregnant, which Krulak vigorously denied. Another explanation would be affirming the obvious: sixteen-year-old boys are devoid of sound judgment.

Applicants to the Naval Academy are expected to have judgment beyond their years, so Krulak hid this marriage when he applied to Annapolis. Legally, of course, the annulment meant that the marriage had never happened. But such an argument is sophistic, as Victor violated the spirit, if not the letter, of the Academy's regulations. In so doing, he failed to meet the standards of the Academy, whose mission is to imbue students with the highest ideals of duty and honor.

Indeed, not only did he hide the marriage from officials at Annapolis, but he also hid it from his second wife and from his three sons. About that marriage, he would say only, "It was a moment in time that went nowhere. I have not thought of her in decades. I don't see this as a significant factor in my life." He would talk no more about it, except to say, "This should not be included in the biography."

This cold dismissal of Krulak's first love is indicative of the hard-edged pragmatism and lack of emotion he would display most of his life. It was also indicative of his propensity to revise information that was not in accord with the biography he wanted.

KRULAK flunked the entrance exams to Annapolis. By then news of the marriage and annulment had no doubt made the rounds in Cheyenne. As soon as the school year ended, Morris and Bess took Victor back to Denver, where he enrolled in the summer session at Denver's East High School. He lived with the Zalls, whose home was only a few blocks from the school.

Morris now appealed to Congressman Carter to give Victor another chance at attending the Academy. He said that his son would attend a preparatory school and would do better on the next admission tests. The congressman agreed to make Victor his principal nominee for entrance in 1930, but now there was some fear that the Academy might reject Victor because of his size. Although he had grown, he was still only five feet four inches tall and weighed 116 pounds. On August 28, 1929, Carter wrote a letter to the superintendent of the Academy asking for a preliminary physical examination by Navy doctors "in order that Mr. Krulak may correct any minor physical defects, if any."

AFTER Victor spent three months at East High School, he and his mother boarded the Union Pacific and headed to Annapolis, where Victor enrolled in the Bobby Werntz Preparatory School, the sole purpose of which was to enable young men to pass the entrance exams to the Academy. Tuition for the October–May term was $125.

About the time he arrived in Annapolis, he took a physical examination at the Academy and was deemed physically acceptable. Officials there believed that he would grow during the four years of tough physical conditioning.

In his application, Victor said that he had completed twelve years of school when in fact he had completed only the tenth grade. He studied hard for the exams, and on May 23, 1930, Congressman Carter notified him that he had passed and that his appointment had been confirmed. With a grade of 4.0 being perfect and 2.5 considered passing, Victor had scored 3.4 in geometry, 3.8 in algebra, 3.6 in English, 3.7 in history, 3.9 in ancient history, and 3.9 in physics, for an average of 3.7. Carter ended his letter by saying that Victor's father knew many people in Cheyenne and he hoped the Krulaks would help in Carter's upcoming reelection campaign.

For Victor, it was not enough that he had been accepted to the Naval Academy. He later told people that his grades had placed him first among all the plebes entering Annapolis that year. The Academy, citing privacy constraints, would not confirm this. Nevertheless, a 3.7 average was more than respectable. Victor Krulak was ready, physically and academically, for the U.S. Naval Academy.

THE year that Victor entered the Academy, Morris told U.S. census takers that his parents were from England, while Bess claimed that her father had been born in Switzerland and her mother in Poland. Morris and Bess had created a new life in the American West. Their son, who would show that in family matters the apple did not fall far from the tree, would create another new life in the East. Although he had been appointed to the Academy as a resident of Wyoming, Cheyenne quickly became a footnote. He was now the man from Denver with deep roots in America. Krulak told people that his great-grandfather had served in the Confederate army, that his grandfather had moved from Louisiana to Colorado to homestead 640 acres of land, and that his father had been born in the Colorado capital. Krulak added that his father had graduated from the Colorado School of Mines and had "started off in silver" before doing "engineering work." Sometimes, even years later, he claimed that his father was "a scientist" and hinted of material success by saying, "My father had capital," and "I spent my summers on a ranch." He told one researcher that his father retired to San Diego in 1928 but lost all his money in the stock market collapse of 1929 and had to return to Denver. The baby book kept by his mother included a diploma from Coronado Elementary School in San Diego showing that Victor

34

graduated on June 10, 1927, and a program of the 1930 Cheyenne High School graduation showing that Victor was a graduate. The provenance of the first is doubtful; the second is a fabrication.

Victor Krulak would tell his own version of his life story until the day he died. To his Jewish relatives in Denver, it was a story that caused immense pain.

# 2

## Rocks and Shoals

On Krulak's first day at the Naval Academy, a towering midshipman looked down at him, smirked, and said, "Well, *Brute*."

It is likely that the upperclassman, pleased with his sense of humor, moved on and forgot the incident. But from that moment on, Krulak was taken with the name and henceforth introduced himself as "Brute Krulak." Over the years, the derisive nickname would evolve into one of great respect and, in some quarters, a certain amount of fear.

"I was scared of a strange world," Krulak said of entering the Academy. He had good reason. Life at "the Severn River High School" or "Canoe U" was rigorous, demanding, and for plebes (freshmen) brutal. Hazing was rampant, and plebes were verbally abused and physically beaten.

The Navy is the most hoary of all the military services, and it is essential that plebes learn Navy traditions. One Sunday evening every month, Brute and the other plebes marched into Memorial Hall and listened as the Articles for the Governance of the Navy were read: "The captain of a ship shall not suffer his ship to run upon a rock or a shoal," "the captain shall not strike his flag nor pusillanimously cry for quarter"—the famous "rocks and shoals" speech that many Academy graduates remember all their lives.

Attendance was mandatory at a weekly "nonsectarian" service modeled on the Episcopal Church liturgy. Because Episcopalianism was the religion favored by many senior officers in all branches of the military, the Episcopalian model was considered most appropriate for a military academy. It may have been during his plebe year at the Academy that Brute first told the story of growing up as an Episcopalian. This would not have been a big leap; at the time, Jews who converted to Christianity often chose the Episcopal Church, which was seen as the "country club church" of the upper classes. (A widespread saying among Jewish children was, "If you can kiss your elbow, you will turn into an Episcopalian.")

In a very real sense, Victor Krulak's life began at the Naval Academy. On the personal side was the fabulist yarn he had concocted about his early life. On the professional side, he was a tabula rasa, and he soaked up everything the Navy threw at him. But he remained spoiled, undisciplined, and self-indulgent. During his plebe year, he was sometimes late for formation, did not shine his shoes, and allowed food to stain his uniform. His size and high energy level gave him the appearance of a water bug as he scooted down the hall, darting in and out of rooms along the way. Accounts of the time reveal him as a prankster and, though details are slim, something of a ladies' man. His grades were undistinguished.

THE year after Brute entered the Academy, his parents moved back to Denver. In the 1932 Denver city directory, information for which was gathered during the summer of 1931, Morris is listed as a jeweler. It seems he had returned to work for his father-in-law.

\*   \*   \*

AT some point during Brute's first two years at the Academy, he met Amy Chandler. Amy was the petite, dark-haired, and vivacious daughter of William D. Chandler, who had graduated from the Academy in 1911 and now taught electrical engineering there. This was the class in which Brute made his best grades. The Chandlers were an old, genteel East Coast family, Episcopalians all. (A family friend was author Herman Wouk, and it has been said that William was the model for Pug Henry, the principled main character in Wouk's novel *The Winds of War*.) Amy's maternal grandfather was a prominent Washington doctor, and her paternal great-grandfather, William E. Chandler, was secretary of the Navy under President Chester Arthur and revered as "the Father of the Modern Navy." The Chandler family lived on a large estate in northwest Washington called Cliveden. (This estate was later bought by socialite Perle Mesta and then by Vice President Lyndon Johnson.) Brute and Amy met at a weekend dance. The young couple danced to "Smoke Gets in Your Eyes," a song from the new operetta *Roberta*. And so it began.

BRUTE's third year at the Academy was pivotal. For the Army-Navy football game, he had anti-Army posters printed and sold them to midshipmen. Although the wording is lost to memory, it was most certainly scatological. But Academy officials were not as concerned about the content as they were about the fact that Brute had *sold* the posters to fellow midshipmen, a commercial act expressly forbidden by Academy regulations. (That Krulak did not know about the regulation was, in the rigid and unforgiving world of the Academy, irrelevant.) He was brought before a disciplinary board, charged with "conduct to the prejudice of good order and discipline," and given 78 demerits — so many that, on November 25, 1933, he was, according to his Academy records, "INFORMED IN DANGER OF BECOMING UNSAT. IN CONDUCT," which usually led to dismissal. An instructor told Krulak that he was not the material from which naval officers were made and that he should consider another career. Despite these events, Krulak remained at the Academy, intent on pursuing a military career.

DURING all this, Brute's friendship with Lieutenant Colonel Holland M. Smith, an influential officer in the Marine Corps, flourished. As a veteran of Belleau Wood, Smith was a revered figure among midshipmen and enjoyed great respect within the Corps.

Smith was stationed in Philadelphia during Brute's first two years at the Academy and often came to Annapolis to visit his son John Victor (whom he called Victor). During Brute's third year, Smith was transferred to Washington, and he and his wife often entertained midshipmen in their home. Because of the impact Smith would have on Krulak's career, we must pause here to consider both Smith and the racial views prevalent within the military at the time.

Smith was a short, stocky man from Alabama, an unreconstructed southerner, an ardent Protestant, and quite conservative. Demanding, profane, and burdened with melancholy, he had thinning hair and an impassive face. His flat, intimidating stare was magnified by austere steel-rimmed glasses. His father was a lawyer and had enough political connections that Holland had been offered a nomination to Annapolis. But his parents believed that attending the Academy would be a "surrender to Yankee ideology," so Smith went to what was then called Alabama Polytechnic Institute (now Auburn University) and then to law school. He joined his father's practice but, by his own admission, was a terrible lawyer. Frustrated, he joined the Marine Corps in 1905 and fought in World War I.

In his autobiography, Smith manifests a patronizing and paternal attitude toward blacks. He was not alone in this regard; many Marine officers were southerners who believed that the Marine

Corps was a club for white men only. (Blacks were not accepted into the Corps until World War II, and then mostly as laborers and in noncombat roles.) Smith's attitude toward Jews is not known, but at the time anti-Semitism was almost institutionalized both at the Naval Academy and in the Marine Corps. As a result, few Jews—enlisted men or officers—were found in the Corps.

In the early 1930s, the Naval Academy formed one of the toughest color barriers in America: no black man had graduated from the Academy since it was established almost ninety years earlier. Robert Schneller, in *Breaking the Color Barrier: The U.S. Naval Academy's First Black Midshipmen and the Struggle for Racial Equality*, says that the Academy was the fountainhead of the Navy's institutionalized racism. Krulak's parents thought that their only son had entered an institution that would grant him access to the American dream. Annapolis would do that, but first Krulak had to experience the worst side of the American military.

From the time he walked through the gate at Annapolis, Krulak no doubt frequently, perhaps daily, heard derogatory comments about blacks and Jews. Add to this the hardened racial attitudes of Navy and Marine officers such as Holland Smith, and it is clear that Krulak had fallen into a veritable witches' brew of racism and discrimination. It was a good time to be an Episcopalian.

DESPITE his flaws, Smith was a passionate advocate of the Marine Corps, always alert to the slightest hint of predation by the Army or Navy against the Corps. To Smith, the Marine Corps was a high and lofty calling, and he frequently urged his son to apply for a commission in the Marines. Because the Marine Corps was in the Department of the Navy, a limited number of men from each graduating class at the Academy were eligible for a commission in the Corps.

Victor Krulak often accompanied John Victor Smith when he

visited his parents, and there Krulak listened to Lieutenant Colonel Smith's eloquent exegesis of Marine Corps values and how no young man could better serve his country than in the Marines. The younger Smith was not convinced. Tall, cool, and elegant like his mother, he was distant from his impatient and forceful father. He favored the patrician gentility of the Navy to the warrior ethos of the Marine Corps and would go on to a distinguished Navy career.

But Krulak was drawn to the dour southerner. Smith, as were many Marine officers of the time, was a skilled horseman and was delighted to find that Krulak knew a great deal about horses and riding. Brute began visiting Smith even when John Victor was not present, and when he announced that he was going to apply for a commission in the Marine Corps, the bond was sealed: Brute had become Smith's surrogate son.

DURING Krulak's third year at the Academy, he also decided to marry Amy Chandler. She was not only the personification of ease, manners, and gentility, but given her family connections, she was also the perfect wife for a young man considering a military career. Years later, after Amy had died and Krulak was living alone in a retirement home, he talked of his marriage as if it were a business merger. "Amy grew up in a naval family. Good and decent people, and very rich. Amy knew how to entertain. She understood the hierarchy of rank; it was second nature to her." As headstrong as Brute, she adored him from the beginning, and he knew he would always be at the center of her life. "She knew what was expected from the wife of a senior officer, and I didn't have to ask her to do anything," he said. "She knew what to do better than I did."

DURING Brute's final year at the Academy, he received considerable acclaim as an athlete. Crew is the oldest college sport in

America, but Krulak had never heard of it back in Cheyenne. As a plebe and almost certainly because of his size, he had been drawn to the sport and was cut out for one role in particular: coxswain. The coxswain of a boat is small, the lighter the better. His job is to steer the boat and set the pace — the all-important strokes per minute — for the eight oarsmen. Maneuvering a fifty-foot-plus shell with a skin one-eighth inch thick is a sensitive and tricky business. The coxswain is also the crew's tactician and must know how to push the oarsmen to their limit.

During his second year at the Academy, Krulak became coxswain on the varsity crew, and then, at the end of his third year, he was elected captain. This was the first time in the history of the Naval Academy that a coxswain had been chosen as captain, an event so noteworthy that it appeared in the *New York Times*, which described Krulak as "brainy" and "a magnetic leader."

Navy had just had one of the best years in its rowing history and had defeated Pennsylvania and Harvard to win the prestigious Charles Francis Adams Cup. (After that victory, the *Times* had called Krulak a "fine little coxswain.") During the competition with Harvard, Brute became friendly with Hamilton "Hammy" Bissell, coxswain of the Harvard crew, who later would play an important role in his life.

The popularity of crew as an intercollegiate sport and the novelty of his being captain caused the *Times* to keep an eye on Krulak. In April of his senior year, the paper again singled him out by saying that he was "full of aggressive energy," that he was "the most important man in the boat," and that "his iron voice has echoed over nearly every waterway Navy rows on."

There is no small amount of irony in all this. Krulak had never participated in a team sport and now was captain of one of the most important teams at one of the most prestigious universities in America. This man who had grown up far from any major body of water was now rowing on some of the most significant rivers and bays in the country. His cocky nature had matured into absolute self-confidence, and his leadership of men almost twice his size revealed the force of his personality.

His prominence in crew notwithstanding, Brute was no athlete. In truth, he could be clumsy and awkward, the best example of which is the story of the sword.

A midshipman must learn the sword salute, a maneuver in which, in approaching a reviewing stand, he moves the sword smartly so that the pommel is in front of his face and the blade is almost vertical. Then he sweeps the sword down and out, the point only a few inches above the ground, as he passes the reviewing stand. In one parade, as Krulak brought up his sword, he knocked off his hat — his "cover," in Marine parlance — and when he swept the sword down, the tip stuck in the ground. He marched on, swordless, covered only with humiliation.

In 1934, the Annapolis yearbook, *The Lucky Bag*, identified Krulak as hailing from Denver and mentioned his "sunny disposition and cheerful good humor," calling him "the little feller" who trashed the rooms of his friends. The yearbook said that Brute never had to study, "because he has one of those minds which penetrates the deepest subject in less than nothing flat," and that midshipmen were always dropping by his room to "find out how some gadget works." Brute took a lot of kidding because of his size, the yearbook added.

But in his final year at the Academy, Brute Krulak's size almost ended his military career before it even began. Academy records show that in November 1933, the Permanent Medical Examining Board (PMEB) found Brute "physically disqualified for commission" because he was "underheight." The Academy's food and tough physical regimen had had no effect on Brute: he was still five foot four and weighed 116 pounds — two inches too short and four pounds too light to meet the minimum size requirements to be commissioned.

The Great Depression had already had an impact on the number of midshipmen being commissioned. Because of military budget cuts, half the previous year's graduating class had not been commissioned. Although they had received a splendid education courtesy of the U.S. taxpayer, the Navy could not afford them. Their compulsory military service was waived, and they were free to join the civilian world.

Of the 464 graduates in the class of 1934, more than one hundred were not commissioned. To the board charged with identifying midshipmen who would not be commissioned, Krulak's physical size, as well as records identifying him as Jewish, meant that his was one of the first names on the list. There were no grounds for appeal.

Nevertheless, Krulak did file an appeal. On April 6, 1934, the PMEB again ruled that he was disqualified for a commission, and on April 27 he was directed to tender his resignation. The next day, however, in an astonishing turn of events, not only did the Navy grant him a waiver, but he became one of twenty-five graduates offered a commission in the Marine Corps. Although his fingerprints are nowhere to be seen, it is almost certain that Holland Smith had a part in this.

The story of how Krulak received the waiver has become part of what Marines call "the lore of the Corps." Almost every Marine second lieutenant who goes through The Basic School, the first professional school attended by new lieutenants, hears of Brute Krulak, the man who wanted to be a Marine so badly that he paid a friend to strike him on the head with a piece of lumber in order to raise the two-inch knot that would enable him to meet the height requirement. Some say that he hit himself with a ball-peen hammer, others that he simply willed himself to be taller.

Brute, of course, was the source of this apocrypha and would repeat the story many times throughout his career. And he may actually have attempted to raise a knot on his head. (He supplied convincing details. "I had my friends draw straws to see who had the opportunity to hit me on the head," he said, adding that the winning midshipman took a piece of wood from the window seat of his room and struck him a stout blow across his crown. A respectable knot was formed. "It hurt, and it did not make me tall enough," Krulak said.) But the real reason Krulak received a waiver was that one of his classmates, John Hyland, who was an inch taller than Brute, received a waiver first. Hyland's father taught at the Academy and had enough influence to secure a waiver for his son. Brute, almost certainly assisted by Smith, boldly asserted that if the PMEB could grant one waiver, it could grant two. The Navy agreed, and thus Brute Krulak became the shortest and lightest man ever to graduate from Annapolis and be commissioned in the Marine Corps.

BRUTE bought a Naval Academy ring of yellow gold, selected an onyx as the stone he wanted for the inset, and then bought two miniatures of the ring—one for his mother and one for Amy, as an unofficial engagement ring. The Marine Corps did not allow lieutenants to marry until they had served two years and done an obligatory tour at sea. Amy would wait.

Amy knew of Brute's Jewish background, but it did not matter to her; she would have married him no matter what his religion was. Even so, Krulak knew enough of Navy and Marine Corps ways that he no doubt minimized the fact that he was Jewish. He continued to insist that, like so many professional military officers, he was Episcopalian.

THE marriage he would hide and the religion he would deny, along with the tendency for exaggeration and the craving for approval (the latter of which is not uncommon in the Marine

Corps) present an off-putting picture of Second Lieutenant Victor Krulak. But two things must be said in Krulak's defense. First, the roots of his actions lie in a childhood about which we know very little. Krulak was not the first, and neither was he the last, to hide a Jewish background or to lie about his past in order to pursue a military career. Second, a man's accomplishments are a better window into who he is than are the misdeeds of his youth. So let us wait a few years before we pass judgment on him.

WHEN Krulak pinned on the eagle, globe, and anchor, he began his career at a pivot point in Marine Corps history. Because America did not feel the need to compete militarily with European countries, the military was stagnant. In the Marine Corps, some captains had ten years or more in grade and would not be promoted until a senior officer died. The year Brute graduated from the Naval Academy, Congress passed a law making selection boards responsible for promotions. This would open the door to more rapid promotions. Still, the Corps remained so austere that Marines cut wood for heat rather than buy coal, and they used ammunition left over from World War I for target practice.

Foremost in the memory of every Marine was the glory that had been theirs at Belleau Wood. The Marines had to build on that glory, or they would not survive. Army chief of staff Douglas MacArthur had talked of absorbing the Marine Corps into the Army, and if the Corps did not develop a unique role, it would be swallowed up by the Army. Some in the Corps wanted the Marines to emphasize small wars, such as the ones they had been fighting in the Caribbean and Central America, while others thought the future was in amphibious warfare.

The year Brute graduated, the Marine Corps published its *Tentative Manual for Landing Operations*, in part because a brilliant but mercurial Marine named Earl "Pete" Ellis had predicted back in 1918 that war was coming with Japan, that it would happen in the

Pacific, that the Japanese would strike the first mighty blow, and that the American military would wage a bitter and protracted island-hopping campaign across the central Pacific before emerging victorious. The Ellis report, titled "Advanced Base Operations in Micronesia" and published in 1920, would prove to be one of the most prescient military studies ever written; it could have been used as an overlay for island landings in World War II.

Looming over military theorists of the time was the memory of the disastrous 1915 amphibious landing at Gallipoli, on the coast of Turkey. Winston Churchill, then first lord of the Admiralty, conceived the Gallipoli plan as a way for the Allies to capture Istanbul and provide a safe sea route through the Dardanelles. But the invasion was repelled by the Turks, and the Allies suffered some 250,000 casualties.

Nevertheless, emerging young Marine Corps leaders such as Holland Smith were outspoken proponents of Ellis's ideas. The big problem for the Marine Corps was boats. The Navy assigned small boats to the Marines so the Marines could practice amphibious landings. But the boats were the wrong kind, there were too few of them, and there was no money to buy the right kind, whatever the right kind might be. If war was coming as Ellis had predicted, America would be even less ready than it had been in World War I.

This was the depressed and confused military world Brute Krulak was entering. It was a world on which he would have a dramatic impact.

# 3

# A Sojourn in the Middle Kingdom

Few things on earth are as useless as a newly commissioned second lieutenant. Although Congress considers him an officer and a gentleman, it would take an act of God to give him the knowledge and common sense possessed by the average gunnery sergeant. The Marine Corps, wisely unwilling to wait for God to get involved in such matters, attempts to short-circuit the process by sending young lieutenants to various schools and minor assignments, hoping they do not sink, break, or blow up something in the process.

As historian Allan Millett points out, military biographies too often treat the prewar or between-the-wars years of a subject as useless filler rather than as an integral and significant part of a life lived within the unique military environment. In the small Marine Corps of the 1930s, when every officer knew every other officer, by reputation if not by sight, both the personality of an officer and his relationship with his brother officers were crucial in his career. Indeed, much about Brute Krulak's early career foreshadows the legendary figure he would become.

Krulak's first assignment was to Philadelphia to attend The Basic School, where lieutenants learned small unit tactics and leadership. Once while serving as officer of the day, Brute was inspecting guard posts and parked his car on the railroad tracks. A train came along and demolished the car. This incident showed that at $124.80 per month, Krulak was not overpaid, and it reinforced the common perception of second lieutenants.

During the ten-month course, Brute met the second officer who would have an enormous impact on his career, Gerald C. Thomas. Captain Thomas wore a Silver Star received at Belleau Wood, and now, though he taught the intricacies of intelligence work, was best known for his daylong lecture on Gallipoli, in which he emphasized the failure of leadership once the assaulting troops were ashore. Thomas told the lieutenants that establishing a beachhead was only the first step in an amphibious landing; the troops had to keep moving, always moving, inland.

"He could think ahead," Brute said of Thomas. "He would pick up the stub of a pencil and write things that were historic about either the future of the Marine Corps or the course of war in the Pacific."

The course in intelligence work was the only part of The Basic School that Brute considered of any merit. It appealed to his sense of drama and his desire for secrecy. He would glide in and out of the intelligence world throughout his military career and beyond.

In June 1935, Brute was ordered aboard the battleship *Arizona*, which spent the next six months steaming between ports up and down the West Coast. He recalled that one night, while the *Arizona* was anchored near Yerba Buena Island in San Francisco Bay, he was granted the responsibility of being senior officer of the deck watch. Because he was an inexperienced second lieutenant, he was assigned to the mid watch—midnight to 4 a.m.— when things of moment rarely happened. During the quiet morning hours, Brute thought the anchor was dragging and ordered a second anchor dropped. An enlisted man knocked off the stoppers, and as the 19,585-pound anchor began pulling links of chain weighing 120 pounds each through the hawse pipe, the ship became one of the noisiest places in San Francisco. Brute was transfixed by the flying sparks and the jangling cacophony. He did look up once to see the captain on the veranda outside his stateroom — nightshirt flapping, arms waving, mouth opening and closing — but he could not hear what the captain was saying.

Brute had forgotten that the anchor chain on a capital ship is lightly attached to the structure — it is secured by brakes and stoppers — and he watched, fascinated, as eighty fathoms of chain, followed by the bitter end, whipped through the forecastle. Again the night was silent, except for the unbelieving wail of the captain: "He lost my anchor. He lost my anchor."

Brute looked up and shouted, "Sir, the anchor is not lost. I know exactly where it is. But I just can't reach it."

The comment set the captain off on another round of imprecations, the most printable of which was, "You will never again hold a position of responsibility on this ship."

If this story is true, it is the first instance of Brute Krulak's willingness to speak to senior officers with a candor that bordered on impertinence, a quality that later would make him invaluable to a series of generals whom he would serve in a staff capacity.

Brute would tell this story for the rest of his life, saying the anchor and the chain were recovered the day after the incident, and always ending by leaning forward and asking in a conspiratorial fashion, "And you know what happened to the *Arizona*, don't you?" — the implication being that it was divine providence that had transferred him from the deck of the *Arizona* before she was sunk at Pearl Harbor, with the loss of 1,177 sailors.

For a number of reasons, this story may be fictitious. First, the enlisted men in attendance would have known to stop the anchor chain before it reached the bitter end. Second, at regular intervals in an officer's career and always when he is finishing an assignment, his superior writes a fitness report (FitRep) that becomes part of his personnel file. This is something of a report card and is the primary basis for an officer's promotion and future assignments. As losing the anchor chain of a capital ship is no small matter, it is reasonable to assume that the incident would have prompted a poor FitRep. But when Brute left the *Arizona* in December 1935, the captain in the flapping nightshirt reported that he was an "outstanding young officer of his rank. A strict disciplinarian. Very energetic, thorough and able. He has the respect of men under his command."

The FitReps of the time had eleven categories by which officers were graded. In most of those categories during Brute's early career, he was rated as "excellent" or "outstanding." He received lower grades in the categories of physical fitness, military bearing, and leadership; he remained too short to look like a real Marine.

From the *Arizona*, Brute was transferred back to Annapolis to coach Navy's crew for the 1936 Olympics. He reestablished contact with Holland Smith and, of course, Amy Chandler. On January 10, 1936, the *Denver Post* reported that Amy Chandler, daughter of Commander and Mrs. William Chandler of Newport and Washington, was engaged to Lieutenant Victor H. Krulak of Denver and the couple would be married in the spring. The Navy rowing crew never made it through the preliminaries.

On June 1, 1936—two years to the day after being commissioned—Brute Krulak married Amy Chandler. The ceremony speaks volumes about how Brute and Amy—and the Chandler family—handled Brute's religious background: the wedding was not in a church, but in the home of Amy's grandmother in Washington, and it was performed not by a priest or pastor, but by a military chaplain. The most significant item of all was buried in the *Washington Post* account of the wedding, a story that was primarily a list of Amy's family members who attended, along with a reminder of her illustrious forebears. The single reference to Brute's family said only that Brute was being transferred to California and en route he and Amy would stop in Denver "to visit the bridegroom's parents who were detained from the wedding by illness in their family."

Krulak later said that the newspaper story was wrong, that his mother had been at the wedding. But the contents of social columns, like those of obituaries, are furnished almost entirely by the families involved. Accuracy is crucial because such stories are cut out of the paper and saved, often passed from one generation to the next. If the *Washington Post* said that the bridegroom's parents were not in attendance, they were not in attendance. Brute, however, would discuss the matter no further. The most likely reason that Morris and Bess did not attend the wedding is that Brute did not want his Jewish parents at this gathering of eminent Episcopalians. This was another significant early instance of Brute's lifelong efforts to minimize his Jewish background—what one of his sons called a "benign conspiracy" to hide his cultural and religious heritage.

When news that young Victor had married a shiksa arrived back in Denver, it is likely that some Orthodox members of the Zall family sat shivah for him.

THE assignment in California was a pivot point, personally and professionally, for Krulak. It cemented his love for San Diego, a city to which he would return and where he would eventually retire, and it formed his interest in what he called "the amphibious business," an interest that would become a grand passion.

Within the U.S. military, only the Marine Corps questioned British military historian Basil Henry Liddell Hart's belief that amphibious landings were "almost impossible" and were no longer a part of modern warfare. Gallipoli, they said, proved only what happens when bad leadership, bad doctrine, and bad technique are combined with a lack of coordination between the Army and Navy. Other branches of the military looked at Gallipoli and turned away. The Marines looked at it and figured out how mistakes made there could be lessons learned for the next war.

By now Pete Ellis's report about Pacific island-hopping and a war with Japan was assuming greater importance. Some Marine officers were coming to see Belleau Wood—Marines moving through a sea of wheat to attack the wood—as not unlike an amphibious landing on a defended island.

But America remained in a pacifist and isolationist mood and, as events in China were about to demonstrate, was more concerned with protecting America's interests than with protecting its honor. Japanese soldiers had been fighting in northern China since 1931, and that struggle was about to affect Americans.

During World War I, Japan had seized a number of German islands in the Pacific. After the war, the League of Nations had awarded Japan mandates over those islands. Now much of the western Pacific, plus all of Southeast Asia, comprised what the Japanese called their Greater East Asia Co-Prosperity Sphere.

Ellis had written that when America and Japan went to war, the burden of winning the land battle would fall on the Marines. The only way to take Pacific islands would be with large amphibious landings. But when Brute arrived in San Diego, the Marines had only a primitive doctrine of how to conduct such landings, and the Navy still had no proper landing craft. Navy boats were between thirty-three and fifty feet in length. They had exposed rudders and propellers that dug into the sand when the boats retracted from a beach. They also lacked speed and maneuverability and often broached in the surf. The Navy and Marine Corps had conducted several fleet exercises—practice amphibious operations—that had been chaos squared. To minimize the loss of boats, the Navy chose only the easiest beaches for these exercises. It seemed that the Navy was unable to design, build, or adapt a boat suitable for the Marines' amphibious landings—or victory.

Krulak's job in San Diego was to supervise experiments with various landing craft. In early 1937, he was in charge of six small boats during the third fleet exercise, FLEX-3, off San Clemente. When he saw combat-equipped Marines climbing over high gunwales and dropping into surf that was often over their heads, he knew there had to be a better way. What heretofore had been of academic interest suddenly was very real. Krulak became fascinated with the most important issue facing the Marine Corps: how to move men from ship to shore. But his involvement was cut short when he received orders transferring him to China.

Amy was two months pregnant when she and Brute boarded the *President Polk* and proceeded toward the Philippines and China. The boat moved at a stately eleven knots, as if intentionally giving Lieutenant and Mrs. Krulak a peaceful journey so they could gather strength for what lay ahead. The couple arrived in Shanghai in April 1937.

MARINES who served in China from 1927 to 1941 believed that those years were the Golden Age of the Marine Corps. A single regiment, the 4th Marines—whose numbers fluctuated between 1,200 and 1,600 men—served in China during those years; these "China Marines" were looked upon with considerable envy.

In 1937, Shanghai was one of the largest and most densely populated cities in the world—a colorful, cosmopolitan, and corrupt metropolis; a place of spies, provocateurs, and intrigue; a place where gunrunners and drug dealers socialized with diplomats and where the British looked down their pale noses at everyone, particularly the Americans. The superior attitude of the British was offset by the fact that they believed generous amounts of alcohol prevented tropical diseases. As the British had been at this outpost business longer than anyone else, the Americans assumed they knew what they were talking about.

Almost daily, there were high teas and horseraces. There were streets such as Blood Alley, where sailors and Marines from a half-dozen countries routinely fought one another. And there was the Lane of Lingering Happiness, the location of 151 brothels (or "singsong houses," as the Chinese called them). Shanghai was, to quote the Chinese writer Xia Yan, "a city of 48-story skyscrapers built upon 24 layers of hell."

There were three parts to the city: the International Settlement, the French Concession, and the Chinese Municipal Association. The International Settlement and the contiguous French Concession sprawled over some ten square miles and contained about half the city's three million people. The International Settlement was bound on the north by Soochow Creek and on the south and east by the Whangpoo River. To the west was Xuxi—"the Badlands"—a place of opium dens, gambling, and shootings, ruled by violent criminals. One writer described it as a "carnival of crime."

The International Settlement was a colonial outpost for various nations, predominantly the United States, Britain, and Italy. There were parties every night—urbane, cosmopolitan gatherings where a half-dozen languages were heard over tables covered with crisp linens and where polished silver gleamed in the candlelight. American officers and their wives were welcome guests at these parties. It was a heady existence for the twenty-four-year-old Marine from Cheyenne and his effervescent wife.

BRUTE, who had gained a modest ability to speak French at the Academy, found a new apartment at 219 rue Cardinal Mercier in the French Concession. His job was as assistant intelligence officer of the 4th Marines, and his primary duty was as a liaison with the French, who, through the Catholic Church, had developed an extensive intelligence network throughout China.

In Shanghai, the duty day ended about 1 p.m., after which horses and parties dominated an officer's life. Sitting a horse well was considered the mark of a gentleman, something usually associated with the gentry of eastern America, and an officer's equestrian abilities were important both socially and professionally. Brute's expertise with horses meant that he immediately became a member of the Marine polo team. Being on the team, even though it was among the worst in Shanghai, was a professional plus. After all, skill at riding was the mark of a gentleman, and officers were gentlemen.

Whether they rode or not, many Marine officers in Shanghai carried a riding crop as a stylish accoutrement to their uniform, and Brute acquired a collection of handmade crops. In July, he was promoted to first lieutenant, bought his own polo pony, and named her Beauty. It should come as no surprise that a first lieutenant could own a polo pony; the lifestyle in Shanghai was such that a captain might own as many as five.

In Shanghai, the Royal Ulster Rifles invited Brute to his first Mess Night, an elegant and structured military dinner. The evening had a profound effect on Krulak, who watched as officers in formal dress, wearing their orders and decorations, marched two by two into the dining hall. Regimental flags lined the walls, and printed menus were at each place setting. The president of the mess ordered, "Parade the beef," and, accompanied by a drum and fifes, an enormous prime rib atop a silver platter was brought into the dining room, where it was presented to the president for his approval. (This practice dated back to pre-refrigeration days, when an important attribute of an officer and a gentleman was his ability to "tell meat"—that is, to know if the meat was safe to eat or if it had "turned.") The president of the mess then sampled the beef and announced, "I proclaim this meat fit for human consumption, and I commend it to the enjoyment of the mess and our guests."

At Mess Night, the rules of deportment were inviolate. Officers could not loosen their collars, nor could they pass out at the table. Officers could not leave the table for any reason until after dinner. The conversation was pleasant and topical, and neither shop talk nor profanity was allowed. Dinner was followed by a glass of port. The decanter was passed from right to left at the head table and from left to right at the other tables. After a series of elaborate toasts, the president of the mess announced, "Gentlemen, please join me at the bar." After a few drinks, the senior officers left the bar, while the younger officers continued drinking, usually to the point where they ended the evening by breaking furniture and throwing one another out the windows.

Krulak was awed by the pageantry of the dinner. He was developing both a sense of history and an increasing pride in the Marine Corps, and he, along with Lemuel Shepherd—who had served in China ten years earlier and in a few more years would become important in Krulak's career—would eventually introduce Mess Night throughout the Marine Corps.

In Shanghai, Brute and Amy had three servants: a cook, a steward, and a "mafoo," who was assigned miscellaneous chores. Brute wore custom-tailored uniforms and bought a car, a Citroën, for $36. Amy's impeccable taste enabled the young couple to buy lamps and silver and linens and silks. Brute acquired a large overstuffed armchair that would be his favorite for the remainder of his life. For the equivalent of $1.50, he commissioned a small circular rug of fine wool on which was embroidered, in bright red, the eagle, globe, and anchor. That rug, as bright as when it was made, was at the foot of his chair when he died.

Brute hired a Chinese tutor to come to his house for an hour every day to teach him Mandarin. Later, he said that most of the teaching sessions consisted of him walking around the dining room table trying to stay ahead of the "garlic burner" who was his tutor. Brute did learn a modest amount of Chinese, including the fact that "Victor Krulak" was translated as "Chu Lai."

Brute traveled to Tsingtao and Peiping and went by Navy gunboat up the Yangtze River to Nanking. The U.S. Navy had a small fleet of shallow draft gunboats on the Yangtze. The United States, along with France, Britain, and Russia, had won treaty rights to patrol Chinese rivers and territorial waters in 1858.

Always in the background were reports of the Japanese military rampaging across the Far East. And there was always the possibility of hostilities between Chiang Kai-shek's Nationalist forces and those of the Communists or local warlords. Gathering and evaluating information, not just on military forces but also on the political and economic situation in China, was an important part of Krulak's job and the foundation for his later reputation as a China expert.

On July 7, the Japanese used a minor incident at the Marco Polo Bridge near Peiping to begin an all-out attack on China. The second Sino-Japanese War was officially under way, and on August 13 the war came to Shanghai: more than two dozen Japanese warships stood up the Whangpoo and began shelling the city. Krulak and Captain Robert Edward Hogaboom stood atop the roof of the Palace Hotel and watched Japanese aircraft dropping bombs on the city, followed by an artillery barrage and then tough fighting as Chinese soldiers put up a stiff resistance. Thousands of civilians were killed.

Hogaboom, who was named for Robert E. Lee, came from Mississippi. A cerebral man, he would become the only close friend Krulak had throughout his Marine Corps career.

*　*　*

THE location of the International Settlement prevented the Japanese from flanking the Chinese defenders. The U.S. government, fearing the Japanese might attempt to violate the neutrality of the International Settlement, sent Marines to the barricades with orders to stop any incursion. But the State Department placed rigid restraints on the Marines, who, under no conditions, were to use heavy weapons; they could use only tear gas and, as a last resort, small arms. Their main weapon, although neither the Japanese troops nor the Marines knew it, was that neither of their countries wanted war with the other. President Roosevelt was focused almost entirely on the rising threat of Nazi Germany, and the Japanese were not yet ready to move against the West. Nevertheless, at a tactical level, tensions between the Japanese and the Marines remained high.

ONE day Brute received word from Lieutenant Commander Ari Nishayama, a Japanese naval attaché whom he had met on the social circuit: "There is going to be a landing." Using amphibious craft, the Japanese would seek to outflank the Chinese.

It is not widely known among civilians, but in most wars there are, on both sides of the conflict, observers from what are called "nonbelligerent nations"—those not participating in the war. These observers are allowed relatively free access to the belligerents' tactics, weapons, and operations. They also accept the inherent risks of being in proximity to combat. Krulak, in a bold and impetuous move, decided that observing the Japanese amphibious landing was part of his job. He approached Lieutenant George Phelan, an aide to Admiral Harry Yarnell, the Navy's senior man in Shanghai, and asked to borrow a tugboat. The Japanese attack began at midnight with an artillery barrage directed at the landing beach on the south bank of the Yangtze between Woosung and Liuho. At dawn, with the U.S. flag flying and accompanied by

Phelan and a Navy photographer, Krulak sallied forth into the middle of the Japanese landing fleet.

As the tug approached one of the larger Japanese warships, there was a flurry on deck, and Japanese sailors rushed to the rail. The shooting stopped. The sailors saluted. Other sailors dipped the Japanese ensign, and a horn sounded. Then Krulak and Phelan, who were in the wheelhouse of the tugboat, came to attention, saluted, and gave a blast on the horn.

Proper naval courtesies having been rendered, the Japanese resumed their assault, and Brute resumed his intelligence gathering.

He was in dangerous waters. Japanese naval guns were firing only a few hundred yards away. Brute recalled that the tug was so close to the action that Phelan took a piece of shrapnel in his shoulder. When the barrage lifted and landing craft were launched, Brute ordered the tug closer. There was something unusual about the design of the Japanese landing craft: their flat bows jutted up and out like an inverted V, and their sterns were pointed. They were powerful, seaworthy, and stable, carrying both vehicles and personnel. Everything about the vessels showed that the Japanese were years ahead of the Americans in the development of landing craft.

"That's it! That's it!" Brute shouted, and his tug moved in tight among the landing craft. He clocked their speeds, took notes, and drew sketches as his photographer clicked away. Again and again, as he absorbed design details of the Japanese craft, he exclaimed, "We don't have that."

When the Japanese craft ran up on the beach, their large, flat bows opened and formed ramps that dropped onto the sand, allowing the boats to disgorge vehicles and personnel on dry land. When the craft hit the beach, they remained firmly grounded; their sterns were not pushed around by the surf, nor did they fall off into a steep list. As soon as the Japanese troops ran onto the beach, the coxswains revved their engines, backed the landing craft off the beach, pivoted smartly, and returned to the troopships for another load.

This was the boat the U.S. Marines needed.

Throughout the day, Brute stayed on station with the Japanese landing force. When he returned to Marine headquarters, he began preparing a report titled "Japanese Landing Operations Yangtze Delta Campaign 1937."

The Japanese would land a second force at Hangchow Bay, also observed by Krulak. During the ten days the operations took place, Brute saw landing craft on the beach being repaired. Because they were upside down, he could see design features not visible earlier. The bottom of each craft had two skegs that enabled the boat to remain stable and upright when driven onto the beach. He took notes — lots of notes.

THE fighting in Shanghai was an intense time for Brute. From his almost daily post atop the Palace Hotel, he took numerous photographs of the war unfolding below him. His scrapbook of that time, embossed with a fiery dragon, is filled with rare photographs that show low-flying Japanese aircraft, bombs falling, explosions, wrecked buildings, and streets littered with bodies. Shanghai was the first of the world's great metropolitan areas to suffer such horrific destruction at the hands of the Japanese. Damage was in the billions of dollars and affected the country for decades. "The Japanese were very aggressive, unthinking, and almost inhuman in the way they conducted operations," Brute later said.

Several times the Japanese army attempted to drive convoys through the International Settlement, but the Marines stopped them every time. One factor in the Japanese reluctance to press the issue may have been that Japanese officers occasionally visited the Marine Corps rifle range to watch the Marines engage in target practice. The Japanese could not hide their amazement when they saw Marines, using World War I Springfield .03 rifles, hitting twenty-inch bull's-eyes from six hundred yards away.

KRULAK's curiosity also led him to another bold and dangerous act. The Fu Foong Flour Mill and the Foh Sing Flour Mill stood on the banks of Soochow Creek. Krulak climbed to the upper level of the mills' towers and observed the combat taking place across the creek, only yards away from his exposed position. The bayonetings and beheadings were unsettling to watch.

At night he worked on his report of Japanese landing operations. The thirteen-page report contained close-up photographs, engineering drawings, and sketches. It included detailed technical specifications, such as building materials, construction details, dimensions, troop capacity, and speed. Krulak analyzed Japanese use of the craft and the problems they encountered, and he recommended improvements for Navy designers.

Once the report was finished, Brute sent it to the Navy office in Washington responsible for developing new vessels. His youthful exuberance and his confidence caused him to believe that once the Navy received the report, it would move rapidly to build proper landing craft for the Marines.

In the meantime, Japanese advances and the savage fighting began to threaten the Americans directly. On September 15, while Brute was "busy with the war," a Marine came to Krulak's apartment and told Amy to pack a small bag: American military dependents were being evacuated to the Philippines. Amy wanted to talk to Brute, but there was no time. ("I never got to tell my wife goodbye," he later said.)

There is some conflict between Brute's version of events and the versions of others. But there can be no doubt that Amy was eight months pregnant when she was taken down to the Bund, the embanked riverfront. At the time, there were no piers in Shanghai, and all movement between ship and shore was done by small boats called lighters. Because of fighting surrounding the International Settlement, the *President Jefferson* could not come up the Whangpoo, but had to remain anchored fourteen miles downstream at Woosung, near the mouth of the Yangtze. Amy and the other dependents were ferried downriver. When the Japanese got word that the dependents were leaving, in one of the few acts of wartime consideration they would ever manifest, they stopped the bombing of Shanghai until the dependents were aboard the *Jefferson*.

Beyond this point, certain details are unclear. Brute was ninety-five when he told this story, and two of his sons contest his version of events. But all agree that this was a very difficult time for the family. Amy had only a few changes of clothing and little or no money. The *Jefferson* sailed along the edge of a typhoon several days out of Manila, making most of those aboard terribly sick.

Upon arriving in Manila, Amy stayed at the University Club until, on October 13 at Sternberg General Hospital, she delivered a son, Victor Harold Krulak Jr. (Had the baby been a girl, she would have been named Amy.) Because the University Club did not accept children, Amy stayed in the hospital for some time — Brute said six weeks — before, through the good offices of General Douglas MacArthur's family (who were known to Amy's mother), she moved into a condemned Army barracks. Robert Hogaboom's wife, Jean, and her two children also moved into the barracks. Brute said that he sent Amy $50 through the Navy Relief Society to cover expenses.

In November, Chiang Kai-shek's troops were forced to withdraw from Shanghai, and the Japanese army began pushing harder against the International Settlement. The Japanese could not take over the Settlement, which remained neutral, without risking war with Britain, France, and the United States. Even so, the position of the Marines in Shanghai became even more delicate.

Brute's commanding officer was Colonel Charles F. B. Price, a man with dark, slicked-back hair and a neatly clipped mustache—a somewhat avuncular fellow, but also a "fighting Marine." Price was angry that Japanese soldiers were shooting Chinese civilians in the back when they sought safety in the International Settlement. He was further outraged that Japanese soldiers were committing numerous rapes and conducting public beheadings.

The fighting around Shanghai continued for ninety-two days, and the city suffered 300,000 casualties. Finally, in November, a truce was signed. After their December 3 victory parade through Shanghai, the Japanese became so belligerent toward the International Settlement that British forces left China. Alarmed, the U.S. State Department ordered all Army units in China transferred out, leaving only the Marines to protect American interests. The disparity in numbers did not trouble the Marines. When the Japanese announced that they were going to take over parts of the International Settlement, Price sent word that if they did, they would have to fight the U.S. Marines. The Japanese seethed but did not enter the Settlement.

With Shanghai conquered, the Japanese pushed up the Yangtze and began what history remembers as "the Rape of Nanking"—what writer Iris Chang calls "the forgotten Holocaust." Some 300,000 Chinese soldiers and civilians were killed in about six weeks, the single greatest atrocity by an army in either the Pacific or the European theater of the war.

On Sunday, December 12, the Japanese bombed the *Panay*, a U.S. Navy gunboat anchored twenty-seven miles above Nanking. The *Panay*, painted a brilliant white, was flying a large U.S. ensign and had two large U.S. flags secured to the awnings of her upper deck. The day was clear and the sun sharp when, at 1:38 p.m., Japanese aircraft attacked at close range and sank the *Panay*. The Japanese then sent in barges loaded with soldiers, who machine-gunned any survivors they could find. Two members of the *Panay*'s crew and an Italian newspaperman were killed, and fourteen others were wounded. Those who escaped did so by hiding in the reeds along the riverbank and later making their way to safety.

Several days later, Brute went upriver to see the *Panay*, her bow jutting above the surface, and was outraged. "I wouldn't have been surprised if we had dropped bombs on the Japanese consulate in Shanghai," he said. "I realized this was not going to end."

The *Panay* was the first U.S. Navy vessel ever lost to enemy aircraft, and when news of the sinking reached the United States, there was disbelief and anger. President Roosevelt sent the Japanese a mild memo of protest. The Japanese did not respond directly but announced that they "most deeply" regretted what they said was a case of mistaken identity. Given that a sailor aboard the *Panay* had taken motion pictures of the attack and that those pictures were at such close range that the facial features of the Japanese pilots could be seen, the claim was ludicrous. The footage was so inflammatory that Roosevelt ordered thirty feet of the film excised before it was shown on Movietone News in movie theaters around the country.

A high-ranking staff officer of the Japanese navy, a man educated at an American university, came to Colonel Price's office, where, in a formal and stilted manner, he read a prepared note of apology regarding the *Panay*. Krulak was there. He recalled that Price sat fuming and then, when the Japanese officer finished, stood up, poked his finger at the officer's chest, and said, "You sons of bitches will not get away with this." The Japanese officer "remained at rigid attention while Colonel Price chewed him out."

This would be the strongest rebuke the Japanese received in regard to the *Panay*.

SINKING the *Maine* in Havana harbor was the casus belli for the Spanish-American War; in fact, the rallying cry for that war was "Remember the *Maine*." But only military historians would remember the *Panay*. Within a few weeks, she vanished from the headlines. FDR knew that America was not ready for war, and in any case, his attention remained focused on Germany.

Because America's reaction was so mild—FDR's memo of protest never mentioned retaliation—historians believe that militarists in Japan and Germany took this to mean that America would not actively oppose Japanese aggression in Asia or German aggression in Europe. The two Axis powers continued on the same course. If there remained any Marines who doubted the prophetic report of Pete Ellis, those doubts now disappeared. The Marines dusted off and reread War Plan Orange, the plan for a U.S. offensive against Japan, not realizing that the fundamental premise of the plan—America would set the terms of war—was flawed.

KRULAK says that around Christmas, "Amy and her baby" returned to Shanghai. The Krulak family was reunited at a time when Japanese occupation was well established and life in Shanghai had returned more or less to what it had been before the war.

Early in 1938, the Japanese government paid $2,214,007.36 as settlement for the *Panay*, three Standard Oil tankers sunk in the same attack, and the American casualties. Then the Japanese resumed working overtime to harass the Marines in Shanghai. Just outside the boundary of the International Settlement and in full view of the Marines, the Japanese frequently bayoneted Chinese prisoners for entertainment. Marines defending the Settlement stopped numerous attempts at encroachment but were careful not to provoke the Japanese. When they took action against Japanese troops, the reason was always obvious and justifiable and never gave the Japanese a reason to take over the Settlement. For example, toward the end of his tour, Brute was made commanding officer of a rifle company. One day he was riding around with a platoon leader checking sentry posts when they came upon a Japanese officer and a dozen or so soldiers trying to force their way into the Settlement. The platoon leader stopped, jumped out of the jeep, strode over to the Japanese officer, and knocked him flat. The humiliated officer turned and led his men away.

On April 5, Colonel Price signed a letter to be inserted in Brute's personnel folder. The letter said that Brute had "prepared a special report on Japanese assault landing operations in the Shanghai area" and that "this special study was undertaken largely upon his own initiative and was pursued with zeal, energy and resourcefulness inspired by personal interest in this professional subject far beyond the normal call of duty." The letter ended by saying, "The result was an intelligence document of great value to the Naval Service and this young officer deserves special credit therefore."

On May 4, the record shows that Krulak was "submitted for special commendation for his excellent performance of duty under hazardous conditions during the late Sino-Japanese conflict."

On September 26, the *Chaumont*, a Navy transport vessel, called in Shanghai. Amy's father had finished his tour at the Academy and had returned to sea duty as skipper of the *Chaumont*. Brute and Amy took young Victor out to the ship so that Amy's father could meet him. Upon his return, Brute wrote his Naval Academy mentor, now Colonel Holland M. Smith, offering to make any purchases the colonel wanted—silver, rugs, furniture, linens—and send them back to America aboard the *Chaumont*. Was Krulak simply offering a kindness to the man responsible for his joining the Marine Corps, or was he fawning over a senior officer whom he knew he would encounter again? Probably a bit of both.

Most of the diplomatic world was deeply concerned about the possibility of war in Europe, but the Marines were concerned about Shanghai, where tensions between them and Japanese troops remained high. On August 13, Gunnery Sergeant Milton "Slug" Marvin was leading a patrol through Shanghai when he saw four Japanese soldiers threatening a man flying the Chinese Nationalist flag over his home. One of the Japanese soldiers pulled a pistol and forced the Chinese man to lower the flag. Marvin ordered the Japanese to move on. When they refused, he swung his rifle butt and knocked the Japanese officer to the ground. Then he arrested the Japanese soldiers and charged them with disturbing the peace.

Despite repeated efforts by the Japanese to destabilize the International Settlement, life and parties and grand old times continued. But it was a fragile peace.

In March 1939, Brute's FitRep said that he was "excellent" or "outstanding" in all categories save physical fitness, military bearing, and leadership. The narrative portion reported, "He is conscientious and energetic. He is quick to recognize any duty and prompt and forceful in its execution." His final FitRep from China was dated May 11, 1939, and he was graded "outstanding" in all categories except military bearing and leadership. Despite his daring acts during the Japanese invasion of Shanghai, his brilliant study of Japanese landing craft, and his ability to instill discipline and respect in the enlisted ranks, Brute Krulak's superiors still believed that he did not look like a real Marine.

In May, Brute, Amy, and Victor Jr. departed China for Marine Corps Base Quantico in Virginia. The sea voyage was interminable to Brute. He was an impatient man and believed that by now the Navy should be well along on plans to develop a landing craft based on the study he had submitted some eighteen months earlier.

Krulak looked back on China with good feelings. He had been present at what many historians believe was the opening stage of World War II. He had seen war firsthand, and had even sailed among a Japanese landing force, an adventure he would describe many years later as "the most exciting experience of all my life." He had begun to mature militarily and had lived a cosmopolitan existence; in fact, the roots of the smooth and urbane general he would become were planted in Shanghai. But, like other Marines who served on the China Station during the late 1930s, he would remember Shanghai for another reason: that was where he learned how the Japanese waged war.

# 4

## Stand By to Launch

MARINE Corps Base Quantico sits on the west bank of the Potomac River a half-hour drive south of Washington. Because at some time during his career almost every Marine officer is stationed at Quantico, the base is called "the Crossroads of the Marine Corps."

Brute Krulak came to Quantico during the late summer of 1939 to become a student at what was then called the Junior School (today the Expeditionary Warfare School). He enrolled at a time when amphibious warfare was about to become more than the specialty of the Marines Corps; it would be crucial to the security of America.

British military historian J. F. C. Fuller, U.S. Army general Dwight Eisenhower, and even Adolf Hitler all said that the most important piece of tactical equipment in World War II—in North Africa, in the Pacific, and at Normandy—was the Higgins boat, the landing craft that took Marines, soldiers, and their equipment from ship to shore. In fact, Higgins boats put more men and equipment on the beach than did all other types of boats combined. Eisenhower, a man not given to hyperbole, told historian Stephen Ambrose that the Higgins boat "won the war for us."

The man usually given credit for the boat and for the doctrine regarding its use is Holland Smith, who, in the prewar years, was responsible for developing the landing craft. But if we zoom in tightly and take a look at the Marine officer most deeply involved in the development of the boat, especially the most crucial design feature, we see Brute Krulak everywhere. Thus a large part of the credit for America's victory in the Pacific, the successful D-Day landing, and ultimately America's triumph in World War II can be traced to a single junior Marine officer. This seems a bold and foolish statement, the type of flat assertion so abhorred by historians, so let us look at those years.

AMERICA had not yet begun the buildup for World War II, and the Marine Corps budget was so austere that the quartermaster computed the number of sheets of toilet paper a Marine should use on a daily visit to the "head" and issued supplies accordingly. Nevertheless, the Marine Corps has always believed that it should be the most ready for war when the country is the least ready.

Hitler's pursuit of lebensraum had resulted in his troops taking over Austria in 1938 and Czechoslovakia in early 1939. The emerging Marine Corps leadership, most of whom had fought at Belleau Wood, knew that Britain's policy of appeasement would not mollify Hitler, and they burned the midnight oil in refining a doctrine that most of the world's military forces considered outmoded: amphibious warfare. The year Krulak enrolled in the Junior School was the year Liddell Hart wrote that landing on a defended coast, always a hazardous operation, was now "almost impossible." The Marines did not believe that Hart knew what he was talking about. Nor did they believe that the "blue-green split" — the division of funds between the Navy and the Marines — was equitable. They wanted more green.

It was at the Junior School that Krulak met Merrill "Bill" Twining, a lawyer and the third man who would have a great influence on his career. Twining's cerebral approach to issues intrigued Krulak, who later said, "Bill Twining was my idol from the time I met him." Twining, Holland Smith, and Gerald Thomas would, in World War II and beyond, become part of the senior Marine Corps leadership, and, along with Lemuel Shepherd, would each play a role in Krulak's meteoric rise.

At Quantico, Krulak and his fellow students listened with rapt attention as Major Gerald Thomas, who had been Brute's instructor five years earlier at The Basic School, spun out his famous lectures on amphibious landings. Thomas's assistant was Captain David Shoup, a former farm boy from Indiana who would receive the Medal of Honor in World War II and become Commandant of the Marine Corps. Shoup and Krulak would have their differences.

An amphibious assault on a defended position is among the most complex of military operations. It is a "hard" landing in which the attacking force will suffer heavy casualties. In fact, if the landing is not well executed, the results can be catastrophic. The two defining characteristics of a successful assault are detailed planning and violent execution. And once a beachhead is established, it is crucial to push inland as quickly as possible. The idea is not simply to seize a beach but to take enemy-held territory.

At the end of the day, the Quantico lectures were merely academic, because nothing taught by Thomas and Shoup could be implemented. The Navy had only eighteen landing boats, and they were the same ones that had been used in 1898 to land in Cuba during the Spanish-American War.

The U.S. Navy reveres tradition. Thus when war is imminent, Navy planning revolves around the last war. What worked in World War I was now proven doctrine. The Navy believed that if war came in Europe, France would hold off the small German fleet and French ports would remain open. Further, Navy transports would haul American troops to a protected dock, just as they

73

had done at Le Havre in World War I, and thereafter the troops would march off the boat, get into trucks, and go to war. There would be no need for those newfangled landing craft the Marines were talking about. Besides, amphibious landings were a simple mechanical operation, and Navy launches were sufficient for the job.

In the Pacific, the Navy remained focused on traditional fleet battles—that is, great armadas of battleships, aircraft carriers, destroyers, cruisers, and frigates slugging it out. Dealing with landing craft was, well, beneath the Navy.

As for the Army, in 1939 its strategy remained centered on large-scale land campaigns, and it would be another year before it expressed any interest in amphibious warfare. Thus had there not been a Marine Corps strategy based on amphibious assaults, the doctrine, organization, and equipment used in World War II would not have been available until much later in the war, and the cost in lives is impossible to estimate.

HOLLAND Smith was now a brigadier general commanding the 1st Marine Brigade at Quantico. He was in charge of amphibious training on the East Coast and had a mandate to refine amphibious landing doctrine and develop a landing craft suitable for hauling Marines and their equipment ashore on a hostile beach. The Navy frustrated his every move and seemed determined to slow his headlong rush toward his destiny in the Pacific.

Brute contacted General Smith soon after arriving at Quantico, and a few days later the general dined with the Krulaks, something he would do often in the coming months. General officers do not socialize with first lieutenants, and nothing better illustrates the special relationship between Smith and Krulak than their frequent dinners. Krulak said that he found Smith "to be a tremendously spiritual man, willing to be regarded as a practicing Christian and anxious to do the things that a practicing Christian is supposed to do." He also said that Smith "was a terrifying man if he elected to be mad....Once he told me that the greatest weapon that one can have is controlled anger, and the greatest defect that one can have is uncontrolled anger."

Smith's fatherly attitude toward Brute was demonstrated one night when a very pregnant Amy came downstairs complaining that a rat was in her dresser drawer. The general ran upstairs, grabbed the rat by its tail, hit it smartly on the head, and tossed it outside. Brute enjoyed telling fellow officers the rat story because what he was really telling them was that General Smith had dined at his house.

IT should be understood that these dinners were not one-sided conversations where the junior officer listened and nodded as the general expounded on various topics. Krulak had thoughts on just about everything and was not reluctant to express them. Both Smith and Krulak had a passionate interest in amphibious landings. The general was intense in discussing how the Marines needed landing craft and some sort of vehicle that could move Marines across the coral reefs that surrounded many Pacific islands. In China, Brute had seen things few Marine officers had seen and could respond with firsthand information about Japanese landing craft and with piercing tactical observations of how the Japanese conducted amphibious operations.

Smith's second-favorite dinner table topic was ongoing Army and Navy attempts to get rid of the Marine Corps. This awareness is a necessary attribute of any senior Marine, but Smith would take it to an extreme that would result in increased interservice squabbling and even have strategic implications. Indeed, Smith's obsessive protectiveness toward the Marine Corps was his greatest flaw (although Marines do not see it as such), and he would pass that obsession on to Brute Krulak.

The constant jockeying of the Army and Navy, and later the

Air Force, to take over or absorb Marine Corps functions may seem tangential to Krulak's story. But Krulak's time with Smith at Quantico, and later in the Pacific, insinuated into his DNA the need for vigilance toward the other services. Krulak would see numerous examples of Army and Navy animus in the Pacific during World War II, in the bitter military unification battle after the war, in Korea, and in Vietnam. And his farewell speech to the Marine Corps would call on all Marines to be alert against the other services. Protecting Marine Corps interests was the core issue of Krulak's thirty-four-year military career, and it came from Holland Smith.

At the Krulak dinners, Smith gained a greater appreciation of Brute's wide-ranging intellect and realized that his surrogate son had become the sort of young officer who could make a general look good. Brute was still a student when Smith asked him if upon graduation he would be interested in becoming the general's aide. Few jobs in the military offer a better chance for promotion than does being a general's aide-de-camp, and most lieutenants would have immediately agreed. Not Krulak.

"I wanted more than that, and I told him so," Brute said, explaining that he wanted a substantive job in addition to being aide. And he did not want to wait until after graduation to go to work for Smith. He wanted to begin immediately.

And he did.

That Krulak was able to carry on as a student, perform the work expected of an aide-de-camp, and keep the demanding and hard-edged Smith happy is a measure of his energy and intellect. But there was something left undone, something Krulak had to resolve. The Navy had remained silent regarding Krulak's study of Japanese amphibious landings in China, and he wanted to know what was being done about his ideas for a new landing craft. Krulak was granted permission to take a day off and go into Washington to visit the Navy office responsible for these matters.

"I went up there thinking I might find someone who knew something of my report and who would tell me the status" of how it was affecting the design of landing craft, he recalled. "Neither turned out to be true." He and a Navy officer searched for an hour before finding the study in the back of a file cabinet. On the cover sheet was a handwritten notation: "Prepared by some nut out in China." The Navy officer thumbed the report, looked at a few of the sketches, laughed, and handed the report to Krulak. "The person who wrote that did not know the bow of a boat from the stern," he said.

Krulak disagreed, saying the Japanese had developed a boat with a blunt bow and a pointed stern.

"How do you know that?" the Navy officer said.

"I wrote this. My name is Krulak."

The Navy officer was not embarrassed.

Krulak found out that the Navy was drifting along with three different designs for landing craft—all modified versions of Atlantic fishing boats—and had not the slightest interest in the proven Japanese design. So he returned to Quantico and for the next week spent his evenings building a two-foot balsa-wood model of what he thought a proper landing craft should look like. Building the bow ramp was the most difficult part, but he solved that by using tiny wires to hold the lowered ramp steady. On the wall over his head as he worked was a framed quote from President Calvin Coolidge: "Doubters do not achieve; skeptics do not contribute; cynics do not create."

When Krulak finished the model, he showed it to General Smith, explaining such details as the "tunnel stern" shaped like an inverted V to protect the propeller, skegs to stabilize the boat when it was run up on the beach, and the bow that pivoted down and out to form a ramp. He explained how there must be sufficient horsepower both to push the heavily loaded boat onto an enemy-held beach and hold firmly as Marines stormed ashore, and then to extract the bow from the sand and pivot in the surf before returning to the offshore troop carrier.

Smith was fascinated by the detailed model, nodding in agreement as Brute detailed various features. When Krulak was through, Smith picked up the telephone and called General Thomas Holcomb, Commandant of the Marine Corps. The conversation was brief, and when it was over, Smith turned to Brute and said, "You are going to brief the Commandant. I will take you over there and sit in on the briefing." Krulak nodded and acted as if he had fully expected that this would happen. With perfect aplomb, he picked up his model and followed Smith to the Commandant's office. This may have been the only time in Marine Corps history that a mere lieutenant briefed a Commandant on the most critical problem facing the Marines.

Krulak recalled that the Commandant was "keenly interested" in the model and that he talked of the Marine Corps's "tremendous shortfall of landing craft" and of keeping pressure on the Navy to let the Corps design its own craft. According to Krulak, the Commandant said that the Navy designs were "totally useless. None of them were worth a damn." After the meeting, Krulak said, General Smith "congratulated me on my hard work and told me to press forward" with developing the much-needed landing craft.

Meeting with the Commandant was important. Although there was an equipment board headed by a general who had day-to-day responsibility for developing landing craft, in reality the two most important men in the Marine Corps regarding this issue were the Commandant and Holland Smith, both of whom now looked on Krulak as the expert on the subject. Krulak had come up with the solution to a most vexing problem and would henceforth be what

Smith called his "boat man," responsible for all matters regarding landing craft.

It is axiomatic in the Marine Corps that several things are fraught with peril. One is a corporal wearing the white duty belt that is the symbol of authority for the corporal of the guard. Another is a general with a map. Perhaps more dangerous than either is a self-confident lieutenant possessed of a big idea and a general's support. Smith had unleashed a tornado of enthusiasm.

Krulak thought that it would be a good idea to show his boat model to high-ranking Navy officers and that the model, along with his pictures and drawings of Japanese landing craft, might influence Navy thinking. The Commandant agreed and set up the meeting. Krulak made his presentation and was dismissed, with Navy officials saying they would consider the proposal and respond at a later date.

SOME people, including a prominent Marine historian, would later say that Brute Krulak owed his career to the generals for whom he was an aide or staff officer. This argument has some merit. Certainly, as Smith's aide Krulak would be given what for a first lieutenant were extraordinary responsibilities, and the man whose early FitReps were a bit weak would be, like many young officers in World War II, promoted rapidly. But another argument is that Krulak was a brilliant officer whose vision and energy made a number of generals look very good indeed. He performed admirably in every staff job to which he was assigned, and the generals for whom he worked showed their appreciation by seeing that he was promoted rapidly.

As 1940 arrived, Brute planned a party to celebrate his twenty-seventh birthday. It was the first of what would become many legendary birthday parties, primarily because he served large amounts of Fish House Punch, a beverage that, like its equally infamous cousin Artillery Punch, had originated during the Revolutionary War. There is no precise recipe for Fish House Punch; one simply mixes rum and brandy with lemons and sugar. The purpose of the last two ingredients is to cover the hammer hiding in the first two. Serving the punch in an elegant silver bowl that had belonged to Amy's mother, Brute presented it as a bright and lovely drink; when consumed, it invariably evoked such perky comments as "It tastes like fruit juice." During the evening, the color of the punch might change from a pale, almost iridescent tan to a deep amber, depending on the proportions of rum and brandy.

Fish House Punch is an insidious drink that, after two glasses, causes a peculiar numbness around the ears. After three glasses, a man believes he is the smartest person God ever created. Then comes the moment when he thinks bugs are crawling all over his body. As the body's systems begin shutting down, the numbness around the ears changes to a humming noise that causes the man to believe he is becoming deaf. Then his vision blurs, and the hinges in his knees go wobbly. The man can slow the loss of motor skills by maneuvering on his hands and knees for a while, and there is a compensatory moment when he feels compelled to talk in a loud voice, even to sing. But finally he is rendered confused and babbling and, mercifully, is possessed of amnesia.

Brute invited some of the highest-ranking officers on base to his party. By then he was well-known in the still-small prewar Marine Corps. There was talk of his intelligence coup in China, of his expertise regarding amphibious landing craft, and, of course, of his friendship with General Smith and his audience with the Commandant. As a result, his first party was widely attended. And because the first one was such a success, so were subsequent festivities. Some of the most senior and most famous Marines of the 1940s, 1950s, and 1960s would be laid low by Brute's Fish House Punch.

At one of the early parties, one guest who had had too much to drink disappeared, along with the turkey that was on the dining room table. When Amy sent everyone in search of the turkey, someone opened a closet door, and there sat the officer, a future Commandant of the Marine Corps, with the turkey between his legs, eating away.

ON October 6, 1940, Amy had her second child, another boy, named William. She had not been able to reach Brute on the telephone to tell him she was about to give birth, so she had walked to the base hospital, admitted herself, and delivered the child.

"I was busy at the office," Brute recalled. "She found she had to go, so she went."

Brute had his job; Amy had hers.

WHILE he was at Quantico, Brute discovered *A Message to Garcia*, a slim little book about Lieutenant Andrew Rowan of the U.S. Army. When the Spanish-American War broke out, Rowan was assigned the task of carrying a message from President William McKinley to an insurgent Cuban leader named Garcia. No one knew Garcia's location, only that he was somewhere in the mountains of Cuba. Rowan's instructions were straightforward: take the message to Garcia. Rowan asked no questions, simply made his way to Florida, hired a small open boat, landed on the Cuban coast at night, disappeared into the jungle, found Garcia, delivered the message, and returned to America.

To Krulak the book symbolized the Marine Corps ethos of following orders without question, of doing an assigned task without asking directions. Over the years, Krulak would buy and give away thousands of copies of the book. And today there is no greater compliment for a Marine than to be known as someone who can "take a message to Garcia."

* * *

By the time Brute graduated from Junior School in June, Denmark, Norway, the Netherlands, and Belgium had fallen to the Germans. Then France fell, and on June 14, the day German boots were heard on the Champs-Elysées, President Roosevelt signed a bill giving the Navy the authority to build a "two-ocean Navy." Army and Navy expenditures rose from $1.8 billion in fiscal year 1940 to $6.3 billion in fiscal year 1941.

With the fall of France, Britain stood alone against Hitler's seemingly unstoppable army. Prime Minister Winston Churchill beseeched President Roosevelt for help. With the fall of France also came the realization that when America invaded Europe, this time there would be no sailing up to the docks at Le Havre.

Brute was assigned to General's Smith's 1st Marine Brigade, where, in addition to continuing his job as the general's aide, he became the assistant logistics officer. Over the next two years, he would write Marine Corps logistical doctrine for amphibious warfare. Such doctrine is infinitely complex and includes such arcane matter as the "combat loading" of a ship—that is, how to load a ship so that the equipment most needed by a Marine landing force is in position to be unloaded first.

But most important, Krulak became Smith's point man in developing amphibious landing craft. In August, he was promoted to captain, and in September Smith wrote a FitRep describing Krulak as "one of the finest officers I have ever known, highly intelligent, gets things done." He was now to prove it.

On October 2, the Navy's Bureau of Ships responded to the presentation Krulak had made the previous year, acknowledging his model of his proposed landing craft but adding that such boats had to be built "in accordance with existing designs." The correspondence closed with the thought that Krulak's ideas "could well be investigated when time permits."

A few days later, Smith's 5,000-man brigade was ordered to Guantánamo Bay, Cuba, where it would grow into the 22,000-man 1st Marine Division. One of its jobs would be to test the new amphibious tractor called the Alligator, a vehicle Smith thought might solve the problem of crossing reefs on Pacific atolls.

Meanwhile, two parallel stories had been gathering force and were now beginning to intersect with the story of Brute Krulak. These stories feature two relatively unknown civilians who would do what the U.S. Navy could not do — design and build the most important naval vessels of World War II. In so doing, they would become two of the unsung heroes of World War II.

The first was Donald Roebling, who had designed an amphibious vehicle he called the Alligator as a post-hurricane rescue vehicle in Florida. The vehicle was powered by a Ford V-8 engine and had tracks that enabled it to climb over obstacles in the water. Even though the Marines envisioned the Alligator as a logistics vehicle, Roebling was reluctant to release the vehicle for Marine Corps testing: the Alligator was for rescue work, not for war. But in May 1938, Roebling relented. A Marine officer went to Florida to put the vehicle through every test imaginable, then recommended that the Navy buy Alligators for the Marines. The Navy refused. Nevertheless, a year later two Marine officers convinced Roebling to design a military version of the Alligator. By the late spring of 1940, Roebling had designed and built a lighter, more powerful model that was quite seaworthy. (Despite his initial reluctance, Roebling personally funded almost all the development costs, more than $60,000, which in 1940 was the equivalent of several hundred thousand dollars today.) In late 1940, the Navy placed an initial order for one hundred Alligators for the Marines. During the war in the Pacific, derivatives of this vehicle, while technically known as "landing vehicles, tracked," or LVTs, were known generically as amphibious tractors, or amtracs.

Parallel with Roebling's story, and more relevant to Krulak's career, is the story of Andrew Jackson Higgins, a builder of small boats in New Orleans, whose story is told by Jerry E. Strahan in *Andrew Jackson Higgins and the Boats That Won World War II.* Higgins was brilliant and hot tempered, a dreamer with a disciplined mind, and a cyclonic personality who had developed impatience into an art form. He had a burning patriotism rarely equaled in the business world, and he trampled anything and everything that tried to prevent him from doing his job *now.* Higgins could take a message to Garcia. He and the Marines were a natural fit.

In the 1930s, Louisiana fur trappers needed rugged, shallow draft boats to navigate streams obstructed by fallen trees, vegetation, and sandbars. In response to this need, Higgins built what he called the Eureka, a flat-bottomed boat with the propeller housed in a protective tunnel. Rather than the conventional pointed bow, the Eureka had a somewhat rounded bow that Higgins called a "spoonbill." It was the strongest part of the boat and enabled the craft to run full speed up on riverbanks and sandbars and over obstacles in the water. The boat had a draft of about ten inches and could reach what was then considered high speed for such a vessel — twenty miles per hour.

Higgins also built "patrol craft" that he sold to the Coast Guard to chase rumrunners. It is a measure of his entrepreneurial spirit that after he sold the boat to the Coast Guard, he convinced the rumrunners to buy faster boats so that they could outrun the Coast Guard. Then he persuaded the Coast Guard to replace his earlier boat with an even faster model. These boats were the forerunners of the famed World War II patrol torpedo, or PT, boats. Both Higgins and the Electric Boat Company built PT boats, and both designs would gain renown because of their bold missions in the Pacific. In addition, one of these boats, skippered by a young Navy officer named John F. Kennedy, would come to Krulak's aid in a daring rescue mission on a dark and dangerous night in the Solomon Islands.

THE Eureka may have been the ugliest boat ever built, but it was so practical that by 1937, it was owned and operated by a half-dozen government agencies. Higgins approached the Navy about considering a version of his boat as a landing craft, but the Navy favored either its own designers or one of the famous boatyards along the eastern seaboard with a long history of building "proper" boats. Why should the Navy consider a southern boatbuilder? In addition, to the Navy Higgins was a joke; his boatyard was not even on the water.

When the Navy requested bids for shallow draft boats, Higgins was not notified. But he found out about the request and sent an intemperate letter to the Navy saying that his Eureka was better than anything any East Coast builder could design. The Navy did not respond.

Yet in all of the Navy and Marines' annual fleet exercises, the landing boats they tested proved to be unmitigated disasters. The Marines needed a specific design, but the Navy still insisted on a boat with a deep V bottom, a relatively sharp bow, and high gunwales—a boat seaworthy enough to move cargo and personnel between larger vessels when at sea and at the same time stout enough to be an assault boat that could run up on a beach. Such multipurpose designs were favored throughout the military and even today are illustrative of a great flaw in military thinking.

In May 1938, the Navy gave Higgins $5,200 to build an experimental thirty-foot landing craft. The boat Higgins built cost almost $13,000, but this was his long-sought chance to get his foot in the Navy door, and he did not mind losing money. He even paid the shipping fee to get the boat to the Norfolk Naval

Shipyard in Virginia. Once there, he was charged an exorbitant fee to use a Navy crane to unload the boat from a railroad car.

The next day, the boat was sailed to Virginia Beach. Upon approaching the beach, the Navy crew prepared to drop a stern anchor as they always did with landing craft, in order to more easily pull the boat off the beach when they were ready to leave. The captain whom Higgins had sent along said the anchor was not necessary. The Eureka cut through the surf, the officers disembarked onto the beach, and as they watched in amazement, the captain backed off smartly, spun the boat around in its own length, and headed back out to sea. A few days later, the captain did the same thing in five-foot seas.

The Navy response was to steal part of the Higgins design and use it in its own boat. But Navy designers missed the point of the tunnel drive and did not shape the bottom properly, thus rendering their "new" boat almost as useless as their old one.

The fleet exercises in 1939 were especially important because it was then that the Navy finally realized that traditional designs would not work for a landing craft. The competition to build a new landing craft came down to two contenders: the Navy's own Bureau of Construction and Repair and Higgins. Each would build one boat to be tested in a head-to-head competition, and the winner would receive a contract to build multiple boats. The Bureau of Construction asked for a thirty-foot boat because that was the size that would fit between the davits on a ship. Higgins suggested that the davits be moved farther apart, angrily saying that the "Bureau of Shit" was asking for a boat too short for its beam. At his own expense, he built a thirty-six-foot boat and paid for it to be shipped to Norfolk. Of course, the Navy was dismayed that the boat was not what it had ordered and dithered about, wondering whether the boat should even be tested.

By now Brute, still a student at the Junior School, was following General Smith's mandate to press on with his interest in landing craft. He talked to Higgins by telephone several times a week. Higgins did not know that Brute was a student and did not care that he was just a lieutenant. "He didn't know the difference," Brute said. "All he knew was that I worked for General Smith."

Higgins was delighted to find someone who seemed to understand what he was trying to do, and Krulak was delighted to find many of the qualities he wanted in a landing craft in the Higgins boat. Indeed, the Higgins boat was very close to what the Marines needed. When Krulak learned that the Navy might not test the thirty-six-foot version, he told General Smith that the boat deserved a chance. Smith agreed, and on September 11 the new Eureka demonstrated that it could easily retract from a beach, that it exceeded the Navy's speed requirements, and that it was in all ways superior to the Navy design.

On November 18, 1940, Higgins was awarded a $3 million token contract to build Eureka boats and PT boats. He wrote to Smith, saying, "I am quite sure that had it not been for the championing of, and the interest of the Marines, that boat would not have been tested." And Smith would later write in his autobiography, "Andrew Higgins, a fighting Irishman, won the opening phase of the boat battle single handed, with loud Marine applause."

The Higgins yard was so small that Higgins did not have room to set up an assembly line for the new boats. He took over unused land in a nearby cemetery, with the result being that almost half of his production facility was on land he did not own.

Now, with Roebling and his Alligator and Higgins and his Eureka in place, we can go ashore at Guantánamo Bay and resume Brute Krulak's story.

# 5

## The Bridge to the Beach

AFTER World War II, General Holland M. Smith said that if Waterloo was won on the playing fields of Eton, the great battles of the Pacific were won in the Caribbean.

He said this because in late October 1940, he and his 1st Marine Brigade arrived at Guantánamo Bay, hacked their way ashore, built an enormous tent village, and for twelve hours a day, seven days a week, practiced how to establish and control a beachhead and how to move inland against enemy resistance. Smith's Marines cursed their chow, their officers, and their decision to become Marines. They were driven so hard that they called themselves "the raggedy-assed Marines," but the training was preparing them for a battle almost as important as Belleau Wood.

After several months, Smith told Brute that the first Alligator built for the Marines had arrived and that Brute would be in charge of determining whether it was capable of carrying men and equipment across coral reefs. Krulak's tests would determine whether the Marine Corps accepted the Alligator for the coming war.

How could a twenty-seven-year-old captain have so much

authority in a matter of such critical national importance? "Because General Smith said so," Krulak explained.

KRULAK now found himself in the enviable position of having a high-ranking mentor—what Marines call a "sea daddy"—and a job that, if performed to Smith's exacting standards, could overcome his early FitReps. This was his chance, and he bent to the task. He spent ten days designing a rigorous testing program, then drove the Alligator through high seas, horsed it around in the surf, and sought out rough beaches to traverse. He found numerous problems with the Alligator's track bearings, transmission, steering, clutches, and treads, which easily broke. When a staff colonel arrived from Quantico to check on the testing and ask what Krulak had found wrong with the Alligator, Krulak answered, "Do you have several hours?"

The colonel chewed Krulak out for being a wise guy.

Then Brute went to Culebra, an island off Puerto Rico, to test the Alligator's ability to cross coral reefs. The testing coincided with a combined Army, Navy, and Marine fleet exercise called FLEX-7, commanded by the haughty Admiral Ernest J. King— the man alleged to have said, "When trouble starts, they call for us sons of bitches." If King did say that, he would have been the first one called. His daughter said that he was the most eventempered man in the Navy: he was always in a rage. He was also a resolute man with an aggressive mind-set and one of the most brilliant naval strategists in American history.

While Brute was testing the Alligator, he went aboard King's flagship, the *Wyoming*, and persuaded Smith to allow him to ask King if he would like to see the new Alligator. King said he would, so Krulak ran the Alligator around the ship a few times, then climbed back aboard, approached the imperious admiral, and said, "Sir, I'd like very much to give you a ride."

The admiral said he was too busy.

"Sir, it will be a short ride."

The admiral relented. Resplendent in his immaculate white uniform, left chest ablaze with row upon row of ribbons, and accompanied by an aide, the admiral climbed aboard the Alligator. After a few maneuvers, Krulak said, "Now let me show you what it will do on a coral reef, Admiral."

King looked at his watch. "I don't have time."

"Sir, it will only take a minute." Krulak accelerated the engine, ran the Alligator hard onto a reef, broke one of the treads, and found himself stranded atop the coral in four feet of water.

During the next few minutes, Krulak learned that the admiral's reputation for being ill-tempered was not without foundation. "The things he said to me were unprintable," Krulak remembered.

Eventually, the admiral paused for breath, took another look at his watch, and, followed by his aide, climbed over the side of the Alligator. In chest-deep water, he stopped, looked back at Krulak, and said, "Captain, have you considered a civilian career?" Then, cursing the entire time, he waded ashore.

Krulak sat atop the broken Alligator pondering an uncertain future.

He need not have worried. Smith's May 5, 1941, FitRep described Krulak as "an outstanding type of young officer. Has no equal in the Marine Corps, of comparable rank."

As FLEX-7 was winding down, Krulak concluded that the Alligator's shortcomings could be fixed and that if his recommended improvements were incorporated into production models, this was the vehicle the Marines should take into a war in the Pacific. Until its existence was later revealed in the *New York Times*, the improved vehicle, called the amtrac, would be something of a secret weapon, taking the Marines across the coral at places of their own choosing and enabling them to ignore the easy beaches where Japanese defenders expected them to come ashore. The irony is that the Marines still saw the amtrac as a logistics vehicle, and it would not be until 1943 that they realized it would make a splendid assault vehicle.

No matter where he was or what he was doing, Krulak overflowed with ideas. While testing the Alligator, he decided that he could waterproof a jeep so the jeep could be driven ashore from a landing craft. His early efforts were less than successful, and saltwater intrusion ruined the jeep's engine. The Marine Corps quartermaster was outraged: who had authorized this, and why was an amphibious jeep necessary? When Krulak was less than diplomatic in his answer, the quartermaster demanded that he pay for the jeep. General Smith interceded, saying that Krulak had only been doing his job.

FLEX-7 was the last combined fleet exercise before World War II and was important for a number of reasons. First, the exercise foreshadowed numerous interservice problems that would arise during the war. For instance, during the exercise the Navy had aerial photos of the beaches on which the Marines would be landing but would not show the pictures to Smith. When Admiral King insisted on selecting the beach on which the Marines would land, he picked a wide, shallow beach backed by a swamp and steep mountains, a combination that would not allow the Marines to move inland. Only when Smith pointed out these problems did King reluctantly allow him to choose the beach.

Belleau Wood had shown how difficult it was for Marines to take a strongly defended position without the help of artillery and tanks, but the Navy had only three landing craft capable of moving tanks and artillery ashore. During FLEX-7, one of these boats capsized, and the tank it was carrying fell into the sea. Had it not settled upright, it would have been lost.

FLEX-7 also revealed to the Army that it had no amphibious background and was not prepared for a war in the Pacific. But like the Navy, the Army believed that moving men from ship to shore was a simple mechanical operation. The Army would eventually alleviate this deficiency by simply expropriating Marine amphibious doctrine.

After the exercise, the Marines realized that serious problems resulted from their being tied to the Navy during an amphibious assault. The Navy wanted control of everything. The Marines had no problem with the Navy running the show until the landing force was on the beach, but then the offensive was up to the Marines, and they believed that they should be in charge. At what point in an amphibious landing the Navy should relinquish control to the Marines was an issue that would plague the two services throughout the war.

Finally, admirals who thought they were generals would attempt to interfere with Marine ground tactics throughout the war. King was one of those admirals. During one planning session when Smith referred to the "beachhead," King snapped, "I'm sick and tired of hearing the word 'beachhead.' It's a beach, not a beachhead. Why don't you Marines get it straight?"

Here the admiral was wrong. A beach ends near the water's edge and may be held by enemy forces. But a beachhead extends landward and refers to a Marine-controlled piece of real estate hosting a body of troops sufficient to launch an inland attack on enemy forces.

Such interservice conflict exacerbated Smith's paranoia about Navy encroachments on the Marine Corps. Again and again, he told Brute always to be conscious of Marine Corps interests and that he believed America was not prepared for the coming Pacific war.

An extraordinary foreshadowing of events occurred during FLEX-7 when an operation called for the Army to defend a beach against a Marine landing. Army general Walter Short was in charge of Army troops and decided not to defend a portion of the beach because he believed the Marines would land elsewhere. Marine general Lemuel Shepherd landed at night on the undefended beach and captured Short's entire headquarters staff. Short responded by telling Shepherd that if this were really war, he and his Army troops could defeat the Marines within several days. Then he used his seniority to nullify the capture of his headquarters.

From this exercise, Short would be sent to Hawaii to assume command of the Army's defense of Pearl Harbor. Lemuel Shepherd would become one of the heroes of the Pacific campaign.

Upon returning from Culebra in the spring of 1941, a group of Army and Navy observers gathered on the beach at New River, North Carolina, to observe tests of a Navy-designed landing craft. Smith was the senior observer, and by his side, always making his thoughts known, was Brute Krulak.

The Navy landing craft stopped about fifty yards offshore, and the Marines on board jumped overboard into water over their heads. Fortunately, all made it to shore. Then came two larger landing craft, each carrying a tank. A cable broke on one of the landing craft, and the tank fell into deep water. Fortunately, the crew scrambled out and swam ashore. Disgusted, General Smith turned to look for the other tank and saw a young officer some distance from shore in water up to his knees. "What are you doing out there?" Smith shouted. "Where is the tank?"

The young officer snapped to attention, saluted, and said, "Sir, I'm standing on it."

Clearly, the Navy-designed landing craft still needed work.

A few weeks later, top military planners told the Marines that the Caribbean island of Martinique, a French territory, might be taken over by the Germans. Hitler's troops could not be allowed to hold an island so close to America, and if the Germans did occupy Martinique, retaking the island would require an amphibious assault. Smith feared that the Navy would give him landing craft that would result in Marines dying needlessly, so he sent Brute to New Orleans to meet with Higgins and tell him exactly what the Marines wanted. No more dillydallying with the Navy—it was time for the Marines to take charge.

Several stories exist as to how Higgins first saw pictures of the Japanese landing craft with the drop bow. In his biography, Strahan says that Higgins was at Quantico in the spring of 1941 and viewed the images there. Another version says that Krulak went to New Orleans and showed Higgins the pictures. It doesn't matter who showed the pictures to Higgins; the important thing is that Krulak took them. And all accounts agree that Higgins was taken with the idea and agreed to build landing craft with a drop bow.

When Krulak told this story, his eyes lit up and he vividly remembered his dealings with Higgins, even though more than sixty years had passed. " 'No' or 'It can't be done' or 'Impossible' were not in his lexicon," Krulak said. "No one can overstate Higgins's contribution to the war."

On all matters regarding amphibious craft, Krulak was the Marine Corps's liaison with the Navy in Washington. On trips to the capital, Krulak tried to avoid Admiral King, but occasionally the two passed in the hall. Each time, the Navy officer's lips tightened and he scornfully reminded Krulak about pursuing a civilian career.

The main issue between the Marines and the Navy was the design of tank lighters—boats that carry tanks. It did not ameliorate King's feelings toward Brute when he learned that Krulak—a mere captain—had the temerity to disagree with far senior Navy officers about the design. Krulak and Higgins favored a "well-deck" design—that is, one where the tank or artillery piece sat below the waterline, with the weight giving the boat stability. The Navy wanted a "flush-deck" design, where the tank sat well above the waterline. During the discussions, Higgins went to Washington, studied Navy plans, and then scrawled across the plans in bold letters, "This boat stinks" and "This boat is lousy." Higgins returned to New Orleans, locked up his design staff, and said no one could leave until a satisfactory design for a tank lighter, including the tricky bow ramp, was finished. By late afternoon, his crew had drawings that were very close to the design used throughout the war.

In May 1941, Navy representatives came to New Orleans to observe tests of the bow-ramped Higgins boat, now called the "landing craft vehicle, personnel" (LCVP). This was the first version of the boat that would take Marines and soldiers to many a hostile shore.

The Bureau of Ships was desperate. War in the Pacific was inevitable, and the Navy could not fulfill its simple mandate of designing and supplying the Navy and Marines with proper boats. Higgins could have an idea, translate it into a design, and build a prototype while the Navy was arguing over details. Now the Bureau of Ships had to swallow its pride and ask for help. When Higgins was notified that officers were coming to New Orleans to observe the LCVP tests, he was asked, almost as an aside, if he could also begin designing a new tank lighter. Higgins replied that when Navy officials arrived, they would see a finished boat.

"That can't be done," the official said.

"The hell it can't. You just be here in three days."

No other yard in America could have done what Higgins did in the next sixty-two hours. He built a tank lighter that performed so magnificently that the Navy promptly said it would award Higgins a contract to build more for additional testing.

* * *

WITH Higgins's tank lighters, the Marines were ready to assault the beaches of Martinique should the Germans take over the island. But the Marines had only enough boats for a landing on that one little island and not enough for a war in the Pacific. The Navy was still anchored, still hoping somehow that its design could be proven superior to that of the rough man from New Orleans.

Higgins, who had little patience to begin with, lost it all in dealing with the Navy. He said that he would build boats for the Navy, but he would henceforth deal only with Marines.

General Emile P. Moses, head of the Marine Equipment Board, began spending time at the Higgins yard in New Orleans, where his primary responsibility was seeing that boats moved quickly from the yard to the Navy. In dealing with major design issues and in considering what features both the tank lighter and the LCVP should have, Krulak was still General Shepherd's "boat man." And, of course, the Navy, which controlled the purse strings, had the final say.

In terms of manufacturing, with contracts for LCVPs, PT boats, and tank lighters, and with a contract that stipulated "every practicable means be taken to expedite completion and delivery," Higgins saw daylight. When there were not enough trains to haul steel from Birmingham, Alabama, to New Orleans, he had steel-laden cars attached to a passenger train. He closed off a block of Polymnia Street in New Orleans—preventing the entry of delivery vehicles, garbage trucks, even residents—but it was for the war effort, and few people complained. When Higgins could not locate a mill to supply bronze propeller shafts, he found what he needed at a Texas oil company. When the oil company owner refused to sell the shafts, Higgins sent workers to Texas to steal the vital parts. Texas state troopers chasing them were stopped at the state line by Louisiana troopers. And two weeks after the Navy gave Higgins oral permission to proceed, Higgins had nine tank lighters ready for shipment.

IT was here that Harry Truman first appeared on the Marine Corps horizon. The obscure senator from Missouri took notice of rising defense costs and decided he would stop widespread corruption and waste in the defense industry. His friend Andrew Jackson Higgins was supplying him with information about how the Navy did business, and Truman decided to use that information and his chairmanship of an investigatory committee, called the Truman Committee, to catapult himself into national prominence.

Truman did not like the Marines. He had commanded an artillery battery in World War I, and like Marshall, MacArthur, and many other Army officers, he was upset by the publicity the Marines received after Belleau Wood. But he was an ambitious man, he recognized an opportunity, and he would hold his nose — for the moment.

DURING the summer of 1941, the Higgins landing craft underwent major tests at New River, North Carolina. Smith and Krulak observed the tests and agreed that the Higgins boat was far superior to anything else available. This was definitely the boat they wanted.

But Higgins knew that having the best boat was not enough. The natural tendency of a boat operator was to retard the throttle when the boat hit the beach. Yet keeping the bow of a landing craft firmly anchored to the beach demanded that the operator maintain full throttle once the bow was on the beach. The engine at full throttle had the additional benefit of causing the prop to blast sand away from the stern, enabling the boat to retract quickly. In July 1941, again at his own expense, Higgins established a ten-day school to teach sailors how to operate and maintain the LCVP.

The Navy refused even to pay for gas used by sailors taking the course. And as late as November 1941, the U.S. Navy told British officials that it could not foresee landing craft being used in a war with Germany. Escort ships and transport vessels would be all that America needed.

ON December 6, 1941, Smith wrote to Higgins, "Often I ponder the question, 'Where the Hell would the Amphibious Force have been without you and your boats?'"

Brute was at Quantico the next day playing host to Amy's uncle, a lieutenant colonel in the Army, when news came over the radio of the attack on Pearl Harbor. Krulak went to Smith's office, where, Brute recalled, the pace was no more accelerated than it had been the day before. The Marine Corps had been operating at a wartime tempo for months. Now the war had arrived. "We knew we would win," Krulak said, "but we had no idea how difficult it would be."

Had Pearl Harbor not happened, it is likely that Andrew Higgins would have remained an obscure southern boatbuilder. But after Pearl Harbor, the Navy could not escape the fact that America faced a brutal island-hopping campaign in the Pacific and the Higgins boat would be crucial to that campaign.

Even so, the Navy continued to fight the man from New Orleans.

In January 1942, amphibious maneuvers involving the Army, Navy, and Marines were held at Fort Story, Virginia, and were a disaster. Many units did not land in designated areas; some even came ashore in areas that were off-limits. Coordination between the Army and Navy was almost nonexistent. The only good news was the performance of the drop-bow Higgins boat. Two design features of the boat were crucial: the bottom design and the drop bow. A modified tunnel design and a skeg protected the propeller and enabled the boat to run hard aground and then retract. The drop bow allowed thirty-six combat-equipped Marines to disembark in nineteen seconds. Strahan summarizes the development of the boat by saying that Higgins was responsible for the underwater configuration and Krulak for the ramp. The boat performed so well that the Navy stole the bow-ramp design and awarded a contract to Chris-Craft, one of its favorite boatbuilders, for 2,100 boats, while awarding Higgins a contract for only 384.

Truman had had enough. He wrote a scorching letter to Secretary of the Navy Frank Knox, saying that officers in the Bureau of Ships were guilty of "negligence or willful misconduct" and had treated Higgins in a "biased and prejudiced" manner. Truman noted that only the "ability and energy" of Higgins Industries had kept the Navy from causing "irreparable injury" to the war effort.

MARCH was a good month for the Krulak family. On March 4, Amy delivered her third son and named him Charles. Brute asked Major General Holland Smith to be the boy's godfather. In Brute's next FitRep, Smith described him as "the most outstanding officer I have ever known in his rank." That rank did not last long. A few weeks later, Brute was promoted to major.

ABOUT this time, Higgins told Truman that if the senator really wanted to stop wasteful spending, he should start with the Navy's insistence on buying inferior boats, the prime example being the tank lighter. Inspired, Truman ordered the Navy's tank lighter and the one built by Higgins to compete head-to-head, winner take all.

The shootout was on May 25, off Norfolk. Krulak accompanied Smith and a gaggle of Navy and Marine officers, along with aides from Truman's office and the White House. All climbed aboard a Navy vessel to go offshore to watch. The aides were there because out of this competition would come an order for more than a thousand tank lighters—or, to use the proper terminology, "landing craft, mechanized" (LCMs)—and millions of dollars were at stake, with millions more forthcoming. There could be no doubt from any quarter that the boat chosen was the best one available.

That Monday morning, a stiff breeze pushed rough seas, and whitecaps were flying. As the two competing boats, each carrying a twenty-ton tank, came out of the inner harbor and rounded the Cape Henry Light, they were running side by side. They turned south into the open sea, and the Navy-designed boat began driving its bow into the waves, shipping large amounts of water. The boat stopped, and crew members began bailing. Then the coxswain, in an effort to catch up with the Higgins boat, applied full power, causing the top-heavy Navy boat to roll from beam to beam. Pictures show crew members on the gunwales, ready to jump overboard. The coxswain decided that catching up with the Higgins boat was not worth the risk of sinking; he reduced power and turned for the safety of the inner harbor. Meanwhile, the Higgins boat passed Little Creek and moved on to Fort Story, where the tank was landed on the beach. The operator retracted from the beach, spun around, and returned to deep water.

It was all over for the Navy. Now the Marine Corps had the backing of Senator Truman and the White House, and in the new post–Pearl Harbor world, the demand for proper boats steamrolled Navy intransigence. Higgins would have future contracts—big contracts—but in July he returned to Washington to renegotiate those contracts so his profit would be less. He said it was not fair for him to make so much money when American boys were in a shooting war.

Higgins finally was allowed to do what he did best: build boats for the Marines. There was no time to enlarge his boatyard, so his crews worked in multiple shifts twenty-four hours a day under canvas shelters. Higgins would build many types and sizes of landing craft, vessels that would carry everything from troops to artillery to tanks, all known collectively as Higgins boats.

Years later, historian Stephen Ambrose was shocked when Eisenhower told him that Higgins boats had won the war for America. Eisenhower went on to explain that had Higgins boats not been available, a new attack strategy would have had to be devised for the Pacific, for Africa, and for Europe. American Marines and soldiers could not have attacked defended beaches in Navy boats, or at least not without unacceptable numbers of casualties. Every major Allied campaign of World War II began with an amphibious assault. In fact, one of the most dramatic and iconic images of the war is of a drop-bow Higgins boat breasting the surf, lurching to a stop on the beach, dropping its ramp, and disgorging a platoon of combat-armed troops onto the shore. Krulak said that Higgins boats "were our bridge to the beach"—and he was right.

By July 1943, Higgins had shattered every existing boat production record: he turned out more landing craft than all the other shipyards in America combined. The most significant military technological advances of the late 1930s and early 1940s were the amtrac and the Higgins boat. Krulak's experiments and testing of the Alligator led to a far better amtrac—to the vehicle that would be used in thirty major Pacific landings. In September 1943, when the Army landed at Salerno and General Douglas MacArthur's forces landed in New Guinea, the Navy owned 14,072 vessels. Of those, 12,964, or 92 percent of the fleet, had been designed by Andrew Jackson Higgins, and almost 9,000 had been built at the Higgins plant in New Orleans. The next year, on June 6, 1944, when the largest fleet in the history of the world invaded Europe at Normandy, the boat that put the soldiers, their tanks, and their equipment on the beach was the bow-ramp Higgins boat. In World War II, the Higgins boat and the U.S. Marines reshaped modern warfare.

It is a matter of considerable irony that the bow ramp, a design Krulak stole from the Japanese, was the key design feature of the boat that would contribute so much to the Japanese defeat. But victory was years away, and before that end was reached, the beaches of the Pacific would run red.

# 6

# The Twelfth of Never

THE Japanese attack on Pearl Harbor shifted America's attention to the vast stage of the Pacific theater—an unknown and puzzling area to most Americans. The sheer size and confusing nature of that stage means that much furniture must be moved about before the Marine Corps and Brute Krulak can make their dramatic entrances.

Today, with the passage of almost seven decades, we look back at what appears to be the historical inevitability of an Allied victory in World War II. But in the spring of 1942, the Allies were losing the war. Hitler was consolidating his victories over a territory that ranged from the Arctic to Libya, from the English Channel almost to the Caspian Sea. During the first months of that year, German U-boats sank hundreds of merchant vessels along the Atlantic seaboard, and by early summer they had sunk 121 ships in the Gulf of Mexico. In the Pacific, Wake Island, Guam, the Philippines, and much of Southeast Asia fell, and on May 6, some 11,000 Allied troops surrendered at Corregidor. (General Douglas MacArthur had already fled Corregidor aboard a PT boat. He ordered citations awarded to the units that stayed behind to fight the invading Japanese. Then he struck the Marines from the list of recipients, saying, according to William Manchester in *American Caesar*, "The Marines had enough glory in World War I.")

In the spring of 1942, the Japanese knew an American counterattack was inevitable but believed it could not come for another year. With this in mind, the Japanese strategy was to neutralize America before it could gather strength for the counterattack. They were well on their way to achieving that goal.

At this point, the Japanese empire covered one-seventh of the world, an area three times larger than the United States and Europe combined. The Japanese navy and air force had proved bigger and better than their American counterparts, and their tactical and strategic victories had destroyed the myth of white supremacy.

Two important events happened in April 1942. The first was a quiet agreement between Admiral King and General George C. Marshall (now Army chief of staff) that the Army would assume the amphibious role in Europe and the Marines would be confined to the Pacific. Europe would be the big show, and the Army would not share the limelight again. The second event was far more widely known: Jimmy Doolittle's daring carrier-launched bombing raid on Japan. The raid gave Americans a spark of pride but had no strategic or even tactical significance.

In May, the U.S. Navy defeated the Japanese in the Coral Sea, and in June it won a significant battle at Midway — great victories but distant triumphs in the far reaches of the Pacific that did little to satisfy America's desire for revenge. Americans knew intuitively that wars are won on the ground and craved proof that *our* troops could stand toe-to-toe with *their* troops and defeat them.

If one word could describe American attitudes toward the war in the Pacific in the early summer of 1942, it would be bewilderment. Many Americans were of European descent and could see the geography of the continent in their mind's eye: England is there. France and the Low Countries are there. That's Italy, the long boot kicking the Sicilian football. And there, in the middle, is Germany. Americans still considered Hitler the real enemy and believed that the United States must protect Britain and take back Europe. Many popular World War II songs were about Europe — about bluebirds over the white cliffs of Dover, nightingales in Berkeley Square, and, most popular of all, Lili Marlene. If any songs were sung about the Pacific war, they have been lost to memory.

But now the United States was forced to fight in the Pacific, in that great unknown ocean dotted with postage-stamp islands bearing strange names. In the coming months, Americans would hear of Guadalcanal, Bougainville, Tarawa, Iwo Jima, and Okinawa. They would search these places out on maps and be amazed at how small and remote they were. Wives and mothers would weep at the thought that their husbands and sons had died in places they did not even know existed. How could such epic battles be fought in such insignificant places? The phrase "South Pacific"—incorrect because many of the islands were north of the equator—was used to describe the distant and unknown region to which American boys were going.

As for books about the Pacific war, other than historical accounts and event-specific works such as E. B. Sledge's *With the Old Breed*, there is nowhere near the body of writing that exists about the much shorter war in Europe. The best account is William Manchester's elegiac memoir *Goodbye, Darkness*, in which a significant part of the backstory is how unknown the Pacific theater was. Manchester paints the Pacific as a paradoxical place, encompassing the most exotic and enchanting islands on earth, and at the same time an insect-infested, disease-ridden, steaming hell. But for most Americans then and now, the Pacific was decidedly secondary.

Guadalcanal was a Japanese-held island in what were then known as the British Solomon Islands. Guadalcanal sat astride the supply line between America and General MacArthur's forces in Australia. The epic fight there would be what military strategists call a "meeting engagement"—a battle fought at a time and place that neither combatant intended.

On July 17, 1942, Bill Twining flew over Guadalcanal and discovered that the Japanese were constructing an airstrip at Lunga Point. Aerial photographs were sent to Admiral King, who decreed that Guadalcanal—code-named Cactus—must be taken at all costs.

The shooting had started, America had called for the sons of bitches, and King stood at the head of the line. Then he turned and called for the *real* sons of bitches: the United States Marines.

General Holland Smith had turned over command of the newly formed 1st Marine Division to General Alexander A. Vandegrift, a polite and soft-spoken man, then taken his staff, including Krulak, to California to continue training Marines in amphibious tactics. Vandegrift arrived in New Zealand only days before being told that his division would invade Guadalcanal in August.

The Joint Chiefs of Staff and America's Pacific commanders wondered whether the Marines were up to the task. MacArthur, usually the most optimistic of battle commanders, said success at Guadalcanal was "open to the gravest doubts." Admiral Robert L. Ghormley, the overall on-scene Navy commander, said the battle would be "attended with the gravest risk" and wanted the invasion postponed.

But fate and destiny were colliding, and the fight was on. Guadalcanal was the first American "forcible entry"—the term used by Marines for an amphibious assault—of World War II. The 1st Marine Division, while it had a well-trained core, consisted in large part of new enlistees, young men who had rallied to the colors after Pearl Harbor. The division was untested, and it was going up against superbly led and fanatically committed soldiers of the Japanese empire, men who thus far had been invincible in battle.

Vandegrift's Marines still carried the vintage Springfield .03. Furthermore, the drop-bow landing craft had not yet arrived, and the Marines would go ashore in the Eureka, crawl over the sides, and drop into the surf. But all that mattered to the Marines was that once again, they would be first to fight. They would avenge Pearl Harbor.

On August 7 — eight months to the day after the Japanese surprise attack — a Navy officer uttered the ominous command that would be heard again and again over the next few years: "Land the landing force." The Eureka boats crossed the line of departure, coxswains twisted the throttles, and with a triumphant bellow, the Marines began one of the most glorious charges in all of history.

There are few examples of major military operations begun and carried out under such unfavorable conditions as at Guadalcanal. The Navy launched the landing craft six miles offshore, a by-the-book maneuver designed to keep large ships beyond the reach of medium-range Japanese artillery. But the Japanese had no medium-range artillery, and each wave of landing craft took two hours to go from ship to shore. Had the Japanese possessed more troops and better tactical perception, they could have stopped the landing before it even got started.

The long ship-to-shore movement was only the beginning of Marine troubles. After the Marines landed and established a beachhead, it would take several days to unload their food and equipment — everything from artillery pieces to bulldozers. But the morning after the landing, Admiral Frank Jack Fletcher, whose aircraft carrier supported the invasion, announced that his ship did not have enough fuel and sailed away, followed a day later by the supply ships. Samuel Eliot Morison, the great naval historian of World War II, said that Fletcher "could have remained in the area with no more consequences than sunburn."

The Navy had abandoned the Marines on a hostile shore.

Although the Marines were bombed and strafed daily, they seized the unfinished Japanese airstrip, renamed it Henderson Field, and used Japanese equipment to complete it. Massive banzai attacks came one after another, and Japanese atrocities were such that after a few days, the Marines stopped taking prisoners. As they had done at Belleau Wood, they killed anything that moved. In one night battle, Marines killed nine hundred Japanese.

Even so, Japanese confidence was so great that their officers drew up surrender documents to be signed by Vandegrift and ordered new dress uniforms to wear to the surrender ceremony. That opinion was shared by some on the American side. Admiral Ghormley sent a handwritten note to Vandegrift authorizing him to make terms with the Japanese. But to Vandegrift and every other Marine at Guadalcanal, the spirits of the Marines who had fought and died at Belleau Wood hovered over this battlefield. The 1st Marine Division would fight to the last man before it abandoned that heritage of valor. These young men—mere boys when they landed—would find that together they could achieve a greatness they had never known as individuals, and they would risk all of their tomorrows to secure this squalid little piece of real estate.

The only people who believed the Marines would win were the Marines. The fight that followed raged for six months, and the question of who would prevail shifted back and forth on a daily, even an hourly, basis. Guadalcanal was a fetid and insalubrious tropical hell, which meant that the Marines fought not only the Japanese but also mosquitoes and malaria, as well as the stench of rotting corpses and squalid swamps. They cursed the U.S. Navy even as they wondered whether it still existed. They waded through tropical streams that had turned into pestilential cesspools, and they prayed that one day they would see home again. Conditions were so terrible that the reports of war correspondents were heavily censored: it would be too demoralizing for people back home to know of the suffering and deprivation being visited upon Marines at what was coming to be known simply as "the 'Canal." Morison would later write that "Guadalcanal is not a name but an emotion."

When the Japanese realized that their initial predictions of victory were premature, they called in reinforcements, elite units that repeatedly hurled themselves against the Marines in banzai charges. Japanese battleships turned their biggest guns on the Marines, and Japanese pilots bombed and strafed the airstrip where a handful of Marine pilots — the Cactus Air Force — earned immortality defending their brother Marines on the ground. Some two weeks after the landing, Army and Navy aircraft joined the battle, and all the while, at the highest levels of those two services, officers asked, "Can Vandegrift hold?"

Almost every Marine on Guadalcanal suffered from malaria, but men stayed on the line until their temperatures exceeded 103 degrees. Marines lost an average of twenty-five pounds each, were weak and sick and half-starving — indeed, they would have starved had it not been for seized Japanese rice supplies — but they kept their honor clean; they fought on as only U.S. Marines can fight, and they killed some 21,000 of the very best soldiers in the Japanese army while losing more than 1,700 of their own.

The Army thought that it had condemned the Marines to anonymity on unknown Pacific sandbars, but on the first of those sandbars, the Marine Corps found glory. Poet Stephen Spender could have been addressing the Marines at Guadalcanal when he wrote of men who "in their lives fought for life... And left the vivid air signed with their honor."

The stakes could not have been higher. An intercepted message from the Japanese commander on Guadalcanal said that the fate of the war in the Pacific hung on this battle. As had been true at Belleau Wood, the real struggle was to determine who was psychological master of the battlefield. Beyond that, if the Marines lost their first offensive ground action of World War II, for the remainder of the war they would be led by Army generals; no Marine would lead anything larger than a regiment, and the postwar assimilation of the Marines into the Army would be guaranteed.

In early October, Krulak was ordered to Hawaii to brief the Army's 25th Infantry Division on how to plan and execute amphibious attacks. The division commander was General Joseph L. "Lightning Joe" Collins, who was about to take his division to Guadalcanal to reinforce the Marines. When the training was over, Krulak went to pay his respects to General Collins. What Krulak envisioned as a courtesy call took what he called an "unexpected and significant turn" when Collins launched into a tirade against the Marines, saying that the Army was going into the amphibious business, that it was tired of relying on the Marines to teach what was a relatively simple procedure.

Here was an example of what Marines call the "lily pad theory," which holds that when a small frog—in this case, the Marine Corps—finds a lily pad and settles comfortably onto what it sees as home, along comes a bigger frog—the Army—which also likes the lily pad and forces the smaller frog off it. In the coming years, there would be more examples.

Mopping-up operations on Guadalcanal continued until February 1943, but by December 1942 most of the heavy fighting was over. What would be the longest single campaign of the Pacific war was ending with a great victory for the Marines. Media coverage of the war was largely by combat correspondents who wrote for newspapers and magazines and who shot footage for newsreels shown in movie theaters before the feature film. These reporters praised the spirit of the Marine riflemen, their bravery and tenacity in this seminal battle. Holland Smith said that the crucial factor in the victory was the Marines' "willingness to die."

Marines who fought at the 'Canal achieved the same iconic status in the Marine Corps as did those who fought at Belleau Wood. After Guadalcanal, officers of the 1st Marine Division designed a dark blue diamond-shaped patch for their uniforms. On the patch was a constellation of white stars representing the Southern Cross. Down the middle of the patch was the number 1, and down the middle of the number, in block letters, was

G
U
A
D
A
L
C
A
N
A
L

No shoulder patch during World War II drew more respect.

BACK home, a new generation of Americans was falling in love with the Marine Corps. One of them was Ralph Kleiger, a cousin of Brute's from Denver. By now the Zalls were as prominent in Denver as were the Chandlers in Washington. The Zall-Kleiger family dominated the wholesale jewelry businesses there, and Max Zall, Bess's brother, was becoming a famous lawyer who would serve as Denver's city attorney for forty years. After years of struggle, Brute's father, Morris, was making a very good living in the jewelry business and, with the help and advice of Max Zall, was making even more money in real estate. Morris had at last realized the American dream: he was a millionaire.

Marine public affairs people sent news releases of Brute's promotions to Denver newspapers, and an inspired Ralph Kleiger wrote to Krulak to say that he was thinking of joining the Marines and could Brute offer any advice. Not wanting to be outed by his Jewish cousin, Brute wrote back that the Marine Corps would be too tough for Ralph, that he should join the Army. Ralph was devastated.

At Guadalcanal, the U.S. Marines destroyed the myth of Japanese invincibility. Great battles still lay ahead, and the outcome of the war was by no means decided. But after Guadalcanal, the Japanese advance was stopped; never again would Japan have the initiative. Guadalcanal was the first step in what Krulak called the "march toward the setting sun" that was Japan.

To Krulak Guadalcanal was blood-etched proof of everything Smith had told him about the Navy's attitude toward the Marines, and more than sixty years later, Krulak still expressed resentment that the Navy had abandoned the Marines on Guadalcanal. This resentment remains almost universal in the Marine Corps. When John Keenan, now a retired Marine colonel and editor of the *Marine Corps Gazette*, was director of the Expeditionary Warfare School in 1999, a Navy officer asked when the Marines would forgive the Navy for Guadalcanal. "The twelfth of never," Keenan said.

In a few more months, Krulak would emerge at center stage to work for Smith. And in the cauldron of combat, he would solidify his relationship with Bill Twining and Gerry Thomas, the famous "Guadalcanal Gang" led by General Vandegrift. The Pacific would be Brute Krulak's stepping-stone to fame and higher rank.

* * *

AFTER Guadalcanal, American forces were divided into a two-pronged thrust toward Japan, with MacArthur driving up the western Pacific, fighting on some islands and leaving others (usually Japanese strongholds), as he said, "to wither on the vine." For him, the Philippines were the focus of the Army's march—a liberation necessary to fulfill his own prophecy—"I shall return."

Marines would drive up the central Pacific, attacking islands that, as one Japanese commander said, could not be taken by a million men in a hundred years. But one by one, those islands would fall.

ON December 9, 1942, Vandegrift turned Guadalcanal over to the Army and left for New Caledonia to make a courtesy call on Admiral William "Bull" Halsey. Halsey had replaced Ghormley as the Navy's senior man in the Pacific. Vandegrift was accompanied by Colonel Bill Twining, whose brother, Army Air Forces general Nathan Twining, was about to take over the new Thirteenth Air Force in the South Pacific. General Twining was in New Caledonia along with numerous senior Army officers, among them Lightning Joe Collins, who was en route to Guadalcanal. Collins was unhappy with newspaper stories saying that the Army was going to relieve the Marines, implying that the Marines had done all the heavy lifting and the Army was coming in to tend to the housekeeping chores of occupation. That this was true was irrelevant to Collins; he believed that Guadalcanal was just another example of how publicity-seeking Marines wanted to embarrass the Army.

During the evening of December 11, a number of the Army's senior officers gathered to drink and talk of Army plans for the postwar reorganization of the American military. As Bill Twining was a Marine and the lowest-ranking officer present, the Army brass—no doubt loosened up by liquor—told him about concurrent plans for the Marine Corps. Before the evening was over, Colonel Twining heard his brother announce that the Army was perfectly capable of conducting amphibious operations. General Twining bitterly attacked the Marines, proclaiming, "We will run the rest of the war so that people will forget there ever was a Marine on Guadalcanal." He said that after the war, the Army would restructure the U.S. military, and in the new order there would be no place for the Marines. The U.S. military would be unified, with the Army Air Forces becoming the Air Force, a separate branch of the service that would absorb the air operations of the Marine Corps. The Army would take over other Marine Corps functions, including amphibious warfare, and the Marine Corps would revert to being a small shipborne police force.

The Pacific campaign was just beginning, and the invasion of Europe was still some eighteen months away, but the Army seemed almost as concerned about doing away with the Marine Corps as it was about doing away with Japanese military forces. As Krulak would later write, this was no mere professional disagreement between the brothers Twining; this was serious business.

WHEN 1943 arrived, money was flowing to the U.S. military in such a mighty river that the Marine Corps, for the first time in its history, could and did spend wildly. It created parachute units, commando-like raider battalions, glider units, war dog units, and even units that planned to use barrage balloons. As Brute said, the Marine Corps "didn't miss getting a foot on any train that came down the track."

Krulak wanted a combat assignment, but Smith considered him too valuable as a staff member to be released. Brute figured that if he had training in a critical area, he might convince the general to change his mind. He persuaded Smith to send him to parachute training at Camp Gillespie, near San Diego, to become what was then called a Paramarine. He entered training on January 9, 1943. His medical records show that he was five feet five inches tall, had a 33-inch chest and a 29 1/2-inch waist, and had bulked up to an impressive 135 pounds. When Krulak began Paramarine training, he had just turned thirty, an old man by Paramarine standards. (Most trainees were in their teens.)

Krulak was a bit of a klutz, a quality that when combined with his light weight, meant he had difficulty controlling his parachute. On one of his final jumps before graduation, he was unable to collapse his parachute and was dragged across the ground into a fence. The resulting injury traumatized the sciatic nerve in his left leg, and from that time on, he was in almost constant pain. If the severity of the injury was known, he would never see combat. Rather than seek medical attention, he asked Smith to assign him to a parachute unit in the Pacific. With great reluctance, Smith agreed.

As Brute prepared to go to war, Amy and the boys returned east to her parents' house in Washington. In the coming years, Brute would be away for long periods as the boys were growing up. It was Amy who played the major role in nurturing, developing, and disciplining her sons during their formative years.

The sacrifices, duties, and obligations of a military wife have no equivalent in the civilian world, and many women are not cut out for the job. Even in peacetime, a military man is deployed for long periods, leaving his spouse to take care of the children and their schooling, to pay the bills, to make sure the lawn is mowed and the oil in the car is changed, and to handle dozens of other tasks usually done by him. During wartime, always hanging over the military wife is the fear that her husband may be wounded or killed in combat. The life of a military wife is so subordinated to her husband's career that when he receives transfer orders, she says, "*We* received orders."

The status of a military wife is directly related to her husband's rank, and she must show the same deference to the wife of a superior officer that her husband shows to the officer. She must master the intricacies of entertaining in a hierarchal society, knowing that a single misstep could affect her husband's career.

But most of all—and this is always mentioned by nonmilitary people—the military wife has no life of her own; her entire existence revolves around her husband's career. Having a job is frowned upon because her full-time job is being a military wife. To many bright young women who marry military officers, the challenges are enormous.

But not to Amy Krulak. She knew far better than most young women of her time what would be expected of her as the wife of a career military officer. And she performed that role to perfection.

TODAY when troops are sent overseas, they are "deployed." But in World War II, they "shipped out," a wonderful and portentous phrase, especially as it was rarely qualified with a specific destination. When a Marine shipped out, all that was known was that he was going somewhere in the Pacific. In Brute's case, however, he knew that he was going to Tontouta, in New Caledonia, to assume command of the 2nd Parachute Battalion and to train the battalion for a war assignment. He had no idea where he would go after that.

Given that the Marines activated only three parachute battalions in World War II, Brute had been given a very prestigious assignment. His elation increased when, upon arrival in New Caledonia, he was promoted to lieutenant colonel. World War II was here, the Marine Corps was increasing to unprecedented numbers, and officers were promoted rapidly. Also working in Krulak's favor was the fact that General Smith continued to write FitReps that sounded as if Krulak could walk on water.

Krulak had been in the Marine Corps nine years and had spent most of that time in staff jobs or as an aide. Now in the Pacific theater, in command of an outfit that would soon be in combat, he was about to become a Marine legend.

THIS is a good place to pause and gain perspective on the differences between the Marines and the Army, on the war in the Pacific, and on the hastening war in Europe. This book is about a Marine, and it is important to show how the Marines are different from other branches of the military, to look at the world through their eyes. And because the Marines were fighting in the Pacific, it is important to compare the situation there with what was going on in Europe.

The first large-scale engagement between American and German troops in World War II was in February 1943, at the Kasserine Pass in Tunisia. The U.S. Army suffered heavy casualties and was pushed back fifty miles. Embarrassed, the Army sent in General George S. Patton, who led a remarkable comeback. Rick Atkinson's Liberation Trilogy, especially *An Army at Dawn*, the first book in the series, points out the ineptitude of Army leaders in Africa and Europe. Atkinson says that it was neither leadership nor superior tactics and strategy that eventually defeated Germany; it was the sheer mass of America's industrial power.

The Marine Corps could not afford a Kasserine Pass, because such a defeat would have heightened Army efforts to prove the Corps ineffectual and hastened efforts to absorb Marine functions into the Army and Air Force. And in the Pacific, it was not industrial power but individual Marines who carried the day.

While the German army was considered the greatest in the world, it had no amphibious doctrine and no landing craft. And that is why, the Royal Air Force notwithstanding, Germany did not invade Britain across the narrow English Channel.

AMPHIBIOUS doctrine was central to World War II in that every major Allied campaign — North Africa, Sicily, Italy, and

Normandy—began with an amphibious assault. The Marine Corps was the only military unit in the world that, by 1942, had an amphibious doctrine and the ability to assault hostile shores. It was Marine Corps doctrine, along with Higgins boats and amtracs, that put Americans ashore.

Marines were being shipped thousands of miles from California to the Pacific, then often sent straight into battle. Although there were many reasons for the U.S. Army to delay its assault on Hitler's "Fortress Europe," Marines like to point out that even with the experience of North Africa (November 1942), Sicily (July 1943), and Italy (September 1943) behind them, it took the Army almost two years to gather the men and equipment it needed in England to travel some fifty miles across the English Channel and invade Europe.

WHEN Brute took over the 2nd Parachute Battalion, he found a group of men with too much time on their hands. The men recently had been caught firing mortars over the officers' club, and they delighted in tossing grenades into the big barrels used to receive human waste. They had even rolled grenades down the camp's streets. Such behavior often was fueled by "yadidak," a hell brew of raisins, pineapple juice, and sugar even more potent than Fish House Punch.

When Krulak arrived, the good times left. The men had heard that their new skipper was called Brute and were curious about why a Marine officer had such a name. When he formed up his men for their first inspection, they decided they had never seen a more squared-away Marine. The creases in his shirt were knifelike and lined up perfectly with those in his trousers. His cap was at the proper angle, and his shoes glistened. His eyes were hard and his face unsmiling. Still, the men believed that Brute wasn't big enough to be a Marine or tough enough to be a Paramarine.

They were soon dissuaded from both beliefs.

When Brute caught two Marines rolling grenades down the street, he slapped them into the brig and gave them bread and water. He followed Holland Smith's style of hard leadership and believed that arduous training combined with iron discipline was the only way to control high-spirited young Marines. One morning he posted orders saying the battalion would conduct a parachute drop followed by a twenty-mile forced march. After Krulak had another bad jump and sustained heavy bruises, a Navy corpsman (medic) suggested the commanding officer ride along on the march. The corpsman was surprised when Brute instead led the hike.

The corpsman talked about Brute's injury and pain during the hike, and as word of Krulak's toughness made the rounds, the Paramarines realized that, size notwithstanding, Brute was a tough and able skipper. One of the men drew a picture of Krulak atop a box waving his fist. The caption had Brute saying that he could "lick any man in the whole battalion under 112 pounds." Krulak had the picture framed, and it would stay on his wall for the rest of his life.

KRULAK studied the personnel folders of the six hundred Marines in his battalion and memorized almost every face and name. When he encountered his men on the street, he returned their salutes and addressed them by name, much to their astonishment.

Brute was not entirely grit and brain. At times he revealed a compassionate side that the Paramarines did not expect. One of his men had a father who was also a Marine. Father and son had not seen each other in more than a year, and when the father passed through Nouméa, also in New Caledonia, Brute gave the son a pass to go visit him. It was an unexpected gesture that the young Marine would never forget.

* * *

As commander of a parachute battalion, Krulak had a big problem: most Pacific islands were covered with dense vegetation and tall trees—a serious impediment to Paramarines. As a result, Krulak believed that the Marines would never conduct large parachute drops in the Pacific (he was right), so he shifted the focus of his training regimen. Officially, he switched to standard infantry training, but unofficially it approximated the training of Marine Raiders—how to conduct commando-like assaults in rubber boats, guerrilla warfare, and operations behind enemy lines. The new training was even more intense than the old.

Late that summer, Gerry Thomas, now chief of staff of the 1st Marine Division, dropped in for a surprise inspection and found Krulak's men using live ammunition in a training operation, a dangerous practice even for highly trained troops. Thomas also witnessed the remarkable trust and affection between officers and men. When he returned to Vandegrift's headquarters, he told the general that Krulak's men were ready to fight; all they needed was a job.

Before Krulak was assigned that job, he was sent to Nouméa, where he was told to subject amtracs to a brutal test regime in plunging surf and over coral reefs. He was ordered to push the amtracs to the limit, even to the point of destroying them, the idea being to find out just how much abuse the machine could take. He was not told the purpose of this dangerous work.

In *Utmost Savagery*, Joseph Alexander's book about the battle for Tarawa, Krulak says, "As far as I knew, no one had yet tried to ride an LVT through both coral and heavy surf, and the picture of what might happen to a fifteen-thousand-pound unsprung iron box when a wave brought it crashing down on a coral ledge was not encouraging to any of us."

Off the tip of New Caledonia, Brute found surf topping six feet and, accompanied by two skilled enlisted Marines, shoved off in an amtrac. Each enlisted man drove through the surf and negotiated the reef. When it was Krulak's turn, he lost control and came down on top of a reef with such force that he almost broke the amtrac in half. He wrote a report saying that amtracs could negotiate heavy surf and cross reefs, but only if the Marines driving them went to special training classes.

According to Alexander, Krulak's report convinced the Joint Chiefs of Staff that Tarawa, which is surrounded by reefs, could be assaulted using amtracs. Krulak's test opened the door for the invasion of that bloody and therefore revered place. The irony is that the study was lost and never found its way back to those in the Pacific who planned the invasion.

In October, Krulak's battalion was ordered to Vella Lavella, in the Solomon Islands. Krulak was summoned to Vandegrift's headquarters, where Twining briefed him about a proposed raid on Choiseul, an eighty-by-twenty-mile island that lay across The Slot—New Georgia Sound. The Japanese knew that after Guadalcanal, the Marines would attack again, probably at the northern end of the Solomon Islands on either Bougainville or Choiseul. Vandegrift wanted the Japanese to think it was Choiseul, where some four thousand Japanese troops were garrisoned. He was sending Krulak's Paramarines there to create a diversion. The purpose of Operation Blissful was to raise so much hell that the Japanese would think a full division had landed.

Marines do not usually create diversions; they simply show up and knock down the door. This was one of the few diversions the Marines would conduct in the Pacific. Krulak's men would be outnumbered five to one, and although they could call on air support and emergency support from PT boats, there would be no reinforcements. Once they landed, they would be on their own.

Choiseul is noted not only for its isolation and glorious flora and fauna, but also for the fact that if a person wanders off the beach just twenty or thirty feet inland, he can be lost forever. The interior is a thick, dank, overgrown greenhouse—unmapped, with only a few narrow trails. It is the most inhospitable of all the Solomons.

Twining gave Brute rudimentary maps of the island and told him he had a week to plan the attack. Krulak's primary source of information was Cardon Seton, a six-foot-four Australian coast watcher who had operated for months behind Japanese lines and had radioed reports of Japanese troop and boat movements to American intelligence officers. Seton had malaria and was burning up with fever when a Navy amphibious aircraft picked him up and spirited him out of Choiseul. His news was as bad as his health. Most of the Japanese forces on Choiseul were in Sangigai and Choiseul Bay, some thirty miles apart, an impossible distance given the terrain. Boats would have to be used to attack the two locations. Before Seton returned to Choiseul, he told Krulak that Japanese snipers understood enough English to recognize military ranks and that they targeted officers. Upon hearing this, Krulak told his men that on the raid, no insignia of rank would be worn and every man would be addressed by his first name. He was to be called Brute. "If any of you men call me colonel," he said, "I will reply loudly, 'Yes, general.'"

THERE is no twilight in the Solomons. One moment the sun is low in the sky, and the next moment darkness slams down. The men who were on Choiseul will tell you that the island is the darkest corner of a dark world.

On the night of October 27, the 2nd Parachute Battalion crossed The Slot and landed at Voza, an abandoned village on the western side of Choiseul. The operation was a logistical nightmare: with the men were generators, radios, ammunition, and enough food for six hundred men for fourteen days, plus hundreds of bags of rice to pay the two hundred natives Seton brought to unload the equipment and take it to a base camp about three miles into the jungle. A Japanese night air patrol spotted the wake of the boats approaching Voza and radioed for bombers to attack the landing force. The bombs fell into the ocean, but the Marines knew they had been discovered.

Sunrise is an event in the Solomons. Almost as if to banish the absolute darkness, the sun explodes over the horizon like a giant searchlight. Just as there is no transition from light to darkness, there is none from darkness to light, and the sudden colors of the Pacific sunrise are heart-stopping shades of purple, orange, blue. But the Marines had no time to appreciate all that. At dawn on October 28, American fighters and bombers attacked Choiseul as if prepping the battlefield for an invasion. Krulak gathered his officers and reminded them of their purpose: to raise hell over a broad front, but not to engage in set-piece battles. They were to hit hard, then get out quickly. Brute began sending out false radio messages that 20,000 men had landed successfully and were moving toward their objectives: the invasion was going as planned. (The real messages were sent to Vandegrift by two Navajo code talkers.)

Because the primary targets were so far apart, Krulak had to violate a fundamental combat rule and divide his force. He would lead the attack on the barge station at Sangigai, some ten miles south, and his executive officer, Major Warren Bigger, would go twenty miles north and attack at Choiseul Bay. The timing was crucial, as the invasion of Bougainville was scheduled for dawn on November 1.

On October 29, Krulak led the first combat patrol of his career. When he arrived on the beach at Sangigai, the point man signaled that Japanese troops were ahead. Krulak crawled forward and saw ten Japanese soldiers unloading a barge. Using hand signals, Krulak moved his men into position, then whispered to the man on either side to pick individual targets and at his signal "kill them all."

Seven Japanese died on the beach, and three fled into the jungle. Krulak's men blew up the barge, then moved inland.

On October 30, Admiral Halsey's headquarters announced that a Marine division of 20,000 men had landed on Choiseul, an announcement that made headlines back in the States and, so it was hoped, would divert Japanese attention from Bougainville. That same day, Marine aircraft accidentally bombed Krulak's hidden boats, thinking they were Japanese barges. As a result, Krulak's men were forced to carry weapons and equipment they had planned to move by boat. The raid put them dangerously behind schedule and was a perfect example of how unexpected events can cause the friction of war.

For his main attack, Krulak had decided on a classic envelopment—striking the enemy simultaneously from two positions—which meant that he had to reach the ambush site near Sangigai before the other part of his force began the attack and pushed the Japanese into Krulak's guns. Heavily burdened, Krulak's men trekked through gelatinous mud, watching out for snakes and spiders while being eaten alive by mosquitoes, ants, and flies. Even though the Marines were as well conditioned as professional athletes, it was a brutal hike.

More than sixty years after the raid, James Christ interviewed surviving members of the battalion and wrote *Mission Raise Hell*. The book is not reliable on all counts, as Christ accepted every veteran's sea story as gospel, but it does serve as a guide. Christ says the attack began at 2 p.m., but Krulak was not in position. At around 2:30, Krulak heard the firefight and was simultaneously ambushed by Japanese snipers. The Marines lay on their backs and shot the snipers out of the trees.

Krulak fell to one knee, blood running from a facial wound, but he quickly stood up and shouted at his men to keep moving. The Marines did as they had been trained: they charged toward enemy guns laying down a devastating fire. Krulak was hit again, a grazing bullet wound under the skin of his left arm. The jungle was being ripped to pieces by gunfire. The enemy was making brilliant use of cover and concealment, and all the Marines had to shoot at were muzzle flashes. Krulak gave runners orders for two platoon leaders to prepare a flanking movement. He was still talking when a mortar round exploded nearby and threw him backward.

Krulak was up against the same Japanese marines who had taken the Philippines. He knew the Japanese would counterattack, and when they did, he wanted to kill as many as possible, leaving only a few survivors to take back word of the Marine attack. He passed the word: "Fix bayonets."

The Marines checked their ammunition, loosened the cotter pins on their hand grenades, and put their Ka-Bars (fighting knives) within easy reach. The Japanese rushed through the jungle— long bayonets pointing the way, screaming, firing on the run— and the Marines cut them to pieces. Although a banzai attack is fast and terrifying, it is suicidal in the face of disciplined troops. Japanese snipers had killed six of Krulak's Marines, but within seconds more than fifty Japanese were dead.

Krulak's attack on Sangigai was an unqualified success. He had confirmed kills of seventy-two enemy soldiers and had destroyed fuel, food, radio equipment, medical supplies, and ammunition at the Japanese base while losing only six men. He also had destroyed a barge and captured Japanese charts showing the locations of minefields and barge routes. Krulak radioed headquarters to send a Navy amphibious aircraft to pick up the charts. Krulak's minor wounds were bothersome, but the old sciatic nerve injury in his left leg had been exacerbated by the long trek while carrying a fifty-pound pack, and he was in considerable pain.

General Haruyoshi Hyakutake, commander of the Japanese Seventeenth Army, could not ignore Krulak's attack. He was not sure that Choiseul was being invaded, but he issued orders for reinforcements from Bougainville to be moved there.

# 7

# The Brute Unleashed

MAJOR Bigger's men had boarded three Higgins boats and traveled up the coast with the intention of landing at the mouth of the Warrior River, then moving inland and attacking the Japanese main base at Choiseul Bay. But Bigger had fallen behind schedule and spent the night in a malaria-ridden swamp.

Now he was a day late making his attack, and Krulak was furious. One of Bigger's patrols was cut off on the beach and threatened by a full battalion of Japanese troops. Unless the Marines could be rescued, they would be massacred. Krulak sent an urgent radio message to the PT base at Vella Lavella asking for help. Only two PT boats were available, and one of those was being refueled; it had seven hundred gallons of fuel aboard, about one-third of its capacity. The two Navy skippers decided that both boats would go and when the partially fueled boat ran out of fuel, it would be towed by the other. The important thing was to rescue the Marines. One of the skippers gave his signature order, "Wind 'er up," and the powerful boats rumbled out of Vella Lavella and roared across The Slot toward Choiseul. The skipper of the partially refueled boat was John F. Kennedy.

By late 1943, Kennedy had recovered from the famous incident of having *PT-109* sunk from under him and was based at Vella Lavella awaiting orders to return to America. While Kennedy will forever be remembered for his actions aboard *PT-109*, the rescue of Bigger's men at the Warrior River far better represents the capabilities of PT boats and the bravery of their crews.

The PT boats were too far north when they fetched the Choiseul coast, and now they were creeping south even as the gas gauge on Kennedy's boat was creeping toward "empty." Meanwhile, Major Bigger had not reached Choiseul Bay, and he and his men were fighting their way through a large Japanese force.

When Bigger approached the beach, the two Higgins boats that had brought him and his men up the coast were waiting behind a nearby island. Aboard one was a young Navy ensign who was in charge. Each boat had a coxswain and a small group of heavily armed Marines whose job was to protect the crew and the boats. Nearshore reefs meant that Bigger and his Marines would have to wade about one hundred yards into the sea. Bigger heard the Higgins boats and ordered his men into the water. As the boats came under fire from the Japanese, the ensign ordered his coxswain to reverse engines and back away. One of the Marines stuck a .45-caliber pistol into the officer's ear and said, "This boat is going in there. With or without your head." The ensign decided that his boats would move closer to the beach.

By then the Japanese had emerged from the jungle, firing away, forcing Bigger's men to wage a defensive battle as they waded backward through the surf. Bullets struck the water all around them. Then the Japanese opened up with small but deadly mortars. Survival depended on getting the Marines aboard the Higgins boats.

So many Marines crowded aboard the first Higgins boat that the overloaded vessel became lodged atop a coral head. A mighty revving of the engine dislodged the boat, but the effort bent the rudder, and the boat could only go in a circle. The rescue was turning into a disaster, when a sudden providential rainstorm hid Bigger's Paramarines from the Japanese. Even so, the Japanese continued to fire mortar rounds through the rain, aiming them toward the sound of the revving engines. Then the second Higgins boat was punctured by a coral reef; it did not sink only because it was lodged atop the reef. When the engine died, heavy swells dislodged the boat and pushed it toward the beach, forcing several dozen Marines to jump into water up to their chests. They heard the other Higgins boat running in circles and knew it would be no help. There appeared to be little hope.

Suddenly, the throaty rumble of powerful engines sliced through the rain, and Bigger's men, fearing the new arrivals were Japanese barges loaded with troops, swung their rifles toward the sound. A sharply raked bow poked out of the rain, and someone shouted, "PT boat." Then the snout of the second PT boat, skippered by Kennedy, emerged from the rain.

The Marines clambered aboard the two boats, filling every space belowdecks and topside, crowding the boats far beyond capacity. More than fifty Marines were aboard Kennedy's boat, including one who was severely wounded. He was placed in Kennedy's bunk, where he would die several hours later. As the boats began edging out of the shallow water and away from the reefs, Kennedy's boat, still under the shadow of Japanese guns, ran out of fuel. It had to be towed back down the coast to Voza, where Bigger would link up with Krulak's main force.

By then the Japanese command had recognized Krulak's hit-and-run tactics and knew they were facing not an invasion, but a small diversionary force. On November 1, the Marines landed at Empress Augusta Bay on Bougainville, and New Zealanders landed in the Treasury Islands. On November 3, Krulak moved his men to the beach at Voza and set up defensive positions. Krulak ordered more than one hundred booby traps placed around his position. Remembering the Japanese penchant for using snipers, he collected single-edged razor blades from his men and placed them in the bark of likely trees. When night fell, exploding booby traps revealed the Japanese probing Krulak's defensive line. The explosions were so numerous that Japanese officers decided to wait until dawn to launch the final attack. Around 1 a.m., Krulak's battalion made an uneventful withdrawal from Choiseul. Brute shook hands with Cardon Seton and climbed aboard the large Higgins boat; he was the last man off the island.

A few hours later, Krulak and his Marines were safe at Vella Lavella. Seton later wrote Krulak that when the Japanese attacked Voza in force at dawn, he heard seventeen booby traps explode.

Krulak's Paramarines were officially credited with killing 143 Japanese—Seton said the number was far higher—while losing only a dozen men (another dozen were wounded). There is little evidence, however, that the raid diverted a significant number of Japanese troops from Bougainville. Allan Millett, in *Semper Fidelis: The History of the United States Marine Corps*, says it was not particularly effective, and Ken Estes, a retired Marine officer and a historian sometimes employed by the Marine Corps, describes the raid as "ineffectual and probably unnecessary."

Even so, Krulak's bravery in going up against a greatly superior force, the enemy casualties he inflicted, and the light casualties he sustained made for a record to be envied. Brute had been tested in battle and not found wanting. But Krulak's need to improve reality was so great that he would embellish almost every aspect of the Choiseul story. This tendency became particularly evident after Kennedy became a U.S. senator and even more so when he campaigned for president. Krulak would make much of their World War II connection, even saying he was present when Kennedy came to rescue Bigger's force at Choiseul Bay. He also told a dramatic story of Kennedy roaring into dangerously shallow waters off Choiseul, shouting to Krulak's men, "Don't worry, Marines. I'm coming in to get you." Krulak said that he told Kennedy afterward, "Thanks, Lieutenant. You've done a swell job. You were very courageous. When we get back to Vella Lavella, I have a bottle of Three Feathers I'm going to give to you."

But, of course, Krulak was not present when Kennedy rescued Bigger. And in *PT 109*, Kennedy's best-selling account of his time in the Pacific, Major Bigger is mentioned as the senior Marine present during the rescue.

Krulak did little to discourage other writers' JFK fictions as well. James Christ, in *Mission Raise Hell*, portrays Krulak aboard *PT-59* (the other PT boat at Choiseul) issuing orders to Kennedy the night the two PT boats came to rescue Bigger's force. Krulak was interviewed by Christ, read the manuscript before publication, and allowed the story to stand. When later asked about this inconsistency, Krulak admitted that he was not present at the rescue. Correcting the record, he said that he did not meet Kennedy until the next night, when Kennedy returned for the extraction of Krulak's battalion from Choiseul. But this, too, was a fabrication, as the PT boats stood off from the Higgins boats to provide a protective screen. The extraction took place in the middle of the night, and the Marines never saw the PT boats; in fact, they did not even know the boats were there.

Nor did the two men meet back on Vella Lavella, as Krulak told Richard Harold Hoy, who wrote a biography of Krulak for his 1974 master's thesis at San Diego State University. Hoy has Brute giving Kennedy the bottle of Three Feathers, a cheap blended whiskey popular during the war. In later years, Krulak often told how, after he became a two-star general, he arrived unannounced at the JFK White House and was admitted to the Oval Office, where he proffered the bottle of Three Feathers, saying, "Mr. President, I owe you a bottle of whiskey." He claimed that Kennedy looked at him and said, "I know." Then JFK opened the bottle; the two men had a drink and talked of Choiseul and the Pacific; and Kennedy said that he would keep the bottle as a token of the old days.

The truth is that Krulak and Kennedy never met in the Pacific. Krulak admits this in an addendum to his oral history, in which he says they met for the first time after Kennedy became president. This addendum was given to the Kennedy Presidential Library with the stipulation that no one read it until after Krulak was dead.

THAT Krulak fabricated so many events around the Choiseul raid is troubling. Almost every man who has ever been in combat has his own version of what happened, and it is accepted that "war stories" are often exaggerated. People put themselves in battles they never fought and say they served under famous men they never knew. They remember with perfect clarity things that never happened. But one is left wondering why a man would so embellish the truth when his deeds were well documented, when his contributions to the Marine Corps were many, and when his historical legacy was so rich. Granted, Brute's deceptions were harmless, but they were in stark contrast to the overall ethical code of the Marine Corps, and he knew he was transgressing.

Throughout his career, Brute was teased about his height. Thus it is easy to fall back on the "Napoleon complex" theory—the idea that because Brute was a small man, he was driven to overcompensate in every way. His insistence on being called Brute shows the image he wanted to portray. He was also running from his Jewish heritage and from a secret marriage. Put all these together, and the result is a haunted and driven man possessed of a psyche filled with spiders and snakes.

When Krulak left Cheyenne and created a new existence, everything about his new life had to be bigger and better than his old life, and no matter how great his accomplishments, nothing was ever good enough.

A few days after Krulak's battalion landed on Vella Lavella, he was summoned to Camp Crocodile, Vandegrift's headquarters on

Guadalcanal. There, on November 9, he was awarded the Navy Cross. Admiral Halsey himself pinned on the medal.

The Navy Cross is second only to the Medal of Honor as a recognition of valor and is the highest award given by the Navy or Marine Corps. For Krulak, the medal was a "spot award" recommended by Vandegrift and awarded by Halsey without going through a board of officers (who would otherwise study the record and decide the nature of the award). A spot award is given when a senior officer wants to decorate someone *now*. The citation for Krulak's Navy Cross says the award was for his "extraordinary heroism displayed against an armed enemy." It goes on,

> Having been wounded in action, Lieutenant Colonel Krulak repeatedly refused to relinquish his command and continued to lead his battalion with skill and determination in a heroic manner against superior forces, greatly contributing to the success of other operations being conducted elsewhere at that time....By his courageous action the Second Marine Parachute Battalion was able to accomplish its mission against great odds. Lieutenant Colonel Krulak's courage, determination, and utter disregard for personal safety is a credit to the Marine Corps and is in keeping with the highest traditions of the Naval Service.

Krulak also received the Purple Heart, which was later contested on the grounds that Krulak's wounds were too trivial for him to receive that award. But Krulak kept the medal, and the incident is mentioned here only because there would later be another, far more serious example of his need for medals and the lengths to which he would go to receive them.

HALSEY was on Guadalcanal to join Vandegrift and his staff in celebrating the Marine Corps's birthday on November 10. Marines everywhere observe this occasion with all available pomp and ceremony. In 1943, Krulak brewed Fish House Punch for the celebration. General Holland Smith, now famous across America as "Howlin' Mad" Smith, was present, as was Gerry Thomas.

Over the next few days, Krulak wrote a combat operation report that was classified "Secret" and sent up the chain of command to the Commandant. The report is significant for its extraordinary tactical insights about jungle warfare and how to fight the Japanese, and those observations were commented on approvingly by officers at every step of the way. But what is even more noteworthy is that a few days later, Krulak wrote what he called an "annex" to the report that caused consternation and anger up that same chain of command.

The essence of Krulak's second report was that the Marine Corps was too small to contain specialized units such as the Paramarines and Raiders. He believed that both should be disbanded and their roles carried out by conventional Marine units. At the time, there was growing sentiment in favor of getting rid of the two units. In fact, Krulak may have known that Vandegrift was considering doing just that, so it is likely that he was currying favor with Vandegrift. Nevertheless, Krulak's immediate superior wrote that the recommendations were "neither appropriate nor pertinent." After Choiseul, however, the men of the 2nd Parachute Battalion were given thirty days of leave, and while they were gone, the battalion was disbanded and the men reassigned to other units. Soon the Raiders would be disbanded as well.

Being both impertinent and right did not endear Krulak to his immediate superiors, a fact that bothered Krulak not in the least, because he enjoyed the approval of far more senior officers. Nothing better illustrates this approval than the fact that Brute, who was returning to Washington for much-needed and long-delayed surgery to repair the nerve damage in his leg, was flying home with Smith and Halsey. Two of the most senior officers in the Pacific theater were going to Washington to report on the progress of the war and invited a junior lieutenant colonel to travel with them.

When Krulak arrived in Washington, he received much media attention. The Choiseul raid, the Navy Cross, and a five-foot-four Marine colonel with a great nickname were great copy. On November 22, *Time* magazine did a story titled "The Brute & Co.," which included a line about Brute's "whimsical understatement" and another quoting him as saying the Japanese were "really very easy to kill" because of their banzai charges. "A man who goes directly into machine-gun fire generally loses his social security," Krulak said.

One newspaper called Brute "the Mighty Atom," another "the Midget of Might." The Washington correspondent for the *Denver Post* wrote an article with a headline that read, "Denver Man's Razor Blades Rout Japanese." The story credited Krulak with "a lion's share of honor for the successful American landing" on Bougainville.

When interviewed for these pieces, Krulak sounded as if placing razor blades in the bark of palm trees caused havoc among Japanese snipers as he and his men were withdrawing from Choiseul. But, of course, the withdrawal had taken place in the darkest part of a dark night, a time when snipers could not even see the ground beneath them.

Brute's parents were immensely proud of the news coverage, but Ronnie Zall, Brute's cousin, was proudest of all. The only dampener was that Bess's parents had learned that Victor was now an Episcopalian, and they were deeply troubled by it.

IN November, while the Marines were fighting through the jungles of Bougainville, Army chief of staff General George C. Marshall submitted a memorandum to the Joint Chiefs of Staff "relating to a single department of war in the post war period." The proposal for remodeling the U.S. military would go through several changes, but always remaining at the center of the plan was the idea of abolishing the Marine Corps.

In retrospect, the most charitable overall interpretation of the plan is that it was created for military efficiency based on the Prussian general staff system (a system that, incidentally, led in part to the German defeat in World War I and would lead to their defeat in World War II). But when one clears away the underbrush and reads the details of Marshall's plan, there emerges a frightening central concept: an all-powerful Army general who would be chief of staff of all branches of the military and who had no civilian buffers between him and the president. Unprecedented power would be placed in the hands of the military.

A not-so-charitable interpretation of the plan is that George C. Marshall believed that democracy was a weak form of government and was contemptuous of civilian control over the military. If one follows this line of thought, it also follows that not since the founding of the Republic had America faced such a threat from the U.S. military. Because the media considered the unification battle a military turf war, and because military historians usually become bogged down in irrelevant minutiae, even today the unification battle remains a little-known part of America's postwar history.

After his newspaper and magazine interviews, Krulak had several surgeries at Bethesda Naval Hospital, the second around Christmas of 1943. He was still on crutches when, in early 1944, he reported for duty at Quantico. His boss was Bill Twining, who would be in charge of postwar planning for the Marine Corps. In fact, for the next three and a half years, Twining would be the chief strategist to preserve Marine Corps turf.

Twining was what the Marines call "dual-hatted," in that he also was in charge of developing, procuring, and distributing myriad items to Marines in the field. Krulak came to his office as a thirty-one-year-old lieutenant colonel, a decorated war hero, the

Marine expert on all things regarding amphibious craft, and, perhaps most important, part of the "Guadalcanal Gang." All this, combined with Brute's normal confidence and domineering manner, meant that he was no doubt quite full of himself.

In January, Vandegrift, now Commandant of the Marine Corps, ordered Twining to form a group to prevent Marshall's plan from being implemented. The first person Twining turned to was Krulak. After the war, others would join the group, which would come to be known as the Chowder Society, but Brute would have the most impact.

Another part of Krulak's job was to improve the Higgins boat and the amtrac. He must have done a splendid job, because his FitRep dated March 1944 said that he was "a brilliant hard working officer" with "professional attainments of the highest order." He was ranked "outstanding" in all categories except physical fitness and military bearing. Given that he was recovering from surgery, the lower ranking in physical fitness is understandable. But even Gerry Thomas, a mentor and close friend, ranked him low in military bearing. Asked why many years later, Krulak explained, "I was little. I did not look like the poster Marine."

On September 11, Vandegrift wrote a letter for Krulak's personnel folder noting that the chief of naval operations had commended the Marine Corps for various improvements to amphibious boats. Since Krulak was in charge of this effort, Vandegrift wrote to him, "Your energy, initiative, executive skill and ingenuity have contributed to the solution of the difficult problems involved in ship-to-shore movement."

But Krulak then made two of the biggest mistakes of his career: he crossed a powerful and influential general, and he wasted more than $8 million of taxpayer money.

BRIGADIER General W. P. T. Hill was a crusty, sandy-haired, square-faced man with twenty-seven years in the Marine Corps.

In early 1944, Hill was appointed quartermaster general, the ultimate bureaucratic job, and set about acting as if every single piece of equipment in the Marine Corps belonged to him personally. With the certitude of a general and the mind-set of a bean counter, he was a most formidable man.

Brute's job was to recommend various items of equipment for Marines in the Pacific. Hill's job was to accept or reject those items. It was natural the two men would clash.

A larger issue was the poor organization of Headquarters Marine Corps, where Krulak sought to take authority away from Hill and move it to Thomas's office. Krulak wanted the Marine Corps to buy waterproof amphibious cargo trailers that could be towed ashore. The trailers cost $12,000 each, and Hill did not want them. Krulak took the issue to Vandegrift, who, because he thought Brute knew more about the logistical side of amphibious operations than anyone else in the Marine Corps, ruled in his favor. Some seven hundred trailers were ordered.

Brute also wanted jungle hammocks issued to Marines. He had used them on Choiseul and approved of their design, durability, and practicality. But Hill disapproved, saying that Marines would have trouble getting in and out of the hammocks and might even have to cut their way out. Brute again went over Hill's head to Vandegrift. The Commandant agreed with Krulak and told Hill to issue the hammocks.

Then Krulak and Hill clashed over Ka-Bar knives. Brute wanted every Marine to have one on his belt; Hill thought that Marines would cut themselves and one another. Vandegrift agreed with Krulak.

Krulak said that Vandegrift's decisions in his favor "were easy because the issues were clear." But now, although Lieutenant Colonel Krulak had won a significant number of disagreements with General Hill, he made the tense situation worse by inundating Hill with letters and memoranda about still more equipment.

Every staff officer at Quantico had his own dictating machine—Krulak's was number 644—and when secretaries transcribed material, the machine's number was posted at the top of the memo. Once, when Brute was in Hill's outer office waiting to see the general, he heard Hill's loud and disgusted voice say, "Here is another one of those goddamn 644 letters." Krulak was walking into a minefield of his own creation.

It was not uncommon to buy equipment that did not perform as expected, and now word was coming back that the amphibious trailers were an unmitigated disaster. They could not be made waterproof, and only a handful would ever be used. Krulak had become the point man in the power struggle between Hill and Thomas, and now Hill wanted Brute's head on a platter. (Krulak was disingenuous in the extreme when he said the imbroglio was because "Hill didn't like me.")

Because Vandegrift had backed Krulak at every turn, any discipline Krulak received would embarrass the Commandant, and that could not be allowed. Although there is no documentation to back this up and Krulak was very circumspect, it is likely that Thomas contacted Holland Smith, now in charge of all the Marines in the Pacific, and Smith found a job for Krulak.

Krulak speaks of this incident in his oral history, and in so doing he demonstrates why military oral histories are almost useless. "I had an opportunity to go back to the Pacific," he told the interviewer, and the interviewer (as is true of almost all military historians when interviewing a general) did not press for details. But the truth is that Krulak barely got out of town without having his career ended.

In October 1944, Krulak returned to the Pacific as General Lemuel Shepherd's assistant chief of staff. Shepherd was bivouacked near Tassafaronga Point, on the north coast of Guadalcanal, and commanded the newly formed 6th Marine Division. He was poised to become one of the most influential Marines of the 1940s and 1950s.

Shepherd was a Virginian with a soft tidewater accent, a spit-and-polish Marine who had been wounded at Belleau Wood, had served in China, and placed great importance on the history of the Marine Corps, Birthday Balls, and elaborate military rituals. He was a man of habits: a cup of tea upon rising, followed by a cold shower. A devout Episcopalian, he said a blessing before every meal. In the field, Shepherd was rarely without his coco macaque, a magic stick in Haitian voodoo and the sign of a Marine who had served in Haiti. Another of the hard-edged southerners who dominated the Marine Corps, he was perhaps even more bigoted than Holland Smith. Even Shepherd's son decried his father's frequent use of the word "nigger."

There is no small irony in the fact that the two generals who would have the most influence on Krulak's career, Smith and Shepherd, were southerners whose feelings about blacks are a matter of record. Both men contributed to the Marine Corps's efforts to subjugate or minimize the role of blacks and possibly also Jews. Yet Krulak idolized them both. As events were about to demonstrate, a case can be made that Krulak had no small part in Shepherd's rise to power. And Shepherd, again and again, would reward Krulak with water-walker FitReps and promotions to some of the best jobs in the Marine Corps.

By joining Shepherd's staff, Krulak became a card-carrying member of the "Central Pacific Gang" and one of the very few officers who also belonged to Vandegrift's Guadalcanal Gang. These two groups would dominate the Marine Corps for more than a decade.

RETURNING to the Pacific placed Krulak in the swirling vortex of great battles and would widen the sphere of his influence in Pacific events. Now that he had escaped General Hill's clutches, his career was on a sharp upward trajectory even as the career of Holland Smith was declining. The reason for Smith's decline only added to Krulak's fundamental belief about Army predations on the Marine Corps. Back on February 21, Smith had been on the cover of *Time* magazine, in part because of his brilliant leadership of Marines as they slogged their way up the Pacific, but also because of his involvement in the major interservice squabble of World War II, the "Smith versus Smith" controversy.

During the invasion of Saipan, an Army division commanded by General Ralph Smith was in the line between two Marine divisions. The three divisions were commanded by Holland Smith. When Holland Smith ordered an attack, the Marines pressed forward but the Army did not, and there was a big sag in the center of the line, a U with the Marines at the top and the Army at the bottom. The next night, some five hundred Japanese marched in a column through the Army lines, and the Marines had to turn and attack them. Holland Smith told Ralph Smith to be more aggressive, to press the attack, and when the Army division remained stalled while the Marines continued to advance, Holland Smith relieved Ralph Smith of command.

Other Army generals were relieved in the Pacific and later in Europe, but they were relieved by fellow Army officers, not by a Marine. The Smith versus Smith controversy outraged the Army, which convened a board that not unexpectedly exonerated Ralph Smith and excoriated Holland Smith. When Robert Sherrod, the famous *Time* magazine war correspondent, wrote an article detailing Ralph Smith's incompetence, the Army demanded that Sherrod's credentials be revoked.

The issue went all the way to Admiral King, who said that Sherrod would retain his credentials. But the Army never forgave Holland Smith, and there is no doubt that the incident damaged Smith's career and tarnished his reputation.

The Pacific theater of World War II provides some validation of Smith's beliefs. For example, Douglas MacArthur's first bookend for the Marine Corps in World War II was when he denied a unit citation to Marines in the Philippines. The second bookend came on September 2, 1945, when MacArthur presided over the formal Japanese surrender aboard the battleship *Missouri* in Tokyo Bay and did not invite Holland Smith to the ceremony. Military historians today say the Marines were well represented aboard the *Missouri*, and they were. But what these historians have forgotten is that "Howlin' Mad" Smith was not on board.

The march of Smith's Marines up the central Pacific remains the textbook example of an amphibious campaign—a campaign that changed the nature of warfare, and one of the longest sustained drives in military history. In a tactical sense, Smith did as much as MacArthur to defeat the Japanese in the Pacific—another reason MacArthur did not want him near the surrender ceremony.

By the time Krulak returned to the Pacific, America's interest in the European theater was all-consuming. Of course, there was some news coverage of Pacific events, but nothing received media coverage comparable to the Army's D-Day landing at Normandy in June 1944. America remained focused on defeating Germany, and almost every battle in Europe was front-page news back home. In December, when the Army's 101st Airborne Division was cut off at Bastogne, hundreds of thousands of Americans followed the fight. Almost everyone knew about the "Battered Bastards of Bastogne," whose commander, General Anthony McAuliffe, replied "Nuts" when the Germans asked him to surrender, and who were surrounded for eight days before being rescued by General George S. Patton. Bastogne later became material for books, movies, and television shows, and the Battle of the Bulge, of which Bastogne was a part, became the great symbolic battle of World War II. Almost forgotten is the fact that the Marines were isolated on Guadalcanal for six months and had no

General Patton to come to their rescue. America remembers Bastogne. Marines remember the 'Canal.

LEMUEL Shepherd relied on Krulak even more than had Holland Smith. On Shepherd's staff, Krulak was first among equals, but his closeness to Shepherd, though not the father-son relationship he had with Smith, was rather like the relationship between a very bright student and his teacher. Krulak was at Shepherd's side constantly and was never reluctant to voice his ideas and opinions. Shepherd, as had Smith before him, knew that Krulak's intellect and vision could make the general look good. Not only did Krulak have the most important staff job, but he was also the general's favorite, almost an alter ego, and regimental commanders soon found that when Krulak spoke, he spoke for General Shepherd. Brute was a man few wanted to confront; he had influence out of proportion with his rank, and there was growing jealousy, even animosity, toward him among his peers. He was so smart, so assertive, and so *right* that he made people angry.

Shepherd gave Krulak the job of planning the role of the 6th Marine Division during the invasion of Okinawa, and as was his way, Krulak went back to the basics. He put the infantry units on a vigorous program of physical fitness and conditioning that included numerous forced marches. He sent them to the rifle range and worked on coordinating tank and infantry units. It was Krulak who brought the division to combat readiness and enabled the units, in mid-March 1945, to sail for Okinawa.

WHILE Krulak was preparing the division for the invasion of Okinawa, another Pacific battle was raging. Although Brute was not there, that battle is important to his story because it shows that the Marine Corps still considered itself a white man's club from which Jews and blacks were excluded.

Today, if America has any memories of the Pacific war, at the top of the list would be Iwo Jima and the flag raising on Mount Suribachi. In fact, the picture of the flag raising remains the single most iconic image of the Marine Corps. But there is another Iwo Jima story known to few Americans.

Of the 70,000 Marines who landed on Iwo Jima, about 1,500 were Jewish. Assigned to the 5th Marine Division was Rabbi Roland Gittelsohn, the first Jewish chaplain ever assigned to the Marine Corps. (The Marine Corps has no chaplains and no medical corpsmen of its own. These jobs are filled by Navy personnel who are assigned to the Marines.) Gittelsohn was in the thick of the battle, ministering to Marines of all faiths, and his bravery and around-the-clock compassion in comforting the wounded earned him three commendations. When the fighting was over, the division chaplain, a Protestant, picked Rabbi Gittelsohn to conduct the single, nondenominational service to honor the Marines who had died on Iwo Jima. Some of the other Protestant chaplains objected to having a Jew preach over Christian graves, and Catholic chaplains opposed any sort of joint religious service at all. Thus, at the most sacred occasion following the invasion — honoring the dead — the chaplains did not unite under the same colors that flew atop Mount Suribachi; rather they flew the colors of bigotry. Three separate memorial services were held: Protestant, Catholic, and Jewish.

Division and regimental officers did nothing to avert this shame. But several Protestant chaplains were so upset that they boycotted their own service to attend Gittelsohn's. His message was so moving, so eloquent, and so powerful that one of the Protestant chaplains made several thousand copies of the printed sermon and passed them out to the regiment. Marines enclosed the sermon in their letters home, and family members passed it on to newspapers. *Time* magazine and the wire services spread the sermon farther. It was published in the *Congressional Record*, and the

Army later broadcast it to American troops around the world. Even today, Gittelsohn's remarks are sometimes read on Memorial Day and frequently pop up on the Internet.

This brief sermon is well worth reading.

*Here lie men who loved America because their ancestors generations ago helped in her founding, and other men who loved her with equal passion because they themselves or their own fathers escaped from oppression to her blessed shores. Here lie officers and men, Negroes and whites, rich men and poor... together. Here are Protestants, Catholics and Jews together. Here no man prefers another because of his faith or despises him because of his color. Here there are no quotas of how many from each group are admitted or allowed. Among these men, there is no discrimination. No prejudices. No hatred. Theirs is the highest and purest democracy....*

*Whosoever of us lifts his hand in hate against a brother, or who thinks himself superior to those who happen to be in the minority, makes of this ceremony and the bloody sacrifice it commemorates, an empty, hollow mockery. To this, then, as our solemn duty, sacred duty do we the living now dedicate ourselves: to the right of Protestants, Catholics, and Jews, of white men and Negroes alike, to enjoy the democracy for which all of them have here paid the price.*

*We here solemnly swear that this shall not be in vain. Out of this and from the suffering and sorrow of those who mourn this will come, we promise, the birth of a new freedom for the sons of men everywhere.*

In 1995, at the battle's fiftieth commemoration at the Marine Corps War Memorial in Washington, an aged Rabbi Gittelsohn read part of his sermon. He later wrote that no one would ever have heard of it had not it been for the bigotry of the 5th Marine Division. This is yet another reason why Krulak would have been inspired to hide his background.

\* \* \*

ANOTHER relatively unknown codicil to Iwo Jima is that Holland Smith had asked the Navy for a preinvasion bombardment lasting nine days to soften up Japanese positions before the Marines landed. Instead, the Navy gave the Marines only three days of gunfire—a shortfall that Smith believed contributed significantly to the almost 30,000 casualties, the greatest Marine battle loss in history and the only battle where Marines lost more men than did the enemy. Smith was vocal about what he saw as one more example of Navy malfeasance toward the Marine Corps. In doing so, he alienated both the Army and the Navy.

OPERATION Iceberg, the Okinawa invasion, began on Sunday, April 1, 1945—a time when Easter and April Fools' Day coincided. To assault this island, which was about sixty miles long, the Navy assembled the greatest naval armada in history—far larger than that assembled for the D-Day landing—with more than 1,300 ships carrying more than 180,000 troops. The island's harsh terrain meant that tanks and heavy firepower could not always be used, and instead the job had to be done by individual Marines, with their rifles and bayonets. The Marines rarely gave ground and never for very long, and they never failed to capture a fortified Japanese position. During the eighty-two days of combat, the 6th Marine Division moved from one end of Okinawa to the other, taking more than two-thirds of the island, the city of Naha, and two airfields. After the capture of Naha, Krulak sent a note to the officer who had led the assault, advising him that he was now the mayor of the city but that he would have to draw his salary from the Japanese.

Brute spent almost as much time with frontline units as he did at Shepherd's command post. For his role in the invasion, he would receive the Legion of Merit, the citation for which praises him for bringing the division to "a state of complete readiness" and for providing Shepherd with advice "of immeasurable value, being always sound, and based upon comprehensive and excellent tactical judgment and a consistently complete grasp of the situation." It also notes that to better acquaint himself with fluid battlefield conditions, Krulak frequently was on the front lines, where he exposed himself to enemy artillery and small-arms fire, and that his coordination of subordinate units "contributed materially to the success of this difficult operation."

In April, while Marines were dying on Okinawa, the U.S. House of Representatives, pushed by Army leadership, began holding hearings on postwar unification plans. The president ordered the hearing stopped, saying that America was still at war and this was no time for interservice squabbling. But the president's order had little effect in the field. During the battle for Okinawa, for example, the Army attack stalled for twenty days in the middle of the island. Meanwhile, the Marines took the Motobu Peninsula, then turned north and went all the way to the tip of the island. Krulak proposed an amphibious landing on the southeast coast that would force the Japanese to withdraw forces from their main line to resist the landing. But Army general Simon Bolivar Buckner Jr., overall commander at Okinawa, had the soldier's conviction about fighting on the ground, about going toe-to-toe with the enemy and slugging it out. He rejected Krulak's seagoing left hook, which caused Krulak later to observe, "General Buckner did not like the water. We liked the water. It is a very useful route to get from A to B." Later, Krulak would write in the *Marine Corps Gazette*, "For the force that has the skill and the courage to use it, the ocean is an immense tactical ally." This statement was not only an affirmation of the Marines' great strength; it was also a slap at the Army.

THE Army did not share the Marines' belief that officers should remove their insignia of rank while fighting on Pacific islands, and each time General Buckner visited Marine units, he was quickly spotted by the Japanese, causing an artillery barrage within minutes to rain down on his position. Usually Buckner moved fast enough to avoid the barrage, and it was the Marines who had to take cover. But on June 18, 1945, the Japanese landed three rounds within seconds of Buckner's arrival, and a piece of coral flew up and killed him.

Command passed to Marine general Roy Geiger. The idea of a Marine commanding Army divisions so appalled the Army that they took only four days to bring in Army general Joseph Stilwell to relieve Geiger.

By then the fighting was over. During the battle on Okinawa, Adolf Hitler committed suicide, President Roosevelt died, Harry Truman became president, and Germany surrendered. While America was still rejoicing over V-E Day (May 8, 1945), the Marines on Okinawa were counting their casualties.

The Navy lost more ships at Okinawa than it lost at Pearl Harbor. Okinawa was the last stepping-stone on the route to Japan, the last stop in the long central Pacific campaign. The Japanese had defended many islands almost to the last man, but neither they nor the Germans at Normandy ever repulsed a major amphibious assault. These amphibious landings, beginning at Guadalcanal, opened up the Axis powers to invasion and defeat. Now, after almost three years of hard fighting, the Marines had wrestled control of the Pacific from the Japanese, and there remained only Japan itself.

In August, as the Marines were girding themselves for the last great battle, Truman ordered atomic bombs dropped on Hiroshima and Nagasaki, and the war was over.

The Marines are not only first to fight; they are also often the last to come home. And so it was in the Pacific. After Okinawa, the 6th Marine Division was ordered to China, to accept the surrender of Japanese troops for the Chinese government and to supervise the repatriation of the Japanese military. On October 11, Shepherd, with Krulak at his side, sailed into Kiaochow Bay and landed on the Shantung Peninsula. He took over Tsingtao, where increasing clashes between Nationalist forces and the People's Liberation Army (PLA) had created a volatile environment. The Japanese, their surrender notwithstanding, were patrolling the streets and keeping order in the face of aggressive Communist forces that had taken over the territory around Tsingtao. The Soviets were aiding the PLA, and it seemed clear that if the Marines did not take charge, the Chinese Communists would fill the vacuum. The Marines' job was to assist Nationalist forces in reestablishing a municipal administration, establishing law and order, and returning China to a peaceful way of life.

Shepherd summoned the Japanese commander, Major General Eiji Nagano, and gave him seventy-two hours to submit a list of all weapons held by his men and surrender those weapons. Nagano agreed. When he came to Shepherd's office, he placed a stack of papers on the American's desk and asked to speak. Krulak remembers that Nagano was quite fearful when he said, "If you oblige us to lay down our arms, the Communists will kill us. I ask you to leave each man his rifle, each officer his pistol, and each individual with five rounds of ammunition. We can't harm you with that small amount of ammunition, but it will save our lives."

Today any general presented with such a proposal would relay the request to his superior, who would go to the Joint Chiefs of Staff, who would contact the secretary of defense, who would contact the White House. But Shepherd was a wartime general not afraid to make decisions. "That's a deal," Krulak remembered Shepherd saying.

Then an emissary from the PLA came to Shepherd's office. He said that the Communists were the legitimate power in China and that the U.S. Marines should deal with them rather than with

Nationalists. The PLA officer wanted to help wipe out the Japanese military in China. Shepherd refused, saying the Marines were in China to ensure peace.

Accepting a surrender was an unusual situation for the Marines, in that they were used to killing every Japanese in sight. In fact, no large Japanese units had surrendered during the long Pacific war, and thus there was no precedent for how Shepherd should manage the ceremony. Shepherd told Krulak to take care of the details.

Krulak decided that the fundamental precept of any surrender is that the losing force must lay down its arms. So he decided to hold the surrender ceremony at the racecourse, a venue big enough to parade the entire 6th Marine Division. The featured part of the ceremony would be the highly symbolic act of General Nagano handing his sword to General Shepherd.

This sort of theater and pageantry was right up Krulak's alley. In addition, he knew that no senior officer in the Marine Corps favored Mess Nights and the highly stylized drama of Birthday Balls more than Shepherd. So Krulak drew up formal surrender plans that revolved around keeping Shepherd at the center of all events. On October 25, before the assembled Marines, the 10,000-man Japanese garrison at Tsingtao formally surrendered. The ceremony was a production worthy of Hollywood.

General Nagano wrote a note to General Shepherd saying the samurai sword he had surrendered had been in his family for 350 years and he hoped Shepherd would not throw it away. Shepherd was so touched that he wanted to return it to the general, but Krulak convinced him not to do so, saying that accepting the sword was a highly symbolic act in the surrender and that it must remain with Shepherd.

A few days after the surrender but before the repatriation process had begun, Nagano met with Shepherd and made a startling proposal. Winter was coming, and the Marines needed coal, which came down the Tsingtao–Tsinan Railway. Even though each locomotive on that route carried an American flag and Marine guards, the trains were under almost constant attack from the PLA. According to Krulak, Nagano said, "My troops have nothing to do while awaiting transportation to Japan. If you will give me back my artillery and a supply of ammunition, I will secure the rail line for you." Shepherd, again without consulting Washington, agreed on the spot. Thus, as early as the fall of 1945, the former enemies were allied against the Chinese Communists.

It was in that heady atmosphere that the Marine Corps birthday was celebrated. The 6th Marine Division had been eating C rations on Okinawa and welcomed the abundance of the Chinese table. Peiping duck was featured at the Birthday Ball. Shepherd awarded Krulak the Bronze Star, the citation for which gave Krulak full credit for the Marine landing in Tsingtao, the occupation, and the surrender ceremony.

As 1945 drew to an end, the Marine Corps had written a new chapter in the history of warfare. An estimated 16.3 million Americans served in World War II, less than 5 percent of them Marines. Yet the Marines had suffered almost 10 percent of all battlefield casualties: 67,207 wounded and 19,733 killed. In addition, the Marine drive up the central Pacific had been so stunning in its scope and its accomplishments that few campaigns in history can be used as a comparison. It had been a nightmare—but also a dream.

THE U.S. Army is famous for leaving expensive equipment on the battlefield, but Marines have always been so light in the budget, and so indoctrinated with the idea of making do with what is available, that the idea of simply walking away from serviceable equipment is anathema. Thus Lemuel Shepherd's Marines in China did as Marines in the Pacific had done: they gathered the jeeps, trucks, amtracs, Higgins boats, artillery pieces, and other pieces of equipment costing more than several hundred dollars and shipped everything back to America. There it was refurbished, repaired, painted, oiled, and sent to the dry air of Barstow, California, to be ready next time America had to go to war on short notice.

DEMOBILIZATION and sharp cuts in the military budget—what politicians call the peace dividend—always follow a war. The Army Air Forces wanted independence as a separate branch of the military, which meant the new Air Force would require a big portion of a diminished budget in order to build air bases and buy airplanes. The Army, jealous of Marine glory in the Pacific, wanted not only to retain its status as America's land army but also to ensure that the Marines never again took to the battlefield in large numbers. These and other dynamics would be resolved under the rubric of "unification" of America's military.

The most revered names in the Army—George C. Marshall and Dwight Eisenhower—aided and abetted by President Truman, were trying to do what the Japanese empire had failed to do: destroy the United States Marine Corps. It was decided that the Marine Corps should be cut from a peak strength of 485,000 to 100,000 and then to 65,000, all the time trying to preserve its combat capability.

Many Marines minimized the threat of the Army's intentions because they believed the great Marine victories in the Pacific would protect them from Army politics. But the forgotten truth is that were it not for a small group of officers, the Marine Corps would have been rendered militarily ineffective by postwar unification plans.

Gerry Thomas was the Commandant's choice to coordinate Marine Corps opposition to Army unification plans. Bill Twining, a calm and scholarly lawyer, headed a board that would conceive and implement the Marine Corps's own plans. Twining, who needed someone to run the board on a day-to-day basis, had the Commandant's authority to summon any officer in the Marine Corps to his side. Twining and Thomas agreed that the assistant not only had to be intelligent, enthusiastic, and tireless; he also had to be a visionary officer who believed passionately in the survival of the Corps.

In late 1945, Brute Krulak received orders telling him to "proceed without delay" to Quantico.

# 8

## Chowder

In World War II, an Army general told Holland Smith, "You Marines are nothing but a bunch of beach-runners anyway. What do you know about land warfare?"

Behind this patronizing comment are two Army beliefs. First, Marine enlisted ranks contain a disproportionate number of borderline psychopaths, alcoholics, social misfits, brig rats, and knuckle draggers—men who in wartime can take the hill but in peacetime often act in ways prejudicial to the good order and discipline of the military. Second, Marine officers are not qualified for high command because so many of them are straight-ahead, uncomplicated men who, though they may lead their men to heroic achievements on the battlefield, lack depth and sophistication in military matters.

Other branches of the military find it faintly amusing that Marines, both officers and enlisted men, are a closed society with insistence on rules that to non-Marines seem more than a little ridiculous. Marines are fanatical about their uniforms, about being "squared away": The rear hems of their trousers must fall *exactly* to the heels of their shoes, and their boots can be laced only one way: the bottom lace is over and under rather than under and over, and the lace from the left must cross over the lace from the right.

Rarely, if ever, are soldiers heard saying "our Army," sailors saying "our Navy," or airmen saying "our Air Force," but Marines often speak of "our Corps" with a reverence impenetrable to those outside this almost mystical tribe—this branch of the military where people are more important than machines, where the lowest-ranking member will tell you that his most solemn duty is to protect the Marine by his side and to uphold the honor of those Marines who have gone before him.

And despite what seems to be a rigid institutional conformity, in combat Marines often show more initiative, more freedom of thought, than do members of the other branches of the military. Marines know the rules of war, but when the shooting starts, they consider those rules as a frame of reference and not a prescription.

What appears to be an institutional schizophrenia is in fact an ineffable synergy that has long attracted a certain type of man: the pure warrior whose sole reason for being is to kill the enemies of America. Such rough men—"an assemblage of warriors," Krulak called them—are rarely found among shoe salesmen, pharmacists, and editors. In fact, much of American society is reluctant to acknowledge the need for such men.

Once a person has been through recruit training at Parris Island or San Diego, once a person finishes Officer Candidates School or The Basic School at Quantico, that person becomes part of a blood-bound brotherhood that stretches back to Belleau Wood and beyond; he is forever part of "our Corps." This is not a matter of conscious choice; it is an immutable law.

When Lee Harvey Oswald crouched in a sixth-floor window of the Texas School Book Depository and fired four shots at President John F. Kennedy, who was in a moving vehicle below, two shots hit Kennedy, one hit Texas governor John Connally (who was sitting in the front seat), and one missed. The four shots were fired in about seven seconds from an old bolt-action rifle, causing the media to marvel at such "impossible" shooting. But Marine drill instructors told recruits that Oswald had grown rusty since he left the Corps, that only one shot should have been necessary.

This off-putting picture obscures an important dimension of the Marine Corps: among Marine officers are men of extraordinary intellect who can hold their own with business leaders, university professors, and statesmen. Certainly, the equivalent of these men is found in the civilian world, but the difference is that Marines are motivated by unadulterated patriotism, and their accomplishments accrue to the benefit of all America.

Civilians who know little of the military would say this is an over-the-top assessment, that there are many civilians whose accomplishments benefit all of America—medical researchers, for example. True, but medical researchers are not being shot at every day. To compare medical researchers, or those in any other job in the civilian world, with Marines who volunteer to put themselves in harm's way, to put their lives on the line in defense of their country, is, well, silly.

Nevertheless, those who would make such comparisons often diminish the accomplishments of Marines simply because they wear a uniform. Many Americans believe that people who wear military uniforms could not succeed in the civilian world. That these men press on, unknown and unappreciated, is a tribute to their sense of duty—to the courage, honor, and commitment that motivate them.

In the post–World War II years, few Marine officers better exemplified this aspect of the Corps than Brute Krulak. He and a handful of relatively junior Marine officers realized that although the very survival of the Marine Corps was at stake, a more important issue was the survival of a fundamental American belief: civilian control of the military. Because of these men, the years 1945 to 1952 were the cleanest and purest in the history of the Marine Corps. The shooting war was over, but the battles these men fought were as important as Guadalcanal, Iwo Jima, and Okinawa, and these battles were even more chilling because they were then and remain today generally unknown to the public. These clashes took place in the halls of Congress when a cabal (there is no other word for it) of military officers—respected and revered men who were aided and abetted by the president—attempted to restructure the American military in a way that would have been prejudicial to America's national interests. And they almost prevailed.

Brute Krulak was a pivotal person in both saving the Marine Corps and ensuring that one of America's core beliefs was preserved.

Upon arriving at Quantico in November 1945, Krulak was given the title head of the research section at the Marine Corps Schools, ostensibly working for his close friend Robert Hogaboom. But Krulak delegated the research job to a junior officer while he quietly began working on the most important postwar job in the Marine Corps.

Already the Army unification plan was being studied by the Military Affairs Committee of the U.S. Senate. This plan and others to follow were infinitely complex in how they saw the political-military mix, the military organization, and the roles and functions of each branch of the service. To sort it all out, we must do two things: first, ignore people and issues that may not be directly relevant to Krulak's story; second, reduce the various versions of the unification plan to core issues. From beginning to end, the heart of the Army plan was how it envisioned the Army as a political-military entity with a chief of staff who would wield power not held by a military man since George Washington.

Even with the perspective of more than a half century, it is difficult to imagine how George C. Marshall, Dwight Eisenhower, and Carl Spaatz, commander of the Army Air Forces, could so enthusiastically sponsor a plan that was, at its very core, not only antithetical to how the founding fathers viewed the military but also would have brought to fruition the worst fears Americans have about the military: the all-powerful "man on horseback." It was an idea that by its very nature gave those who opposed it the moral high ground—and, as is often the case with those who hold the moral high ground, events that can only be described as providential would accrue to their benefit.

Truman was an unapologetic Army loyalist. As FDR's vice president, he had seen the flotilla of admirals that always seemed to be in the White House and vowed that on his watch the White House would cease to resemble a wardroom. His wartime alliance with the Navy and Marines had vaulted him into the national spotlight and was responsible for his being selected vice president. But that was an alliance of convenience, and now he dismissed the Marines as the Navy's "little Army." As a senator, he had served on the Military Affairs Committee and was a strong proponent of unification. Later, as a vice presidential candidate, he wrote an article for *Collier's* magazine titled "Our Armed Forces Must Be Unified."

Marshall, Eisenhower, and Spaatz clearly saw the overweening ambition inherent in their plan, because when they codified their ideas in a series of papers known as the JCS (Joint Chiefs of Staff) 1478 papers, the papers, in an arbitrary and unnecessary classification, were stamped TOP SECRET. Indeed, few military secrets were as closely held.

In one paper, Spaatz described Marine amphibious landings and Marine close air support as "patently an incursion" into the role of the Army and the Army Air Forces. Eisenhower, now Army chief of staff, said that the Marines had merely duplicated the role of the Army during World War II. He recommended that the Marine Corps be limited to about 50,000 men and said that if another war came, the Marine Corps should not be appreciably expanded. Neither Eisenhower nor Spaatz saw any use for Marine Corps aviation, which should be absorbed into the proposed new Air Force.

Putting these views on paper would prove to be a major strategic error for the Army and the Army Air Forces. Another error was underestimating the resolve of the Marine Corps. Still another was Army generals believing, in their arrogance, that they could hoodwink Congress. Finally, the Army did not realize that the Marine Corps had become part of the warp and woof of America. Indeed, the picture of Marines raising the flag on Mount Suribachi was already one of the most reproduced photos in history.

KRULAK was part of a loose and informal group of officers who worked behind closed doors. Because he was senior, Bill Twining is usually given credit by military historians for the unification fight. Only months before he died, when Krulak was asked how one might distinguish between Twining's work and his own, he said, "We worked elbow to elbow, mind to mind." Pressed for a sharper distinction, Krulak paused then said, "I was the leader. Twining was senior, and he was the smartest, but he was not greatly articulate. Plus, I had a sincere interest and the conviction that our cause was correct. I had to fight for the Marine Corps."

IN the beginning, Krulak's job was to conduct research and collect information for reports and studies that would be presented to Congress. He was the tactician, the man who coordinated the efforts of others, and was first among equals on the staff. His intellect, his visionary thinking, his willingness to make hard decisions, his seemingly inexhaustible energy, and the ease with which he conveyed sometimes unpleasant truths to Twining—along with his assertive and domineering personality—made him ideal for the job. Over the next two years, a cascade of reports, studies, and recommendations would come from his desk.

Krulak and the officers with whom he worked, most of whom were lieutenant colonels, were seen as Machiavellian, even sinister, by many of their superiors and most of their peers. They had ill-defined jobs and were rarely in their offices—what Marines called "skylarkers"—and many Marines believed that their own careers would be tainted by associating with Krulak's crowd. This unification business clearly involved national politics, and such matters were best handled by senior military leaders. In addition, Krulak and his colleagues could not talk about what they were doing, and all the cloak-and-dagger stuff made other Marines uncomfortable. General O. P. Smith, a cautious and scholarly man who was then in charge of the Marine Corps Schools and the person to whom Krulak and Hogaboom reported (at least on paper), saw some of the documents prepared by Twining's group and was horrified. The blunt assessment of Army plans caused him to order all copies of the documents confiscated, given a high security classification, and then burned. He famously dismissed the work of the group as "wheels within wheels."

But Krulak reveled in the drama, the subterfuge, the idea that he was part of great events. He believed that if the Marine Corps was pushed off this lily pad, there was no place to go.

The nickname for Twining's group was inspired by a popular comic strip of the day called *Barnaby*. The eponymous main character was short, cherubic, and always getting into trouble, and he bore an uncanny resemblance to Krulak. Barnaby had a fairy godfather named Jackeen J. O'Malley and belonged to a social club called the Elves, Leprechauns, Gnomes, and Little Men's Chowder & Marching Society. One day an officer down the hall from Krulak pinned an episode of *Barnaby* on Krulak's door. He had underlined "Little Men's Chowder & Marching Society" and added an arrow pointing to Barnaby, identifying him as "Krulak."

Thereafter, Twining's band of merry men was known as the Chowder Society, and the members, when in public or with officers not sympathetic to their cause, referred to their output as "chowder."

The Chowder Society was an ad hoc group that fluctuated in number from three or four to as many as ten. There were no meetings, only individual members whose work was collected and organized by Krulak. Members joined and later moved on, but Krulak was there at the beginning, and he was there at the end.

The Chowder Society did not lack ambition. It was taking on the president, the Army, Eisenhower, Marshall (who was about to become secretary of state), powerful members of Congress, and — most painful of all — brother Marines.

Over the years, much apocrypha has grown up about various members of the Chowder Society. Who did what? Who was the pivotal person? Other than Krulak, only one person should be singled out, and that is Lyford Hutchins, a shadowy figure who sometimes disappeared for days on end. When he reappeared, he would empty a briefcase onto Krulak's desk, and out would tumble documents so sensitive that Krulak would wonder whether they had been purloined. It was Hutchins who obtained a copy of the JCS 1478 papers that gave Krulak the blueprint for Army unification.

On January 7, 1946, Krulak celebrated his thirty-third birthday with a party and plenty of Fish House Punch. Some of the guests murmured quiet asides to "chowder," because Krulak was drafting a stinging response to the JCS papers. The thirty-four-page response never specifically mentioned the documents, because to do so would have given away the fact that the Marines knew about them and also would have been a serious breach of security. Commandant Vandegrift read the rebuttal; wrinkled his brow at the inherent rebuke of Marshall, Eisenhower, and Spaatz, the most venerated names in the military; but then signed the document and forwarded it to the Army.

The Army was not used to having anyone question the wisdom of its famous generals and fired back with such bitterness that Twining summoned Krulak for an emergency meeting. Was it wise to confront the Army with such bluntness? Krulak answered that the unification debate was not a lofty exchange of ideas, but a "cat fight where the stakes are the preservation of the existing U.S. military structure as well as the survival of the Marine Corps as a national institution." He said that the Marine Corps should step up both the tempo and the language.

Twining agreed. When Vandegrift was asked to testify before the Senate Naval Affairs Committee, Twining and Krulak realized they had a national stage on which to reveal the Army's intentions. As Krulak sat down to write Vandegrift's speech, Twining said, "Make it tough. Tell the truth." This would not be an address couched in the elaborate formalities and artful obfuscation sometimes found in congressional testimony; it would be clear and unequivocal and would focus on Army motivations. For much of the next few weeks, Twining and Krulak worked on the speech — Krulak writing, Twining editing.

Vandegrift had proved his courage on Guadalcanal, for which he had received the Medal of Honor. But he was beginning to realize that he had little stomach for politics. He was disturbed by the force of Krulak's speech and the veiled references to the JCS papers.

On May 10, Twining and Krulak joined Vandegrift for the ride to the Capitol. Through much of the drive, Vandegrift expressed reservations about what he was about to say, but he delivered the speech as Krulak had written it. Subsequently known as the "Bended Knee" speech, it remains one of the most powerful and eloquent addresses ever given to Congress by a man in uniform.

What the committee members expected to hear that day is not

known, but what they got was an opening broadside saying the Army-backed unification bill was fundamentally and deeply flawed in that the Army was deliberately seeking to usurp congressional prerogatives. Few things upset Congress more than the idea that someone is trying to take over its lily pad, and Vandegrift had its undivided attention when he moved on to specific Marine Corps interests. "This bill gives the War Department a free hand in accomplishing its expressed desire to reduce the Marine Corps to a position of military insignificance," he said. He knew this to be true because the idea came from "the highest quarters of the War Department," a reference to the JCS papers.

After going down a list of Marine Corps accomplishments over the years, Vandegrift resumed his attack on the Army, saying that before World War II, America had had the world's top-ranked Marine Corps at an annual cost of $1,500 per Marine and the world's eighteenth-ranked Army at a cost of $2,000 per soldier. In Washington, every issue sooner or later revolves around money, and to document Army financial inefficiency was the unkindest cut of all.

As Vandegrift drew to a close, he lingered on a crucial point, one that placed a great burden on Congress:

In its capacity as a balance wheel the Congress has on five occasions since 1828 reflected the voice of the people in casting aside a motion which would damage or destroy the Marine Corps. Now I believe the cycle has repeated itself and that the fate of the Marine Corps lies solely with the Congress.

He ended with the most famous part of the speech:

The Marine Corps thus believes it has earned this right—to have its future decided by the legislative body which created it—nothing more.... The bended knee is not a tradition of our Corps. If the Marine as a fighting man has not made a case for himself after 170 years, he must go. But I think you will agree with me that he has earned the right to depart with dignity and honor, not by subjugation to the status of uselessness and servility planned for him by the War Department.

After Vandegrift's speech, the questioning was, as Krulak put it, "spirited and sympathetic." A senator who had been briefed in private about the JCS papers posed a planted question: "Are there documents or papers drawn up by the Joint Chiefs of Staff which confirm your fears about the Marine Corps being rendered ineffective?"

"Yes, sir."

Over the next few days, the Army plan was ridiculed by the media. Barely more than a week after Vandegrift's testimony, House and Senate leaders said publicly that the Army bill would not pass if it meant stripping the Marine Corps of its historic functions.

Truman was furious, and his animosity toward the Marine Corps began building up a head of steam that, when released, would have enormous and unforeseen consequences. But he put on a conciliatory face. He said that a revised unification plan would be worked out and that it would include "preservation of the Marine Corps with all its prerogatives."

Krulak doubted that Truman—whom he privately referred to as "the former commander of Battery D"—would keep his word. His skepticism was justified when the president set about resurrecting the Army plan by ordering the secretary of war and the secretary of the Navy—the Marines were not invited—to meet and summarize for him the areas where they agreed and disagreed. He would arbitrate the differences. But the secretaries could not agree on what they agreed on, and in July Truman acknowledged what Congress already knew: the Army plan was dead for that session of Congress.

The Marines knew that they had won a skirmish, but the big battle was still ahead.

KRULAK was also a crucial player in a parallel story. At 8:45 a.m. on July 1, 1946, an atomic bomb exploded on a tiny island at the northwestern tip of the Marshall Islands called Bikini Atoll. Military equipment and various domestic animals had been placed on the island, and dozens of ships were anchored in the nearby lagoon. The purpose of this first peacetime explosion was to determine what damage would occur to equipment, animals, and ships. The resulting devastation was so terrible, especially when piled atop what observers knew about the effects of the atomic bombs dropped on Hiroshima and Nagasaki, that the military was convinced there was no defense against such a weapon.

If there were any whispers of going slowly, of waiting until there were some quantifiable long-range predictions about the lethality of the new weapon, those whispers disappeared in August when *The New Yorker* gave writer John Hersey an entire issue of the magazine to write about the new atomic age. Hersey's famous article provided the military with what it lacked: lethality computations. The Department of Defense considered Hersey's figures "unofficial" and not something on which policy should be based. But it nevertheless used them in its own assessments and was not pleased with what it found. Against an enemy possessing atomic weapons, ships approaching a hostile shore would have to be so widely dispersed that they would not be able to conduct an amphibious landing. Plus, the landing would have to be conducted at a speed that was orders of magnitude beyond the top speed of any ship in the Navy inventory.

The fallout from Hersey's article was that never again could there be such a concentration of ships, aircraft, and men as there had been during the World War II invasions of Pacific islands and

Normandy. Once again, amphibious assaults were thought to be an outmoded form of warfare.

But assaulting hostile shores is the raison d'être of the Marine Corps, and an alarmed Commandant formed a board of three generals and directed them to develop concepts and principles for waging amphibious warfare in the future. Vandegrift told the board to consider "revolutionary measures."

The board had a large staff, but Lemuel Shepherd, its senior officer, believed there was only one man in the Marine Corps whom he could, with absolute confidence, depend on: Brute Krulak. Krulak was deep in the unification battle, was teaching occasional classes at Quantico, and had no spare time. Even so, he could not say no to Shepherd. The two men worked out an arrangement whereby ideas considered by the board's staff would be sent to Krulak for his reaction. During the coming months, dozens of ideas crossed Krulak's desk, but one in particular seized his attention, an idea that he enlarged and developed. He ignored a host of technical and practical difficulties to look over the horizon and see the ultimate potential of a strange and fragile device then in its infancy: the helicopter.

In the late summer of 1946, as Krulak waited for Congress to return from its summer recess, he pored over congressional testimony regarding the unification proposal and, as is sometimes the case when considering a complicated and nuanced subject, realized at a new and deeper level the inherent treachery of an Army plan that sought to suborn civilian control of the military. Making sure the Marine Corps survived unification was, of course, crucial to Krulak, but his goal fit snugly within the bigger and more important goal of upholding the Constitution.

When Congress returned, the unification fight would resume and would be bitterer than ever. A vengeful and hot-tempered

Truman was lying in wait, and against such formidable opposition the Marine Corps had to present a cohesive front. But Krulak was about to lose the Commandant's support, which would make the Chowder Society more vulnerable than ever.

AFTER the "Bended Knee" speech, Truman had given Vandegrift such a brutal tongue-lashing that the Commandant's zeal for political infighting waned even more. Truman believed that by muzzling the Commandant, Marine Corps opposition to the Army unification plan would cease. If Twining's group decided to press on, they would be in uncharted waters, a small group of relatively junior officers attempting to circumvent the desires of the commander in chief—risky business indeed.

But the Chowder Society comprised men who loved the Marine Corps above all else, men who believed the game was worth the candle. When Congress convened, the Chowder Society, bloodied and alone, would rise and fight again.

NORM Hatch was a Marine warrant officer who in World War II had been a combat photographer. In the late summer of 1946, he was "dual-hatted" as chief of photographic operations for the Marine Corps and a member of the director of public relations' staff.

One day he looked up from his desk to see Brute Krulak, who in effect said to him, "The Corps is likely to go down the drain if something radical isn't done quickly." Krulak wanted a documentary that would show Congress the importance of the Marine Corps and let it know what was at stake in the unification battle.

He had come to the right place. Hatch was known throughout the Marine Corps for the film footage he had shot on Tarawa and Iwo Jima, and later at Nagasaki. Krulak would write the script for Hatch's combat footage, and the documentary would be called *Bombs over Tokyo*.

The film was "quick and dirty," but for its intended purpose, it was brilliant and even today could serve as a model for propaganda films. The first three minutes and forty-two seconds are a paean to the Army Air Forces, telling of the devastation wreaked on Japan by American airpower and how, by the end of the war, the sound of B-29s caused "abject fear" among Japanese. Aerial photographs of B-29s are seen against the musical backdrop of "Into the Wild Blue Yonder" and "America the Beautiful."

Then the film explains that the bombing of Japan was accomplished only because Army Air Forces bases were close enough to Japan for B-29s to make the round-trip. And those bases were on islands captured by Marines.

The remaining twenty minutes explain that amphibious operations are the most complex operations in the military repertoire, so risky that if they are stopped on the beach, the results can be catastrophic. And there could have been no bombing of Japan were it not for three and a half years of amphibious landings by Marines. The film includes dramatic footage of Higgins boats being rammed onto a beach, their bows dropping, and Marines charging ashore.

The voice-over says that all this did not start in World War II; it started in 1776 when Marines made an amphibious assault on the Bahamas. The rousing ending tells how the Marines "marched toward the setting sun" and drove a wedge up the central Pacific in the "greatest amphibious offensive in the history of warfare."

Krulak and an assistant spent several weeks lugging a 16-millimeter projector and a movie screen all over Washington to show the film. Krulak used his considerable powers of persuasion to convince the Armed Services Committees in both houses, numerous congressmen and senators, and powerful civilian advisers to the White House such as Clark Clifford to sit down and watch the documentary.

WHEN Congress reconvened, Truman ordered Clifford to meet with Army and Navy leadership and come up with a new unification bill. The meetings took place throughout the autumn of 1946. The Marine Corps was not represented but did learn that the self-interests of the participants were preventing progress. That changed shortly before Christmas when Truman issued an ultimatum that forced an agreement, and on January 16, 1947, the new plan was announced without notifying the Marine Corps.

It was during this period that Krulak found himself at an event, probably a holiday party, attended by Eisenhower and numerous high-ranking Army and Navy officers. Eisenhower had made it a point to know the sources of Marine Corps opposition to the unification plan. At some point in the evening, Krulak was introduced to Eisenhower. The iconic general looked sternly at Krulak and asked, "Just what is it that you Marines really want?"

"The right to fight for our country, sir. That's all," Krulak responded.

Eisenhower turned and walked away.

THE new unification concept dropped the idea of the single military chief of staff, retained the idea of three military departments—Army, Navy, and Air Force—and codified the Joint Chiefs of Staff, an idea that had sprung up in World War II as a matter of necessity. What troubled the Marines about the plan was its vagueness; nothing was said about the roles of the separate services, meaning nothing ensured the continued existence of the Marines. The roles and missions of the military—who does what—were left to the discretion of the president, who would set forth these duties by executive order. A president, were he so inclined, could sign an order that would reduce the Marine Corps to, as Truman later said, "a Navy police force."

The plan left the Marines without legal protection, which meant that the other branches of the military could continue to minimize the roles and functions of the Marine Corps. America's founding fathers had seen enough of British armies in the colonies and wanted no standing army in their new country. Article I, Section 8 of the Constitution says only that Congress shall have the power "to raise and support Armies" and "to provide and maintain a Navy." But if the Marine Corps were to survive, its existence and functions must be protected by law, and the only way that could be done was by lobbying Congress.

Vandegrift had recovered from Truman's ire and reentered the fray by appointing a board to gather material and prepare for congressional action when the Army bill reappeared. The group was called the Edson-Thomas Board, named for Generals M. A. "Red Mike" Edson and Gerald Thomas. (That some military historians say the formation of the board marks the origin of the Chowder Society overlooks the fact that Twining, Krulak, and others had been working on unification issues for more than a year.)

Most members of the board concentrated on Marine Corps survival, while Thomas and Krulak continued to focus on national security issues, specifically too much military involvement in national politics and the need for legislation that spelled out the roles and missions of all branches of the military.

When Truman sent the new bill to Congress on February 26, 1947, it contained no specific duties for any branch of the military. The Marines decided not to fight the bill in the Senate Armed Services Committee, which was dominated by friends of the Army, but to wait and wage their battle in the House. Krulak began writing another speech for Vandegrift, one that was modeled on the "Bended Knee" speech but would place greater emphasis on the hazard to America created by the new bill's concentration of power.

In the Senate hearings, Eisenhower spoke in favor of the German political-military system, saying that his own role in World War II had made him, in effect, a secretary of national defense for Europe. He said that national defense should come from one brain. This extreme position was not questioned because it came from the man who had planned the Normandy invasion and whose forces had retaken Europe.

EVENTUALLY, through heavy lobbying by the Marines, the Commandant was invited to testify at the Senate hearings. Krulak wrote the speech and presented it to Generals Twining and Edson, both of whom agreed that it was, as Krulak said, "a worthy sequel" to the "Bended Knee" speech. But Vandegrift remembered his trip to the woodshed and did not want to cross Truman again. He thought the speech intemperate, and rather than asking Krulak to soften it, he asked someone else to write a new speech, one that acquiesced to the president's unification bill. When that speech was finished, Vandegrift submitted it to the Navy Department and the president for approval. Vandegrift would no longer defend his Marines, and his acceptance of the bill was seen as Marine Corps acceptance.

Then up stepped General Edson to testify before the Senate committee. Edson was a legendary Marine, a hero of the 'Canal, where his Raiders had defeated the very best Japanese troops at Bloody Ridge. To protect the Marine Corps from presidential retribution, Edson put in a request for retirement before he testified. His statement was largely the address Krulak had written earlier for the Commandant. But Edson had thrown himself on his sword for nought, as the committee approved the Truman-backed bill on July 9. Vandegrift, however, had become so indecisive that he took no action on Edson's request for retirement, leaving Edson twisting in the wind.

With victory almost certain, the Army made another major tactical error. It did not want the unification bill to go before the House Armed Services Committee, believing, rightly, that the Marine Corps had friends on the committee. Instead, the Army steered the bill toward the House Committee on Expenditures in the Executive Departments, which was chaired by Congressman

Clare Hoffman. The congressman from Michigan had no military bases in his district and had never shown any interest in military affairs, and the Army believed that he would assign the unification bill to a subcommittee chaired by a congressman who was a friend of the Army. What the Army did not know was that Hoffman was close friends with the father of James Hittle, a member of the Chowder Society, who persuaded the congressman to listen to the Marines' case. The Army was subsequently stunned when Hoffman announced that he would not turn the bill over to the subcommittee, but that his committee would consider the issue.

In the meantime, the Chowder Society had alerted the Veterans of Foreign Wars to the importance of the unification issue. In April, the two-million-member organization publicly urged Congress to spell out Marine Corps roles and responsibilities in the proposed legislation and not to leave the Marines subject to interservice squabbling or presidential whim.

When the hearing convened, numerous Army proponents, including Eisenhower, were put on the defensive when the committee asked them sharp questions about the excessive power of the new secretary of defense, the potential for military leadership to become a general staff along the lines of the Prussian model, usurpation of congressional authority, and threats to the Marine Corps's existence. Now the War Department plan was in danger.

Krulak drafted amendments to the bill that would limit the authority of the secretary of defense and protect the Marine Corps. Pushed by Krulak, Hoffman brought up the existence of the JCS 1478 papers and said that the unification bill would not pass until he could study the papers. The Army refused to release them, but not even Truman could deny the committee chairman access to them. He ordered the Army to turn the documents over to Hoffman's committee. Once the committee members read the papers, any doubts about the implications of the Army bill vanished.

Eisenhower testified before the committee and was disingenuous in the extreme, saying that he had never proposed a reduction in the size of the Marines or a curtailment of their duties. "I am nonplused to find out why I have been considered an enemy of the Marines," he said. When Hoffman's questions made it clear that the congressman had read the JCS papers, Eisenhower began backpedaling, seeking to minimize his contribution to them.

By May, Truman was so angry that members of the Chowder Society were slowing down the progress of his bill that he ordered Vandegrift to "get those lieutenant colonels off the Hill and keep them off." In response, Vandegrift dissolved the Edson-Thomas Board. But Truman's gag order had an unexpected effect: indignant congressmen complained that now they were permitted to hear only one side of the debate. The congressmen forced Truman to back down and summoned General Edson to testify. This put Edson in the untenable position of not only opposing a bill that had been accepted by the Commandant but also of opposing his old comrade from Guadalcanal.

Edson again submitted his request for retirement, and this time Vandegrift accepted. Edson's testimony was all the more powerful because the committee knew that this legendary Marine officer believed so much in his cause that he willing to retire in order to testify.

Following that testimony, Edson handed Hoffman a draft unification bill written largely by Krulak. The bill retained traditional civilian control of the military and articulated the roles and missions of the Marine Corps. After listing the proposed responsibilities of the Corps, the bill contained the seemingly innocuous phrase "and other such duties as the President may direct." This phrase meant that future presidents could turn to the Marines for special assignments not permitted to other branches of the military, and it meant, metaphorically, that if the president of the United States felt the need to dial for help, the Commandant of the Marine Corps would pick up the phone. The phrase is an example of both the subtlety of Krulak's thought process and his belief that the Marine Corps was the most capable branch of the U.S. military.

After a House-Senate committee made several changes to Hoffman's bill, it passed and was signed into law on July 26 as the National Security Act of 1947. Upon the passage of the bill, one of the first things Krulak did was return to Norm Hatch's office to say that numerous congressmen had told him that *Bombs over Tokyo* had been instrumental in their votes to preserve the Marine Corps.

SEVERAL things were now clear to Krulak. First, he again realized that as long as Congress sided with the Marines, the Corps was safe. Second, although the act was a major success for the Marine Corps, it contained compromises that meant the Corps remained vulnerable in that most critical of areas: the budget. The president, the secretary of defense, and even the secretary of the Navy could exert such a budget squeeze on the Marines that they would not have the manpower to perform the duties outlined in the act. And if the Marines were called upon in a time of crisis and could not respond, their survival would be at stake. Eventually, the Army would win. Minimum manpower requirements for the Marine Corps had to be obtained.

Third, both the Navy and the new Air Force wanted to take over Marine aviation. But Krulak knew that Marine air was "organic": not only was it part of the unit to which it was assigned, but its sole purpose was to support ground units. Finally, the act did not allow the Commandant of the Marine Corps a seat on the new Joint Chiefs of Staff. It was clear that the Marines were still viewed by the other services as second-class citizens. This was reaffirmed by a bitter Eisenhower, who said that the Marines were "so unsure of their value to their country that they insisted on writing into the law a complete set of rules and specifications for their future operations and duties," a protective device he considered "silly, even vicious."

ON the evening that the National Security Act was passed, members of the Chowder Society met as a group for the first time. The meeting was at Krulak's house, where the officers celebrated the fact that America and their Corps had prevailed in a great battle. Krulak served Fish House Punch, and almost everyone drank too much as they replayed various skirmishes of the long battle. Then the Chowder Society was dissolved, and Krulak began to devote his full attention to developing the helicopter as another way to conduct an amphibious assault.

# 9

## Flying Low

EVEN while he was the central figure in the unification battle, Brute Krulak was developing the helicopter as an instrument of war. Before helicopter doctrine was developed and before the Marine Corps had its first helicopter squadron, he was teaching helicopter tactics at the Amphibious Warfare School.

In one of his classes, he stood in front of several dozen young officers, flashed on the screen a picture of an LVT, and said, "I want you to envision elevating that LVT ten feet and increasing its speed twenty times. That is what the helicopter will do." He explained how in World War II Marines had conducted frontal assaults and flanking attacks but now could move in a third dimension to go over or around a defending force and attack from unexpected directions. He was teaching what, in a few more years, Marines would call "vertical envelopment."

Helicopters are ubiquitous today, in both the military and civilian arenas, but in 1946 the contraption remained a curiosity. Germany had helicopters as early as 1942 but thought them almost useless for military applications. The U.S. Army had a few toward the end of World War II. Although the Army used them for reconnaissance, observation, and medical evacuation, it considered them so primitive, fragile, and unreliable that they were viewed more as an experimental curiosity than as tactical equipment. In the postwar years, the American helicopter industry almost died, because the fundamental problem of how to maintain control of the craft throughout the flight regime had not been solved. Helicopters could go up, down, and sideways, but they still had problems moving forward.

With helicopters, Krulak followed the same line of thinking he had pursued with landing craft: he went to the source—Igor Sikorsky, who is credited with building the first American helicopter—and asked him to come to Quantico. "He did not know much," Krulak said. "But he knew more than anyone else."

Sikorsky was trying to sell helicopters and sometimes overstated their capabilities. His primary concern was making existing helicopters more reliable rather than thinking of the revolutionary advances envisioned by Krulak. After Krulak picked Sikorsky's brain, there was no other source of information for him.

Krulak recommended that the Marine Corps establish an experimental helicopter squadron, but Shepherd's board was not ready, and the idea was put aside. Shepherd and Twining knew that Krulak functioned best when given a task and then given free rein, but there were probably times when they wondered what they had created. At a time when helicopters flew at about 80 miles per hour, Krulak talked of helicopters flying at 150 or even 200 miles per hour. At a time when helicopters carried a pilot and two passengers, he talked of helicopters carrying a dozen combat-equipped Marines, maybe even two dozen. And rather than considering the current range of the helicopter—about fifty miles—he taught tactics that assumed a range in excess of two hundred miles.

Only the Marine Corps was thinking of the helicopter as an assault vehicle capable of carrying armed men into combat. The Navy thought that the helicopter might have possibilities, but there was no call for haste in developing those possibilities. The Army Air Forces saw the helicopter primarily in terms of hauling cargo or rescuing downed pilots.

IN mid-1946, Lieutenant Colonel Marion Carl, a World War II ace and now a test pilot, flew a Sikorsky helicopter to Quantico to demonstrate it to student officers. Because Krulak was at the center of helicopter development, the pilot phoned him in advance and asked, "Would you like to ride?" When Krulak agreed, Carl said, "Be at the parade deck at ten hundred."

Krulak arrived as the helicopter was being demonstrated and was waved to a parking lot behind a barracks. The chopper landed, and Carl directed Krulak to put a canvas sling over his head and under his arms. The engine groaned and the blades whirred, and with a laborious *thump-thump-thump* the helicopter rose about twenty feet and emerged from behind the barracks with Krulak dangling below. It motored slowly around the field as young student officers watched in amazement.

Glen Butler, in an unpublished manuscript about helicopters in the Marine Corps, says that while Krulak was being hauled through the air, Ed Dyer, a member of the board studying the helicopter, and Bill Twining were watching through the window of their office. They had been considering recommending that the Marine Corps adopt helicopters, and now, impressed with the practical potential of the machine, Dyer turned to Twining and said, "Bill, let's go with this thing, quit fooling around."

"Okay," Twining said.

KRULAK and Dyer wrote the first textbook for Marine helicopter pilots and war planners. Usually doctrine and tactics are developed after a weapon is available, but Krulak believed that doctrine should drive, not follow, the development of the helicopter. He dreamed up scenarios and wrote how the helicopter could be used, a process that caused Dyer much frustration, as Dyer's job was to act as a technical brake on Krulak's flights of fancy. (When Krulak wrote of "the precious ability to rise and descend vertically and to hover," Dyer explained that helicopters could not do that—they needed forward speed before they could climb. He crossed out "and to hover" and amended the sentence to read "the precious ability to rise and descend almost vertically.") This does not mean Dyer was an obstacle to the Marines' use of helicopters; in fact, he favored helicopters as much as Krulak did.

By early 1947, Krulak and Dyer had finished a mimeographed document titled "Amphibious Operations—Employment of Helicopters (Tentative)," a work then so futuristic it seemed like science fiction. Later, after it was revised, Marine leadership directed that the document be used in Marine Corps classes on how to employ the helicopter in combat.

In May 1947, Krulak was appointed assistant director of the Senior School, a command and staff school at Quantico. His job involved supervising instructors, keeping the curriculum updated, and teaching. But Krulak's interest remained in helicopters and in traveling around the country taking part in amphibious exercises. He constantly preached the helicopter's possibilities as a new tool of warfare.

He was gratified when an experimental squadron, Marine Helicopter Squadron One (HMX-1), was established on December 1, 1947. In Ed Dyer, the squadron had a commanding officer, but it had no helicopters. For the first few months of its existence, the purpose of the squadron was to develop techniques for amphibious assaults and to consider other ways in which the helicopter might be used.

In February 1948, the squadron received five Sikorsky helicopters, each of which could carry a pilot and two Marines. Training for air assaults could begin. Even though the Marine Corps was the last branch of the U.S. military to have operational helicopters, Marines would lead the other services in the tactical employment of this wonderful machine.

In 1948, the Army, Navy, and Air Force were squabbling over their roles and missions. To resolve these differences and to carve out the shape of the new Department of Defense, Secretary of Defense James Forrestal summoned the Joint Chiefs of Staff to Key West, Florida. The meeting was crucial in that the military still was deflating in the aftermath of World War II. Money was tight, and the outcome of the meeting would determine the budget for each branch of the military. The Marine Corps was not invited and had no voice in what history remembers as the Key West Accords.

When the meeting was over, the Marine Corps mission was limited to amphibious operations, a role that meant the Marines could never again participate in an extended ground campaign. And given that amphibious operations were, in the new atomic age, considered a thing of the past, the Marine Corps might not have a job if war came. Further, now that the Marines had such a limited mission, the secretary of defense would be justified in cutting the Marine Corps's budget, diminishing even more its ability to fight. For the Marine Corps, the Key West Accords were a disaster.

It is a measure of how slowly helicopter development was proceeding that in 1948, when Krulak's helicopter manual was revised, it opened with this quote from Krulak: "The evolution of a set of principles governing the helicopter employment cannot wait for the perfection of the craft itself, but must proceed concurrently with that development."

Krulak's prophetic vision regarding helicopters is particularly significant when we remember that he was not a pilot. Long after

Krulak retired, new generations of Marine helicopter pilots would shake their heads in awe that a ground officer had been the midwife for the birth of helicopters in the Marine Corps.

WITH the revised manual in hand, Krulak began pressing for the five helicopters of HMX-1 to land aboard a Navy ship, each pick up two Marines, and then make a simulated assault from the sea. Considerable skepticism greeted the idea. Marine pilots had no experience landing on a moving vessel at sea, a very delicate maneuver requiring the helicopter, both on takeoff and landing, to have an over-the-water speed equal to that of the carrier. At the time, helicopters remained so unstable that if a pilot wanted to do something as simple as flipping a switch, he had to do it quickly. In addition, helicopters flew only in cloudless skies and often were grounded by wind and rain.

To allay Navy fears about a potential disaster, Krulak ordered the precise dimensions of an aircraft carrier to be laid out on a field at Quantico, had Marines dress as Navy deck crews, and then had the helicopter crews practice landing and taking off.

In May, Krulak and Dyer put their ideas into practice during a joint Navy-Marine exercise. Marine pilots landed on a carrier, then put sixty-six Marines ashore. This was a small-scale exercise, but one that proved helicopters could be used in an amphibious assault.

Army officers at nearby Fort Lee, Virginia, heard of the exercise, called the Marines, and said that the Army was rethinking this helicopter business and would like to send a few officers over to HMX-1 to interview Marine pilots. Afterward, maybe the Marines could fly their helicopters over to Fort Lee and demonstrate helicopter performance. The Marines were glad to oblige.

By late 1948, the tests and exercises conducted by HMX-1 had resulted in enough data for the Marine Corps to publish a revised fifty-two-page manual on amphibious operations that centered

Earliest known picture of Victor Krulak. After Krulak became a general, a friend saw this picture and said, "You couldn't salute then and you can't salute now." (Courtesy of General Victor H. Krulak)

Victor and Morris Krulak in Cheyenne, circa 1928. (Courtesy of William Krulak)

THE HANDS THAT HOLD
ARE THE HANDS THAT WON
"THE NAVY FOREVER"

Coxswain Victor "Brute" Krulak and the Naval Academy rowing team in 1933. Krulak was captain of the team the following year. (U.S. Naval Academy)

Lieutenant Brute Krulak and Amy Chandler on the occasion of their wedding at Amy's home in Washington, DC, June 1, 1936. (Courtesy of William Krulak)

Bess and Brute, San Diego, 1936. (Courtesy of General Victor H. Krulak)

Amy and Brute with their three sons in 1943 shortly before Brute shipped out to the Pacific. (USMC)

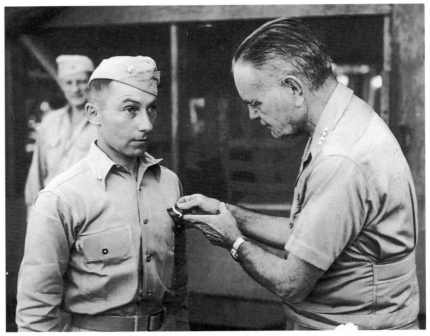

Legendary Admiral William "Bull" Halsey pinning the Navy Cross on Lieutenant Colonel Victor "Brute" Krulak, Guadalcanal, 1943. (USMC)

Colonel Brute Krulak and General Lemuel Shepherd on Okinawa, 1945. (USMC)

Iconic Marine photo of Brute Krulak suspended below a helicopter in a 1946 flight at Quantico. This flight prompted the Marine Corps to organize its first helicopter squadron. (USMC)

A drawing of the "Brute" done by one of his Marines while the 2nd Parachute Battalion was training, 1943. (Courtesy of General Victor H. Krulak)

Lieutenant William Krulak and Lieutenant General Brute Krulak, Vietnam, 1965. (Courtesy of William Krulak)

Brute, Victor, and Amy upon the occasion of Victor's being commissioned as a Navy chaplain, September 30, 1965. Vic left for Vietnam soon afterward. (USMC)

General Krulak and his youngest son, Lieutenant Chuck Krulak, in Vietnam, 1966. (Courtesy of the Command Museum, MCRD San Diego, Lieutenant General Victor Krulak Collection)

Note the body language of each man in the 1967 photograph. Krulak is lecturing President Lyndon Johnson about how the president is prosecuting the war. Immediately after the picture was taken, LBJ stood up, put his hand in the small of Krulak's back, and pushed the general from the Oval Office. (Courtesy of the White House)

Bill, Victor, Brute, and Chuck at Brute's retirement in 1968. (Courtesy of General Victor H. Krulak)

Retirement photograph of Lieutenant General Victor H. "Brute" Krulak. (USMC)

To celebrate the Marine Corps birthday in 2008, General Angela Salinas, commanding general of MCRD San Diego, presents a slice of cake to Brute Krulak. To Krulak's right is his youngest son, Chuck; his oldest son, Vic; and his longtime assistant, Judy Moore. This was Brute's last public appearance. (USMC)

on the helicopter. The paternity of this document cannot be determined, because historians can only speculate about the half-dozen or so officers who may have had a role in its writing. But they invariably mention Krulak as one of the primary authors. Later, when the Army published its first helicopter manual, it did little more than put an Army cover on the Marine Corps manual.

NOT everyone in the Marine Corps shared Shepherd and Twining's vision regarding helicopters. From the beginning, helicopters created a great schism in the Corps, because of the money involved. The Navy controlled the Marine Corps budget, and that budget allowed for only a certain number of airframes, be they observation aircraft, attack aircraft, transports, or helicopters. Proponents of fixed-wing aircraft dominated Marine Corps aviation, and they did not want to sacrifice aircraft of known performance for these rickety new fling-wing contraptions. No branch of the military had more budget constraints than the Marine Corps, and everything about the helicopter was expensive: initial purchase, maintenance, and pilot training. For every helicopter brought into the Marine Corps inventory, a fixed-wing aircraft had to be removed. It was senior generals who decided to buy helicopters and form a squadron, but because Krulak was the most visible and most junior officer involved in the implementation of helicopters, it was he who received much of the ire and derision of other Marines.

WHILE Brute spent most of his time toiling for the Marine Corps, his wife, Amy, kept the family going. As is sometimes the case with firstborn sons of career military men, the childhood memories of Victor Krulak Jr. — whom the family called "Nick" but everyone else called "Vic" — are rarely pleasant. Vic has few warm memories of his childhood, and he would grow up scarred and tormented by his youth. Many years later, he began a long conversation about his father by saying, "Did you ever see *The Great Santini*? I did, and I said to myself, 'What's the big deal? That's the way it was for us.'"

Of his father, Vic said, "I never really had a conversation with him. I just reported at meals."

Vic was a sensitive boy and spent his earliest and most formative years with his mother, whom he remembers as warm and loving. He sees his father, however, as cold and remote, a demanding man whose approval he could never win. Brute's middle son, Bill, has the same view, albeit to a lesser degree.

Vic remembers the time his father ordered him upstairs to get something. He doesn't recall what it was, only that it was something inconsequential, something like a pencil.

"Where is it?" Vic asked.

His father's voice turned cold. "Go upstairs and get it," he said. "And on the way, stop and read *A Message to Garcia*."

Once, when Vic complained about the number of chores he had to perform around the house, Brute said, "Of course you have to do these chores. Why do you think your mother and I had you boys? It was so you could do all the work."

Vic said that he was not joking.

Brute arranged for Vic to ride in one of the Marine helicopters, a unique experience and, one would think, an adventure that carried serious bragging rights. But the ride terrified Vic, a reaction that caused Brute considerable consternation.

CHUCK, the youngest son, is different from Vic and Bill in that his childhood memories are pleasant. In fact, his earliest memory is one of pleasing his father. In 1948, he was six years old, red-haired like Brute and with a sunny disposition. He was called "Cardie" by his family and "Chucky" by enlisted personnel. Chuck recalls that his father loved dogs and had bought a large mixed-breed puppy named Daisy. The dog grew far larger than anyone expected and by all accounts was bumptious and uncontrolled. When Daisy died young, Brute announced, "We have to bury her, and we have to put up a gravestone." Brute and his sons buried Daisy in the woods behind the house. He told each boy to think of an epitaph, and whoever came up with the best one would have the honor of writing it on the concrete grave marker. Chuck won with this:

*Daisy*
*Our Dog*

Chuck smiles when he tells the story. After he became a Marine officer, he visited Daisy's grave. And decades later, when he became Commandant of the Marine Corps, he returned to search the woods for the gravestone.

EVERY day, Brute came home carrying a bulging briefcase. The family had an early dinner, and then he disappeared into his study and worked late into the night.

On Saturday mornings, Brute walked into the boys' bedroom wearing white gloves. The boys snapped to attention, and Vic, being the oldest, reported that the room was ready for inspection. It rarely passed.

Corporal punishment, often administered for failure, called for the perpetrator to drop his trousers and bend over while Brute spanked him with a belt. Crying was not allowed until the boy returned to his room. But Vic feared tongue-lashings more than he did spankings. His father's vocabulary and the scorn he could load into a simple phrase were withering. The humiliation was heightened when Brute would order Vic to go to his room and write an essay listing his shortcomings, telling how he had failed his father. The experience so scarred Vic that when he was seventy and recounting those days, his voice trembled when he said, "Neatness and spelling counted."

Neither Bill nor Chuck remember having to write these essays of shame, but all three sons remember the most unusual form of punishment administered by their father: he would twist his heavy Annapolis ring so the stone faced the palm of his hand, then thump his miscreant sons on the head. Vic grew up fearing that ring.

ON Sundays, the schedule in the Krulak household relaxed a bit. The day went one of two ways. Amy brought Brute breakfast in bed, and he stayed there until late in the morning reading various newspapers while the boys marched single file about a mile down the road to the chapel. Or Brute, accompanied by Vic, went to the stables at Quantico, where they met the Hogabooms and another dozen or so families and took long horseback rides through the wooded Virginia countryside. The officers and their ladies wore proper riding attire and rode English fashion, and they contracted with the officers' club to deliver brunch to an open area called the "remount pasture." There everyone dismounted and enjoyed the leisurely brunch and socializing before returning to the stables.

Amy was afraid of horses but sometimes went along because riding was something Brute enjoyed. As Bill and Chuck grew older, their presence was sometimes required as well. On one family outing, Amy was thrown by her horse. Though unhurt, she was dazed. "Get back on the horse," Krulak snapped. "You are scaring the children."

Krulak always sat a big gray jumper named Gracias. "I did better with that horse, and the horse did better with me," Krulak said. He rode Gracias to three championships in the Texas Cup, the annual open jumping competition at Quantico. Gracias lived for thirty-two years, and when she died, Krulak buried her in the remount pasture and placed a commemorative stone over her grave. The stone is there today, just off the main road at Quantico.

\* \* \*

During these years at Quantico, the Krulaks frequently dined with Amy's parents in Washington. They also hosted parties there. In fact, many of the richest stories about Krulak's Fish House Punch originated during these years, including one about a woman who passed out on the floor. When her husband went upstairs to get her coat, he did not return but instead hid in the closet, reaching out and pinching women on the derriere as they walked by.

These were heady years for Brute, as he had become, as a relatively junior officer, one of the best-known names in the Marine Corps. Legendary Marines such as Bill Twining, Gerry Thomas, and Lemuel Shepherd attended his dinner parties—formal occasions where, after dessert, the ladies withdrew and the officers stayed at the table to drink port. At one such party, Krulak, at the head of the table, picked up the decanter and, out of deference, passed it to Shepherd on his right. Shepherd, ever aware of proper procedure, said that Brute should pour himself the first glass, then pass the decanter to his left as dictated by the protocol of Mess Night.

Many heroes of World War II, such as David Shoup, who wore the Medal of Honor, also attended the festivities. At one of these events, while Shoup was sitting in a chair talking with Amy's mother, he stretched out his legs and put his foot atop her sofa, a social error she would not forget.

At another event, a family dinner, Amy's younger brother, a boy only a few years older than Vic, stopped all conversation when he looked at Krulak and said, "Hey, are you a midget?" If his nephew could say this to his face, what might fellow officers be saying behind his back?

In early 1949, Louis Johnson, a close friend of President Truman, was appointed secretary of defense. Johnson shared Truman's dislike for the Marine Corps and set about slicing the Marines' budget until only 74,279 Marines were on active duty. That number would decrease in the next year. In July, Brute was transferred to Camp Pendleton, about forty miles north of San Diego and only a few miles from where his first mentor, the now retired Holland Smith, lived. Krulak was at Pendleton only a few weeks when he bought a dachshund he named Noodle.

The reasons people pick certain breeds of dog for household pets are as unfathomable as the reasons for their loyalty to those breeds over the years. Krulak later said that he admired the attributes of a dachshund, which he listed as "obedience, affection, and intelligence." Perhaps. But for people who own large dogs, a dachshund is beyond comprehension. The dog has a ratlike head, an elongated sausage of a body, and stumpy little legs that cause it to waddle rather than walk. The dachshund is a hyperactive animal with a shrill bark and a petulant disposition, neither a dignified nor a respected member of the dog world. Nevertheless, over the next sixty years or so, Krulak would own thirteen of the creatures. He said he liked them because they were "loyal and obedient."

THE ever-diminishing budget and ever-shrinking Marine Corps meant promotions and careers slowed overall, but not for Krulak. In November, he was promoted to full colonel; he was thirty-six and had been in the Marine Corps fifteen years. At the time, there were very few slots for colonels, and officers promoted to that rank were handpicked by Corps leadership. Krulak's promotion caused considerable animosity among the numerous lieutenant colonels who were not advanced. Their anger was heightened when Krulak was given a job as regimental commander, one of the best jobs in the Marine Corps, especially as, in this instance, the 5th Marines to which Brute was assigned was the only infantry regiment in the 1st Marine Division.

Several weeks later, the regiment had a parade. The band struck up martial music as the regiment formed. Krulak, of course, was front and center on the reviewing stand; behind him were the wives and families of his officers. The adjutant was facing in the wrong direction when he called "Officers Center," a mistake that caused Krulak to interrupt the ceremony with the peremptory order, "Do it again." This time Brute deemed the procedure acceptable, but the regiment had its first taste of its new commander. So did the wives and families.

From the day he assumed command, Krulak's leadership theory was the same one he had learned from Holland Smith in the Caribbean and from Lemuel Shepherd in the Pacific: training, training, and more training. He ordered the 5th Marines to begin a series of amphibious landings, including several at night, on the coast of Southern California. For students at the Army's Command and General Staff College, he put on an operation called Demon III, during which he borrowed a Navy helicopter to shuttle his command group two at a time from boat to shore. The regiment trained so hard that the wife of one of Krulak's officers came to him and complained, "My children have forgotten what their father looks like." But when the exercise was over, Krulak's 5th Marines were combat ready.

Demon III ended in early June 1950, about the time President Truman visited Quantico to observe a simulated amphibious assault by helicopters. During that visit, Truman did two memorable things. First, he chided Joseph L. Collins, the Army chief of staff, about the Army being so far behind the Marine Corps in developing helicopter tactics. Second, after watching the helicopters perform, he walked over to an artillery piece, patted the barrel affectionately, and said to a Marine general, "I like this better."

LEMUEL Shepherd had just been appointed Commanding General, Fleet Marine Force, Pacific (CGFMFPac), the senior Marine in the Pacific and commander of the largest field command in the Marine Corps. Shepherd was of the old school in that he considered operations officer the most important position on his staff. He wanted an operations officer whom he could trust, a man not afraid to make big decisions, an able man and loyal. He wanted the man who had served him well at Okinawa, in China, and at Quantico. Once again, he wanted Brute Krulak.

KRULAK was aboard a Navy ship en route to Hawaii to assume his new job when, on June 25, the Communist forces of North Korea launched a massive attack against South Korea, surprising not only the South Koreans but also the American military, which believed the first major engagement of the cold war would be when Soviet tanks barreled through the Fulda Gap into Germany. For many in the American military, the first question was, "Where is Korea?"

In response to the invasion, the United Nations, in accordance with its charter, engaged in its first collective action. Some sixteen nations would send troops to Korea. Aside from South Korea, the United States would provide the largest contingent. But America was not ready for war. The Marine Corps had about 74,000 active-duty Marines, and only a few thousand of them were combat ready, most of them in Krulak's former command, the 5th Marines.

Once again, furniture was being moved about on a great stage. Shepherd would have administrative, but not operational, control over the Marines who would be sent to Korea. The Marine Corps was talking about forming a second helicopter squadron, the motto of which would be "Equitatus Caeli," loosely translated as "horsemen of the sky" or, as a military man would translate the phrase, "cavalry of the sky." In Korea, using the new concept of vertical envelopment, the Marines would once again show the Army how war should be waged, both on the ground and in the air. Krulak's job as operations officer would put him squarely in the forefront of this radical evolution.

# 10

# MacArthur Asks
# for Help

No one has written more perceptively of Douglas MacArthur than Eric Larrabee in his wartime biography of Franklin Roosevelt, *Commander in Chief*. Larrabee says that MacArthur mishandled the defense of the Philippines, allowed his air force to be destroyed on the ground, was slow to take the initiative in New Guinea, was a latecomer to the idea of leapfrogging various islands (although he later took credit for the idea), misrepresented his achievements, patronized and disparaged the Allies, tampered with the historical record, tried to undercut Allied strategy, and flirted with political enemies of his commander in chief. In addition, some of his boldest actions were forced on him by the Joint Chiefs of Staff, and throughout the war his speech and actions bordered on insubordination.

In *The Coldest Winter*, David Halberstam writes that this dismal record continued in the postwar years, when MacArthur—an American legend, the senior general in the Army, and a great administrator of postwar Japan—allowed soldiers under his command to spend more time drinking and whoring than they did training. Now war was upon them, and they would bring little credit to the Army.

\*    \*    \*

DESPITE his flaws, MacArthur had a pragmatic side. Only a year earlier, General Omar Bradley, beloved by the American people for his leadership in the European theater of World War II, took a swipe at the Marine Corps by saying he could not foresee a time when America would conduct another amphibious landing. But MacArthur disagreed, saying, "The amphibious landing is the most powerful tool we have." And that meant, despite his demonstrated animosity, he needed the Marine Corps.

BECAUSE America has a profound aversion to a standing army, in peacetime we always diminish the military to the point where, when war comes, we are woefully unprepared. Nevertheless, the Army, Navy, and Air Force assumed they would be assigned the job of putting out this little Korean brush fire and there would be no job for the Marines. In those hectic days after the war broke out, Marine Corps Commandant Clifton Cates could not even get an audience with his superiors in the Defense Department. On June 28, he ran into the chief of naval operations (CNO) in a Pentagon hallway and wanted to know why the Marines were not being considered for Korea.

"What do you have?" asked the CNO, the implication being that if the other, superior services were not ready for war, the Marine Corps could not possibly be either.

The Commandant said that he had Marines on the West Coast ready to go. The CNO was so skeptical he waited two days to send a message to Lemuel Shepherd asking how soon Marines could sail for combat in Korea.

A lesser-known but in some ways more important part of the Marine story took place in Hawaii, at Shepherd's headquarters. Krulak had arrived there on June 28 and had barely had time to unpack when, two days later, Shepherd's chief of staff, Gregon Williams, showed him the note from the CNO. Williams, in Krulak's words, displayed "much agitation, much emotion," over the message, which asked, "How soon can you sail for combat employment in the Far East: (a) A reinforced battalion: (b) a reinforced regiment?" (A reinforced battalion has about 1,200 men and a reinforced regiment about 3,600 men.)

"We have to answer this," Williams said as he handed the note to Krulak. The agitation and emotion Krulak described came from the fact that Shepherd was fishing on a remote lake in Jackson Hole, Wyoming, and it would take several days for word to reach him that hostilities had broken out in Korea. (He would not arrive in Hawaii until July 2.) But his office had just been queried by the CNO on a matter of national significance, and Williams had to answer *now*. Williams knew of Krulak's long relationship with Shepherd and figured that he had some insight into his superior's thinking.

This encounter between Williams and Krulak was one of the most important moments in the history of the Marine Corps. In fact, the future of the Corps depended on how Shepherd's office answered the query from the CNO.

Krulak made no phone calls and consulted no one; he simply took the CNO's note, sat down at a nearby desk, and wrote, "(a) 48 hours. (b) Five days, including a Marine aircraft group." He handed the response to Williams, who stared at it, then at Krulak, then back at the note. "How do you know this?" he asked in amazement.

"I don't," Krulak said. "But if we can't, we're dead."

Krulak in Hawaii and Cates in Washington, though they had not communicated, agreed on this point. The difference in their thinking—and it was an enormous difference—was that Cates was satisfied with sending a brigade, a token representation of Marines, while Krulak had far bigger dreams.

It did not matter that to ship out the reinforced regiment would require most of the Marines on the West Coast. Krulak believed that the only thing that mattered was that when the war trumpets sounded, the Marines must be first to fight. The Army had no combat-trained soldiers in America who could leave for Korea immediately. And because no other branch of the U.S. military was ready, this Marine imperative had become crucial to national defense.

MacArthur sent Army units from Japan to Korea, but the first troops to sail from America would be a Marine brigade. They would turn out to be some of the finest Marines in history, men whose actions would have pleased the Marines who fought at Belleau Wood.

After sending the message over Shepherd's name to the CNO, Krulak suggested sending another message, one that would place Marines at Camp Pendleton on wartime alert and prepare them for deployment in the Far East. The Commandant simultaneously sent the same message. The exchange gained the Marines two precious days before the official order came down from the Joint Chiefs of Staff to mount out an air-ground Marine brigade for combat deployment.

Even with America at war — on July 1 some four hundred Army infantry troops landed at Pusan — the new Air Force played interservice politics by attempting to strip the Marines of their aircraft, insisting that only the Air Force should be in the skies over Korea.

The three-year-old Air Force was dominated by bomber generals from World War II who wanted to use heavy bombers to level North Korean positions. But the Air Force of 1950 was so unprepared that many of its pilots did not have the proper instrument training to fly in the harsh weather of North Korea. Air Force bombers would crash with some regularity into Korean mountains before the Air Force made Korea a fighter war, with American Sabre Jets against Korean MiGs. Similarly, while the Navy could put ships off the Korean peninsula to fire big guns at

Korean positions, war in the Pacific had demonstrated that an entrenched enemy could survive days, even weeks, of heavy shelling with relatively little damage. Thus the Korean War, like all wars, would be decided on the ground.

Shepherd arrived in Hawaii, agreed with all Krulak had done, and ordered him to round up an airplane: they were going to California to ensure that the Marines mounted out as quickly as possible.

It speaks volumes that Shepherd chose Krulak to accompany him on the trip. In the coming months, Krulak would take full advantage of his closeness to Shepherd. When the general told Krulak that he wanted something done, rather than saying, "This is a job for the chief of staff" or "This is a job for the logistics officer," Krulak either did the job himself or went to the staff members involved and told them what Shepherd wanted. For decades after he retired, he retained the persona of the perfect staff officer, in that he minimized his role in events in which his boss was a central figure. "I thought that the fact I was always at Shepherd's side said enough," he noted. But after he became elderly and in failing health, he said, "Many times Shepherd turned to me and said, 'What do you think?' He trusted my advice. And I knew that if I made a recommendation that almost always he would follow it."

Shepherd and Krulak landed in California, where the 5th Marines were ready to go — "ready" being a relative term in that each battalion had two, rather than the required three, rifle companies. This meant that when the 5th Marines — soon to become part of the 1st Provisional Marine Brigade — landed in Korea, it would have around 450 fewer men than it should have had. But all that was important was getting Marines to Korea.

Shepherd and Krulak returned to Hawaii for a brief stopover before proceeding on July 7 to Tokyo, where MacArthur was planning a counterattack. During the flight, Krulak presented three ideas he said Shepherd might consider as goals for the trip. First, Shepherd should get firsthand tactical knowledge of what was taking place in Korea. Second, Shepherd should make sure that when the brigade arrived, it would be employed as a unified command—that is, with Marine aviation still attached and not pulled away by the Air Force. This was crucial, but even more so was the third goal, persuading MacArthur to commit more Marines to Korea. A brigade would be swallowed up by the Army. Krulak envisioned a full division with an air wing, more than 20,000 men, enough Marines to make a difference. The problem was that while Shepherd had administrative control over the Marines in the Pacific, he did not have operational control. He could not ask that Marines be placed in battle; only MacArthur, as theater commander and head of United Nations forces, could do that.

Krulak believed that MacArthur would ask for Marines because the soldiers under his command, though they were brave men, were not ready for war. By now news was coming back that MacArthur's garrison-softened soldiers were being kicked across Korea like old tin cans. July 1950 was one of the worst months in American military history. Not only was the Army dealt defeat after defeat, but documented cases exist of soldiers throwing down their arms, taking off their boots (the better to traverse rice paddies), and fleeing south.

In anticipation, Krulak drafted a note for MacArthur's signature requesting the Joint Chiefs of Staff to send the 1st Marine Division with its supporting air elements to Korea.

KRULAK and Shepherd realized that if MacArthur asked for a division, there was only one man to lead the amphibious assault on North Korea: Lemuel Shepherd. No one in the Army had the experience of the man who had led a division on Okinawa. Given his skill and proven expertise in amphibious landings, and given the fact that he was the presumptive next Commandant (Shepherd expected to be named Commandant in about eighteen months, when Cates's term expired), Shepherd was no doubt quite confident when he arrived in Tokyo.

On July 10, Shepherd and Krulak met with Army general Edward "Ned" Almond, MacArthur's chief of staff, and chatted for a few minutes. Almond liked his creature comforts and the prerogatives of being a general. What he lacked in command experience he made up for in arrogance, a combination that would result in the needless deaths of many Americans. Almond and Shepherd had attended the Virginia Military Institute together, a bond that was even stronger than that connecting graduates of West Point or Annapolis.

MacArthur waved Shepherd and Krulak into his office, where he introduced to them in broad terms his plan for an amphibious assault at a place called Inchon. It was a plan of frightening audacity, and the Army, even though it professed to have considerable expertise in the amphibious business, could not round up the men and equipment by the time MacArthur needed them. As Krulak had anticipated, MacArthur raised the crucial issue of bringing more Marines into the fray.

Krulak's memory and Shepherd's oral history agree on what happened next. MacArthur said, "The way to do this deal is to envelop the whole thing, to make a landing. But I can't do it without a division of Marines." Then MacArthur indulged in a royal pause and asked, "Do you think you could provide a division of Marines?" Before Shepherd could answer, MacArthur tapped on a large map of Korea mounted on the wall and said, "General Shepherd, if I just had the First Marine Division right now, I'd land it here at Inchon and break the back of the North Korean offensive."

"General, why don't you ask for the First Marine Division?" Shepherd replied.

"Do you think I can get it?" MacArthur asked, meaning, *Is the division trained and ready to embark?*

"If you ask the Joint Chiefs for a division, I will do my best to see that you get it," Shepherd answered. "And a supporting Marine air wing as well."

MacArthur nodded, pointed to his flight deck–size desk, and said, "Sit down here and draft the message to the JCS. I will sign it."

Shepherd did not want Krulak to present the prepared draft and asked if he could use an adjacent office. There Krulak pulled out the draft from his pocket and rewrote it on a pad from the desk. When MacArthur read the message, he nodded and wrote, "Send this out" on the bottom, then handed it to Almond.

For two reasons, the importance of this moment cannot be overstated. First, when Shepherd promised MacArthur a division, he promised something that did not exist. Second, there was no other option for Shepherd. America was at war, and had Shepherd said the Marines were not ready, that could well have marked the beginning of the end for the Marine Corps.

On July 14, some 6,000 men of the 1st Provisional Marine Brigade climbed aboard Navy ships in San Diego and embarked for Japan, where they were scheduled to receive brief but intense training before going to Korea. To the Army's way of thinking, this brigade was more than enough; a division was unthinkable. But now MacArthur was asking for a division. The Joint Chiefs of Staff dithered, and MacArthur had to send two more requests, each time escalating the level of urgency, before the Joint Chiefs caved in and, on July 22, ordered that the 1st Marine Division be brought up to wartime strength.

Commandant Cates was furious that such a commitment had been made without consulting him and within hours was having what Krulak called "spirited exchanges" with Shepherd, saying that Shepherd had seriously overextended the Marine Corps and that it was he, Cates, who had to deliver. Reluctantly, Cates ordered that every available Marine be assigned to the 1st Marine Division. He reassigned cooks, administrative personnel, logistics personnel, and every warm body he could find to the proposed division. A battalion on duty in the Mediterranean was ordered to set sail immediately, go halfway around the world, and be on station off the coast of Inchon at a given date in September. That not being enough, Cates asked Truman for permission to call up the Marine Corps Reserves, and within hours men across America toiling away at civilian jobs received the word: Mother Green is calling you home.

And those Marines answered the call. Some were too old, some were a bit infirm, some were deemed to be critical at their regular jobs, but they were Marines, and they showed up at dockside. When staff wanted to see their medical records, many said that their records had been misplaced. History does not record the number of Marine stowaways on Navy vessels leaving California for Korea, but they were numerous. Some were so young that a few weeks later, the Marine Corps sent out a notice that no Marine younger than eighteen could participate in the upcoming operation, an order that caused frantic searching of records to weed out the youngsters. Some of the reservists had never been to boot camp, so on the fantail of the boat, they were issued rifles, targets were tossed into the sea, and they learned to shoot as they traveled into battle.

By now the U.S. Army had been pushed across Korea and was squeezed into a small perimeter around the coastal town of Pusan. The Army was in so much trouble that the Marine brigade received orders at sea diverting it from Japan and sending it straight to Korea. There the Marines became a "fire brigade" to prevent the Army from being pushed into the sea. Army leadership assigned the Marines a sector of the Pusan Perimeter and ordered them to "hold the line." The Army did not understand that the spirit of Belleau Wood hovered over the 5th Marines. The Army did not understand that it is not in the nature of Marines to "hold the line"; it is in their nature to take real estate away from the enemy.

And that is what they did. The Marines took so much real estate so fast that a few days later, they were ordered to halt: there was no one on their flanks.

HELICOPTERS were the secret weapon of the Marine command staff at Pusan. The Marines had not been in the line twenty-four hours when commanders began making reconnaissance flights in rickety two-seaters. It was the beginning of a new day in command relationships. Now commanders could not only have a bird's-eye view of combat; they could maintain direct contact with battalion, even company, commanders in a way never before possible. As one writer for the *Marine Corps Gazette* put it, the military brain now had more control over the military muscle. And the crews of the two Marine helicopter squadrons that came to Korea had been trained, and their tactics developed, at Quantico by HMX-1.

ONCE the Marines stabilized the Pusan Perimeter, they turned it back over to the Army and pulled out. They were needed across the peninsula, where a forcible entry was being planned. They would join up at sea with the battalion from the Mediterranean and become part of the newly formed 1st Marine Division. They would lead the assault at Inchon.

CONGRESSMAN Gordon McDonough of California was so pleased with the Marine performance at Pusan that on August 21 he wrote a letter to President Truman praising the Marines, stressing their importance to America, and suggesting that it was now time for the Commandant of the Marine Corps to have a seat at the table with the Joint Chiefs of Staff.

For three years, ever since the unification battle, Truman had managed to keep a lid on his animosity toward the Marines. But now Truman's temper got the best of him, and without consulting his staff, he wrote a reply: "I read with a lot of interest your letter in regard to the Marine Corps. For your information the Marine Corps is the Navy's police force and as long as I am President that is what they will remain. They have a propaganda machine that is almost equal to Stalin's."

Congressman McDonough inserted Truman's letter into the *Congressional Record* and released it to the press. Once again, America reaffirmed its love affair with the Marines. Truman's comments caused such a public outcry that he was forced to apologize to the Marine Corps.

By now some members of Congress had had enough of Truman's belittling and decided it was time to introduce legislation that would fill the gaps left in the National Security Act of 1947. Senator Paul Douglas and Congressman Mike Mansfield, both former Marines, introduced Public Law 416. Douglas delivered a speech in which he said that Truman, notwithstanding the clear intent of Congress, had attempted to destroy the combat effectiveness of the Marine Corps. He said that the Joint Chiefs of Staff were opposed to the Marine Corps as a combat organization and that it was time for Congress to codify its beliefs about the Marines.

The Joint Chiefs of Staff so vigorously opposed what became known as the Marine Corps bill that it would be more than a year—not until after Krulak returned from Korea and became personally involved in the fight—before the legislation passed.

History would record that getting the 1st Marine Division to

Korea and Truman's intemperate note were two of the best things that ever happened to the Marine Corps.

PUSAN was only a warm-up for the Marines; the main event was Inchon. No other military force in the world was capable of doing what the Marines planned to do at Inchon: assemble an amphibious force at sea and send it ashore against an enemy that had demonstrated its superiority over the U.S. Army. MacArthur deserves credit for conceiving the Inchon landing, but it was successful only because it was led by Marines.

Shepherd and Krulak were not warmly received by those Marines when they flew to Camp Pendleton. Rarely in history had the Marine Corps been pushed to come up with so many men in such a short time, and some staff officers of the 1st Marine Division were not pleased. "There were many whose conservatism exceeded my enthusiasm," Krulak recalled. But Shepherd squared away the footdraggers by reminding them that war was the primary purpose of the Corps and ordering them to assemble the necessary troops, support personnel, and pilots—and, oh, by the way, do it *now*.

The amtracs, Higgins boats, trucks, and artillery pieces that had been parked in Barstow, California, for the past five years were shipped to Pendleton and loaded aboard ships. There was no time to water test the Higgins boats and amtracs; that would come when the boats were lowered into Flying Fish Channel on the approach to Wolmi-Do Island and Inchon.

In August, as the Marines were steaming from the Mediterranean and California, converging toward their destiny in Korea, Shepherd and Krulak returned to Tokyo for another meeting with MacArthur, this time to go over the invasion plans in great detail. MacArthur called the invasion Operation Chromite.

When Krulak told MacArthur that Inchon was the worst possible site for an amphibious assault, the general's staff was horrified. Much has been written about MacArthur's staff, which consisted of sycophants, more like a royal court than a military staff, and on the rare occasions when they disagreed with Mac-Arthur, it was in the most elliptical fashion imaginable. But here was this baby-faced junior colonel, this toy Marine, who had the temerity to tell MacArthur about thirty-three-foot tides at Inchon, about Wolmi-Do Island sitting astride the landing approach to Inchon, about the narrow channel leading through thousands of yards of mudflats to the seawalls (there was no beach), and about the vicious eight-knot current ripping through the channel. Krulak even mentioned his experience at Okinawa and asked Mac-Arthur to reconsider his choice of Inchon, to look at sites to the south better suited for an amphibious assault.

MacArthur was bemused. He had graduated from West Point a decade before Krulak was born. But he listened, perhaps because he was about to drop a bomb on Shepherd. After Krulak finished, MacArthur, unmoved, said that the landing would be at Inchon.

Then he turned to Shepherd and, using Shepherd's nickname — something he never did even with his closest staff members — said, "Lem, I know you want the job commanding the amphibious force. But I'm committed to Ned Almond on this one. I told him he could have command."

For one of the few times in his life, Krulak was speechless. He prided himself on planning for every contingency, but the idea that anyone but his boss would command the amphibious assault had never crossed his mind. Shepherd had as much experience at amphibious landings as any man in uniform, and MacArthur was giving the job to a staff officer with limited command experience.

Shepherd also was speechless. MacArthur smiled and threw Shepherd a bone. "I understand the great complexity of this operation, and I would like you to come out and join me and my staff aboard the *Mount McKinley* and be my personal adviser and

205

mentor on the essence of what we are doing here. I'll make you any sort of plenipotentiary you want, but I want you to come."

Shepherd had one question: "May I bring Colonel Krulak?"

MacArthur nodded his agreement, not realizing he was letting the noses of two camels into his tent. If they were advisers, these two assertive and demanding officers believed, they should advise.

FOR the next few weeks, Krulak spent every waking minute preparing for the Marine landing. General O. P. Smith, who commanded the 1st Marine Division, was a Texan who had graduated from the University of California at Berkeley, a scholarly, careful, and prudent man known behind his back as "the professor." But Smith's quiet exterior covered the soul of a fighting general, and he clashed often with Shepherd and Krulak. It was bad enough that Shepherd frequently offered "advice," but Krulak, who had horrified Smith back at Quantico during the unification battle, had entirely too many "suggestions." When Shepherd and Krulak met with Smith, the meetings were, to use Krulak's understated word, "heated." Krulak also clashed frequently with Ned Almond's staff over details of the proposed landing. The Army officers had the defensiveness of those who had learned all they knew about amphibious operations from the Marines, and here was the Marine who had written the book on amphibious procedures trying to advise them.

Almost everything that can be written about the September 15 landing at Inchon has long since been written. But several stories should be told.

On the morning of the landing, MacArthur was surrounded by generals and admirals. Krulak was by far the most junior officer on the bridge, where he stood next to Almond and engaged him in what Krulak called "an incredible conversation."

The hours leading up to what is known as H hour, the moment the landing force commander broadcasts the portentous order,

"Land the landing force," is very dramatic, what with ships maneuvering up a narrow channel, aircraft dropping bombs and strafing enemy positions, the resulting fire and smoke, the hellish cacophony, and in this case the knowledge that what was soon to come was one of the most fragile amphibious landings ever undertaken. Krulak and Almond watched as Marines and their equipment moved out in heavily loaded LVTs for the assault. With understandable pride of parenthood, Krulak said, "The LVT is really a wonderful machine."

Almond looked down his Army nose, paused, and said, "Can those things really float?"

Krulak's eyes widened, and he sought out Shepherd to repeat the conversation. Over the years, he would tell the story dozens of times, always with the greatest incredulity and always ending with, "Here is the fellow who is technically commanding the landing force at Inchon, and he asks if LVTs can float."

On September 18, Marines were mopping up the last pockets of resistance at Kimpo, the strategically important airfield between Inchon and Seoul, when Shepherd and Krulak landed in a helicopter and laid claim to being in the first U.S. aircraft to land at the vital airfield. Krulak was doing what he had done at Okinawa — going ashore ostensibly to "survey the situation" but in reality to do as much micromanaging as he could get away with. The helicopter enabled him to micromanage to his heart's content.

TAKING Seoul away from the North Koreans was a primary objective of the Inchon landing, and MacArthur wanted the world to believe that the job had been accomplished by September 25 so that he could send out a message saying that three months to the day after the North Koreans had invaded, he had sent them packing. But on the twenty-fifth, there remained bitter fighting around Seoul, and it would be several days before MacArthur could officially hand over the city to South Korean president Syngman

Rhee. MacArthur did not like helicopters, and there was no nearby airfield on which he could land his personal aircraft, the *Bataan*. He would have to drive to Seoul, but the primary bridge on the route into the city had been destroyed.

Marines flew in pontoons from all over the Far East, and they finished building the improvised bridge only a few hours before MacArthur arrived. A large number of Army troops, all in Class A uniforms, were in Seoul for MacArthur's triumphant arrival. General Smith and a few Marines were there, dressed in utilities (what the Army calls fatigues), but most of the Marines had been ordered to stay out of sight. MacArthur did not want others to share his glory.

As far as Krulak's story is concerned, the important thing about the Korean War was the growing and innovative use of helicopters. As a staff officer, Krulak was not expected to jump into a helicopter and fly over areas where people were shooting at one another. But to the dismay of Marine ground commanders, he was everywhere. A helicopter would land, and there was Shepherd's operations officer striding toward them with probing questions, followed by "suggestions" as to how they might better employ their Marines.

Given the use of helicopters today, it must be emphasized that the first helicopters the Marines brought to Korea were the equivalent of fixed-wing aircraft in World War I—that is, they were delicate and unreliable. If it rained, the pilot had to stick his head out the window in order to see. The helicopters operated on the ragged edge of their maximum capability in that they had a 5,000-foot ceiling and were operating over terrain as high as 4,000 feet. Plus, helicopters remained mechanically unreliable, and when something broke, they often crashed.

Captain Victor Armstrong was the executive officer of the first Marine helicopter squadron in Korea, and he often flew senior officers over the battlefield. Starting with Inchon, he flew Krulak many times while furious combat raged below. "He wanted to follow the tactical progress of the battle," said Armstrong, who retired as a major general. "But he also wanted to see how the helicopters were doing. He was fascinated by helicopters and asked a lot of questions." Armstrong said that his pilots had great respect for Krulak. "We listened to him intently," Armstrong said. "He was a very eloquent speaker" about the potential of helicopters.

In Korea, the Army used helicopters largely for medical evacuation. In fact, one of the enduring images of the Korean War is of the small, bubble-canopy Bell helicopters used by Army MASH units. The distinctive sound of those two-bladed helicopters led to the nickname "choppers." But following Krulak's doctrine, the Marines used helicopters for reconnaissance, intelligence gathering, flank security, courier service, to lay communications wire, and to evacuate the wounded. Almost all of these jobs were being done for the first time with helicopters. And very soon, under Krulak's direction, these machines also would be used in a daring and startling fashion.

PART of Krulak's job as operations officer was to decide who was entitled to use the handful of Marine helicopters, and he decided that he should have frequent use of one of the machines—sometimes on missions assigned by Shepherd, sometimes on his own, looking for the disposition of enemy troops or seeking the best route for an advance. "There is no substitute for looking at the ground," he said.

For Krulak, the helicopter was truly a gift from above. If he could not be everywhere at once, as he would have liked to be, he could certainly give that appearance. He flew constantly, sometimes ordering the pilot to land so that he could jump out and offer his observations to ground commanders.

\*   \*   \*

IN mid-November, Krulak returned to his duties in Hawaii. Because of his many helicopter flights, Shepherd recommended him for the Air Medal, adding a FitRep declaring that Krulak was "an outstanding officer in every respect who has proven to be invaluable on the staff of FMFPAC during the Korean War. Fully qualified and capable of performing both staff and command duties and has demonstrated these qualifications to a marvelous degree in peace and war."

After spending a few days in Hawaii with his family, Krulak was ordered back to the States to brief students at Quantico about Inchon. In those pre-jet days, Krulak flew twelve hours to reach California and another twelve to reach Washington. He walked into his mother-in-law's house, greeted everyone, and then excused himself to take a much-needed shower. A few minutes later, his mother-in-law knocked on the bathroom door: he had an urgent phone call.

Lemuel Shepherd was calling to say that the Marines had pushed their way almost to the Chinese border, then celebrated Thanksgiving with turkey and dressing. For many of the Marines, it was their last meal. That night, during a driving snowstorm, several Chinese Communist divisions attacked from the north. Now the 1st Marine Division was surrounded at a place called the Chosin Reservoir, and Shepherd wanted Krulak back in Korea immediately.

Krulak dressed and raced for the airport. Some forty hours later, he joined an anxious Shepherd at Koto-ri. Krulak was about to become part of one of the most significant events in Marine Corps history: the heroic breakout from the Chosin Reservoir. General O. P. Smith would find eternal glory as the leader of that valiant effort, but just as Krulak had played a crucial role in reshaping the Pacific battlefield with the Higgins boat, he was about to reshape the battlefield in Korea with the helicopter.

# 11

## Windmills in the Snow

THE correct name is Changjin. But this was an unexpected war, and on the old Japanese maps used by the 1st Marine Division, the lake in the northeastern part of North Korea was called the Chosin Reservoir. And that is how the epic fight of the Korean War is remembered: the Battle of the Chosin Reservoir.

Korea has been called "the forgotten war," and today if people know anything at all about it, they usually know of the Chosin Reservoir. This is the place where one Marine division was surrounded by an estimated seven enemy divisions and emerged covered with snow, frostbite, and eternal glory. This is the place where the quiet and retiring O. P. Smith proved he was among the great fighting generals of the Marine Corps.

On the morning after Thanksgiving, Smith realized that Douglas MacArthur, who had predicted that the Chinese Communists would not enter the war, had pushed the Marines into the greatest ambush in military history. Now they were surrounded by a numerically superior force with no one to bail them out. It was march or die. Smith passed the word to his Marines: "We're coming out fighting, or we're not coming out at all." Back home in

America, people read of this epic battle and the question was not "Can the Marines hold?" but rather "Will the Marines survive?"

And then it was into the breach. Amid savage combat, the 1st Marine Division broke out of the encirclement and for thirteen days fought its way seventy-eight miles along a one-lane road to the port of Hungnam. The fighting was hand to hand, day and night, in subzero temperatures, and when it was over, the Marines had virtually destroyed every Chinese unit in their path.

Smith famously said that his Marines were not retreating; they were attacking in a different direction. But, of course, it was a retreat, albeit not a classic one, because the Marines brought out their wounded, most of their dead, and all of their weapons and equipment. And along the way, they inflicted at least 37,500 casualties on the enemy and suffered 4,418 casualties themselves. Once again, a remote and inhospitable land, a cheap and heretofore unremarkable piece of earth had become some of the most expensive real estate in the world: it had been paid for with the blood of United States Marines.

Fourteen Marines were awarded the Medal of Honor for their actions during the breakout, and the survivors of that battle, "the Chosin Few," stand with those Marines who fought at the 'Canal and at Belleau Wood.

A quick comparison, painful as it is, must be made with Army troops west of the Chosin Reservoir. The soldiers there were brave, but they were not well trained or well led, and an Army regiment was virtually destroyed. Soldiers broke and ran, leaving their dead and their equipment in the snow. While the Marines were creating legends, the Army was bugging out.

DURING the breakout, the valor of the Marines on the ground was such that the role of helicopters is not widely known. But Glen Butler's unpublished manuscript reports that during those harrowing days, Marine helicopters flew hundreds of missions and continuously dropped supplies, including vital radio batteries, to isolated units. Without helicopters, Marine casualties would have been far greater.

Whenever weather permitted, and sometimes when it did not, Brute Krulak was overhead, reporting everything he saw to Shepherd, who in turn passed along Krulak's suggestions to Smith.

The Marine Corps famously keeps a lengthy "shit list," and because of Korea, Ned Almond will forever retain a top spot. Smith was fighting for his life while being continuously nagged by Almond about tactics and strategy. Disagreements between the two men were so open and so acrimonious as to be rare in military history. Had Smith obeyed Almond's orders to disperse his various units, the Chinese attack would have found his division scattered across a big part of North Korea. But Smith ignored Almond—as well as Shepherd, who often sided with Almond—maintained unit integrity, and fought his way out.

The differences between Smith and Almond went far beyond the operational arts. Almond lived in a luxuriously appointed trailer with a separate dining room that included white table linens, silver, and fine wines. Soldiers acted as waiters and served fresh fruit and vegetables flown in daily from Japan. Smith, a Christian Scientist, was an austere man who slept in the field with his Marines and ate the same food they did. Almond had an apparent disregard for the lives of his men, while Smith's highest priority was taking care of his Marines. The two men could not have been more different.

Halberstam, in *The Coldest Winter*, says that the Marines' breakout from the Chosin Reservoir was a "classic moment in their own exceptional history, a masterpiece of leadership on the part of their officers, and of simple, relentless, abiding courage on the part of the ordinary fighting man." Smith's Marines fought their way to Hagaru by December 4 and to Koto-ri by December 7. As the Marines left Koto-ri, one young Marine hung this sign on a tank: "Only 14 More Shooting Days Until Christmas."

When the 1st Marine Division reached the port of Hungnam, Shepherd and Krulak were sitting in a jeep on the outskirts of town, waiting. When the Marines saw Shepherd, they stood taller and were singing "The Marines' Hymn" as they marched past, continuing on through Hungnam and down to the docks to load the equipment they had brought with them.

Almond sent word to destroy the equipment, an order that was devastating to the Marines. This equipment could be patched up and painted and used in the next war. But Almond was the boss, so the Marines did as they were ordered and boarded the ships.

BECAUSE some fifteen years later, in another war, she would become important to Krulak's story, we must introduce war correspondent Marguerite "Maggie" Higgins here. Even though Higgins had covered World War II, Army objections to her covering the Korean War were such that it took MacArthur's personal approval for her to be near the front lines. In 1951, Higgins became the first woman to win a Pulitzer Prize as a war correspondent, and when she came home from Korea, she was among the most respected and admired correspondents in America. Her reportorial abilities would only improve by the time, years later, she arrived in Vietnam.

EVEN though it seemed to O. P. Smith that Shepherd was spending most of his time in Korea, Shepherd did return occasionally to headquarters in Hawaii. Krulak noticed that when his boss was there, he visited the naval hospital almost daily to spend time with wounded Marines. "Where were you wounded?" he would ask, and the Marine would name a place or a battle in Korea. Shepherd more often than not responded with something like, "Well, hell. I was standing there watching you attack that hill."

More than a decade later, Krulak would follow Shepherd's example of attending to Marines wounded in battle.

\*   \*   \*

GENERAL Smith's leadership in Korea was so exemplary that Army commanders said the 1st Marine Division would have the honored position at the center of the line when United Nations forces launched the spring offensive. On February 24, 1951, Army general Bryant Moore, who was to command the offensive, died of a heart attack, and Smith, with the endorsement of Eighth Army commander General Matthew Ridgway, took over the job.

On the rare occasions when a Marine general commands Army troops, there is serious heartburn back in Washington. Senior Army officers did not believe then and do not believe today that a Marine general, no matter his battlefield accomplishments, is capable of commanding a corps. (A corps usually consists of two or three divisions. A division is about ten thousand men.) And there was the matter of Smith's name: a fresh reminder of the infamous "Smith versus Smith" brouhaha on Saipan a few years earlier.

Eight days after Smith assumed command, he was relieved of duty. The Army flew in General William Hoge from Europe to take over.

On April 26, General Gerald Thomas arrived to assume command of the 1st Marine Division, and two months later he asked Krulak to be his chief of staff. It would be in that job that Krulak had the opportunity to put into practice all that he had earlier written regarding helicopters. Not only would helicopters reshape the Korean battlefield, but their use would become the template for the Army's tactical helicopter operations in Vietnam.

ONLY a few days after taking over as Thomas's chief of staff, Krulak went to Thomas and laid out plans for a shore-to-shore amphibious landing that would envelop the eastern flank of a Chinese Communist force. It would be a relatively simple operation, in that the Marines would be moving troops some forty miles down the coast to the town of Kojo, familiar terrain as the Marines had landed there a year earlier.

215

Thomas liked the idea and set up a meeting in Seoul with Army and Navy officers, who agreed that Krulak's plan was a good one. But they would need six weeks to organize the operation and marshal the needed equipment. What did Krulak, who would command the landing force, think of this?

"I have just one observation, and it has to do with the planning and marshaling time, which you have characterized as six weeks. I would feel that it is a bit long."

After a long pause, an Army general asked, "Colonel, what would you consider an appropriate time for planning?"

"Seventy-two hours."

The Marines around the room were smiling and nodding in approval. But the Army representatives ended the conference, saying they would take up Krulak's plan with their superiors. A few days later, MacArthur vetoed the landing.

"Why it was vetoed by MacArthur, I'll never know," Krulak recalled. "MacArthur was not a strategist; he was a politician. In fact, he was the finest politician ever to wear the Army uniform. Almond, well, he wasn't much of anything."

In July, Shepherd wrote a FitRep for Krulak saying, "I consider Col. Krulak the most competent officer who has ever served under my command. He not only excels in professional assignments but takes an unusual interest in all unofficial and social activities of this command. Fully qualified for promotion to general officer rank."

Given that Lemuel Shepherd was a legendary Marine general, and given that in all probability he would be the next Commandant, the FitRep was guaranteed to get the attention of a promotion board.

In September, HMR-161, the first helicopter transport squadron in the Marine Corps, arrived in Korea with fifteen new Sikorsky helicopters and sporting the motto "Equitatus Caeli." Krulak intended to see that the squadron lived up to its motto. He was bubbling over with notions of putting into use the doctrine he had helped write and knew that Thomas would turn him loose to do so. For Brute Krulak, Christmas had come early.

CLIFFORD V. Brokaw III was a 1950 Yale graduate who upon graduation was commissioned in the Marines and sent to Korea. He was wounded in June 1951 and afterward sent to regimental headquarters as the assistant operations officer—a twenty-two-year-old second lieutenant doing the job of a captain. For a reserve officer who had no intention of pursuing a military career, all this was a grand adventure, especially when, for various reasons, he became the de facto operations officer and thus the right-hand man of Colonel Herman Nickerson, the regimental commander.

For several months, Brokaw was in almost daily radio or telephone contact with Krulak, who, he says, was a legend in the Marine Corps. For a man with such an outsize persona, Krulak's voice over the radio or telephone was understated, even soft, but there was no doubt about the intellect behind it.

One day Brokaw and Colonel Nickerson were at an observation post when a helicopter landed and out stepped a short Marine officer wearing eagles on his collar. The unsmiling officer walked up the hill as if he owned it, introduced himself as Brute Krulak, and with no further conversation pointed to a distant hill that maps identified as Hill 844. "We are going to attack that hill with a helicopter assault," he announced. "We are going to attack, and you are going to provide the troops."

Brokaw remembers that Nickerson looked at Krulak in the way field commanders look upon staff people and replied, "In a pig's eye. It is ridiculous to bring helicopters into contact with the enemy. If you do that, we won't have helicopters to lift ammo."

Krulak said that each of the new Sikorsky helicopters could

carry six riflemen and that now the Marines could ride into battle in a new fashion.

"Get the hell off my hill," Nickerson snapped.

SUCH a giant leap into an operation does not take place without a baby step, without a practice mission. Helicopters in Korea were called "flying windmills," so it was appropriate that, on September 13, when seven helicopters, each carrying 800 pounds of supplies, began shuttling to resupply a Marine battalion seven miles away, it was called Operation Windmill. Some 18,848 pounds of cargo were moved in, and 74 casualties were taken out.

On September 20, despite heavy fog, 224 Marines landed on Hill 844 for the first helicopter-borne landing of combat troops. To support the Marines, helicopters later flew in 17,772 pounds of equipment and supplies, followed by a company of Marines to relieve a South Korean unit on the front lines.

Now the Marines were ready for the ultimate test. In October, Brokaw sat down to write the operations order for the first helicopter assault in history—the first combat application of the theory of vertical envelopment. A battalion of 959 men would be moved fifteen miles, and when they landed, they would be in combat. Brokaw looked around the headquarters tent and asked, "What is the name of this operation?"

When he received only blank stares in reply, he turned to a grizzled gunnery sergeant and said, "What do we call this?"

"Why don't you call it Operation Bumblebee? Them things ain't supposed to fly either."

And that is the genesis of what military historians consider the first significant use of helicopters in combat. It was not the sort of combat assault Americans later would see in Vietnam, where troops were inserted under fire into a "hot" landing zone. Rather, it was a defilade operation, in which helicopters flew through valleys over friendly territory and were not exposed to enemy fire until the last moment. Nevertheless, it proved that helicopters could insert combat troops into a battle.

The Marines and their helicopters were making headlines around the world. Moving Marine battalions by helicopter would become routine in the next few months, and the operations first envisioned by Krulak five years earlier stood up to the rigors of combat so well that in the years after Korea, the Army would jump on this lily pad. Army helicopter units liked "Equitatus Caeli" so much that they, too, called themselves the "air cavalry." And because of the movie and television program *M*A*S*H*, and television coverage of and movies about Vietnam, the public would believe that the Army was the first service to use helicopters in combat.

WHEN Krulak was ninety five, he made one of his last public appearances, at the San Diego Zoo, where he was the guest of honor at a luncheon commemorating his decades as a board member. He arrived in a wheelchair, and during a brief speech, as he had done so many times in the past, he recounted the good fortune that had marked his life and career. He illustrated his point by describing two events that he said occurred in Korea.

In the first story, he was in the field spending the night with a Marine unit, sleeping on the ground in a sleeping bag, when a habu—a venomous snake whose bite is so toxic "there is no known antidote"—crawled inside his sleeping bag. Here he paused and asked rhetorically, "What happened?" then smiled mischievously and said, "Well, the habu did not wet its pants." After the laughter died down, Krulak said that he lay very still, and after a while the habu crawled away.

Krulak should have reported this event to herpetologists, as the habu is usually found in the warm climates of Okinawa and Southeast Asia. This would have been the snake's first known appearance in Korea. And though the habu is a venomous pit viper, in toxicity it ranks below the cobra, mamba, and even the North American rattlesnake and copperhead.

This dramatic and overblown war story is important because it was important to Krulak and because it shows that he could never stop fabricating.

In the second story, Krulak was in the field with a Marine unit that was under fire. He stuck his head over a log to look around, then ducked out of sight. A young private lying beside him asked, "Sir, are you scared?"

"Damn right," Krulak responded.

Seeking to emulate the colonel's bravado, the private stuck his head over the log and was killed by a sniper. "I said to myself that the difference in my being alive and his being dead was only two feet," Krulak told the audience. "That had to be luck."

Others might wonder whether Krulak, when he stuck his head up, gave away their position to the sniper, who just waited for the next head to appear.

WHILE he was in Korea, Krulak received a letter from a cousin back in Denver wanting to know how he might go about joining the Marines and going to Korea. Krulak told him the same thing he had told another cousin during World War II: The Corps is too tough for you. Join the Army. The second cousin was as devastated as the first, perhaps even more so because the Denver newspapers carried occasional stories about Krulak, and it was clear that he was a very important man in the war. More important to Krulak was that he did not want to be outed by his Jewish cousin.

IN October, General Thomas wrote a FitRep saying that Krulak was "probably the best officer of his rank in the Corps" and that he was "ready for any assignment."

About that time, General Shepherd arrived in Korea on an inspection tour. During a private meeting with Thomas and Krulak, he said, "The president will soon announce that he is appointing me as the next Commandant." He told them that his first order of business would be to reorganize Headquarters Marine Corps. Such a move would anger many of the lieutenant colonels and colonels who had been promoted as high as they would go but still had a few years before retirement. (Such staff officers are said to be "retired on active duty" and are referred to as the "ROAD Gang.") They would almost certainly slow-walk every change put forth by Shepherd.

The three men talked of how reorganizing Headquarters Marine Corps would be brutal combat on its own. The difference was that at headquarters, friend and foe wore the same uniform, and it would be only when a man felt a knife in his back that he would realize he was in the presence of an assassin. Shepherd needed trusted and able friends to implement his changes. He wanted Gerry Thomas as his chief of staff and was creating a new job for Krulak: secretary of the general staff.

During the days of the Chowder Society, Krulak had proved that he could survive and prosper in bureaucratic battles. He relished the close-quarter combat of headquarters, the maneuvering, the high stakes, and most of all the chance to make changes — to make things bigger and better, to create a new Marine Corps. He loved the drama of move and countermove, and with the backing of the Commandant and his close adherence to the French military expression *de l'audace, encore de l'audace, et toujours de l'audace* (audacity, more audacity, and ever more audacity), Washington was going to be a grand romp.

Besides, it was a good time to leave Korea. Soon Truman would halt all offensive actions and order American troops to hold on to the real estate south of the 38th parallel. Holding on to real estate is not what Marines do best. Krulak knew that when the Korean War was over, a new vocabulary, a new list of iconic names, would be added to that long list of places sanctified by Marine blood—places such as the Punchbowl, Fox Hill, No Name Ridge, the Hook, and, of course, the Frozen Chosin.

For his own performance in Korea, Krulak had been recommended for the Distinguished Service Medal, an award usually reserved for more senior officers and usually presented upon their retirement. The recommendation said that Krulak had devised a "brilliant new method of deployment of forces in modern warfare by utilizing transport helicopters in vertical envelopment to move and supply troops in the rapid seizure of vital objectives." In Korea, helicopters had moved from being a curiosity to being a proven and valuable tactical tool.

The chance to go to Washington, especially in a new and powerful position, would give Krulak the opportunity to set right his embarrassing departure from there in the late summer of 1944, when General W. P. T. Hill had run him out of town. It was the only known retreat of his military career, and, as he said, "The elephant, the red man, and the Krulaks never forget."

When Shepherd became Commandant in early 1952, his most important responsibility was to correct the omissions of the National Security Act of 1947 so that the Marine Corps would be guaranteed the budget to carry out its functions. Legislation had to be passed to protect the Corps from an anti-Marine president such as Truman and from future Joint Chiefs of Staff who, for whatever reason, might seek to diminish the Corps.

The Joint Chiefs remained the most vocal and bitter opponents of the Marine Corps bill, which made the Corps a separate military service within the Department of the Navy. The bill also gave the Commandant a seat on the Joint Chiefs—when matters affecting the Marine Corps were being discussed. And, most important, it set the Marine Corps structure at a minimum of three divisions and three aircraft wings.

Shepherd ordered Krulak to look after Marine Corps interests in this matter, and it was in that capacity that Krulak wrote the crucial language for Public Law 416. Mike Mansfield, now a senator, called in every chit owed to him and made passage of the bill the most important act of his senatorial career. Signed into law in June 1952, it made the Marine Corps unique in the American military by specifying that it would always have a minimum of three active-duty combat divisions and three active-duty aircraft wings. This legislation was even more important than the National Security Act of 1947, as it proved that Congress stood ready to preserve and strengthen the Marine Corps. Congress did this for one reason: confidence that in times of national peril, the Corps would perform as expected. "Performance is what it is all about," Krulak wrote.

Passage of the bill meant that the Marine Corps would never again have to look over its shoulder at the other branches of the military. Never again would it have to fight for the right to fight.

Or so the Marine Corps believed.

KRULAK was embarrassed when, in 1952, the secretary of the Navy asked for more details regarding his recommendation for the Distinguished Service Medal and, after studying the reports, refused to award it. The secretary concluded that what Thomas and Shepherd called "exceptionally meritorious service" was in fact within the normal scope of Krulak's duties. Brute felt that he deserved the medal and collected ten endorsements supporting his contention. The secretary, however, stood fast and said that Brute could instead be awarded a Gold Star in lieu of a second, less significant decoration, the Legion of Merit. Krulak had no choice but to accept the Gold Star.

IN 1953, the chief of naval operations proposed rewriting General Order No. 5, the fundamental document that governs distribution of authority within the Department of the Navy. The CNO wanted to command the Marine Corps, its forces, and its headquarters and to have the right to decide how many personnel and what equipment the Corps needed.

Given Shepherd's great feeling for the history, customs, and traditions of the Marine Corps, it is understandable that he fought the CNO and the secretary of the Navy with perhaps a bit more intensity than the average Commandant would have. When they could not resolve their differences, they did what commanders often do: order subordinates to find a resolution. The Navy sent in an admiral; Shepherd sent in Colonel Brute Krulak.

Five months later, after many long and acrimonious sessions, Krulak had won concessions on three of the four points at issue. The Commandant of the Marine Corps would command the Marine Corps, its forces, and its headquarters. But the two men could not agree on the crucial matter of who would establish Marine Corps manpower and materiel levels. "The power to feed is the power to starve," Krulak said. Marines had to control Marine resources.

The issue was sent to the secretary of the Navy, who, doubtless influenced by the intent of Public Law 416 and probably influenced by Senator Mansfield, ruled in favor of the Marine Corps. For the first time in history, the Commandant had full authority over his Marines and reported to the secretary of the Navy rather than to the CNO.

The important observation here is the symbiotic relationship between Krulak and his superiors. Krulak had made Shepherd look good at Okinawa, at Tsingtao, and especially in Korea. Now Krulak had been one of the prime movers in a development that would make Shepherd's Commandancy a luminous one in Marine Corps history.

ONE of the things for which Shepherd is revered in the Marine Corps is that as Commandant, he redressed a great wrong. Shepherd visited Belleau Wood and found that there was still no marker showing that the Marines had fought there, no marker showing that the wood had been renamed the Bois de la Brigade de Marine, and no marker saying that Marines were buried there. The American Battle Monuments Commission continued to refuse even the use of a Marine Corps emblem in the cemetery.

Shepherd changed that, adding a striking bas relief in bronze on a black granite slab that still stands today at Belleau Wood. The inscription reads, "May the gallant Marines who gave their lives for Corps and Country rest in peace." Underneath the inscription is the eagle, globe, and anchor. And it is no coincidence that the spigot on a nearby fountain is a devil dog. Legend has it that any Marine who drinks from the fountain will have twenty years added to his life.

BEFORE we continue with Brute's career, we must pause and note that on March 28, 1954, Morris Krulak died. The obituary noted that Morris was a retired wholesale jeweler who had been born in Philadelphia.

Bess Krulak was financially comfortable, having inherited more than a million dollars at Morris's death. She often said that Victor did not make enough money in the Marine Corps and that she was going to save every penny she could and build a very big nest egg for her only child.

By now Brute's uncle Max Zall was one of the best-known people in Denver. He had made a fortune as an oil and gas lawyer and had become co-owner of a refining company before he became Denver's city attorney. Once, when the city could not find buyers for special improvement bonds, Max wrote a check for the entire bond issue. The *Denver Post* described Max thusly: "A pragmatic, not idealistic, lawyer and politician, Zall conducts his business close to his bright red vest and wears his Gucci shoes and heavy turquoise watch and ring with easy grace."

* * *

KRULAK's tour in Washington was similar to his other tours, in that he participated in so many important events that it is almost impossible to impose a cohesive time line on his activities. While he was involved in the passage of the Marine Corps bill, he was also point man for the slow and bloody reorganization of Headquarters Marine Corps. Overcoming bureaucratic inertia was extremely difficult, as Shepherd's proposed changes would redistribute power and would, in the case of General W. P. T. Hill, quartermaster of the Corps, take away much of his power.

General Hill was what today's Marines call a "Doctor No": he rejected almost every new idea that crossed his desk. He was parsimonious, as a good quartermaster must be, and well-meaning, but he had held his job since 1944 and had become an autocratic and feared figure who personified the obstacles to Shepherd's reorganization plans. Krulak was not intimidated, even though he was seriously outranked. Given that Krulak had been handpicked by the Commandant and given a mandate to energize headquarters, the difference in rank, while observed and respected, was virtually ignored. Every leader who wants to make significant change needs a "resident son of a bitch" who can make hard decisions without regard to rank or personality. Krulak wielded the bureaucratic knife that for several years caused much bloodletting at headquarters. Shepherd let Hill know that although he had made an important contribution, it was time for him to consider retirement. Hill waited several years, so the Krulak influence would not be so obvious, then stepped down as he had been encouraged to do.

NOT long after Krulak returned to Washington, he bought a new, two-story brick colonial house at 4651 Dittmar Road in Arlington, Virginia. It was the only time in Krulak's career that the family lived together in a civilian community, and most of the boys' childhood memories—at least their best memories—would be of their four years in that house. Bill, the middle son, says that here the family lived a life close to the *Leave It to Beaver* television show, that they felt "normal" and not part of the nomadic tribe whose only home is the military.

The boys went to civilian schools, and most of their friends were sons of civilians. Bill had a paper route and a shoe-shine route. Brute brought work home every night, but even so the family usually had dinner together. On Sundays, they attended an Episcopal church. Yet Krulak remained so demanding that "our life was all about receiving affirmation from dad." That affirmation never came, but as adults Vic and Bill would find approval from a surprising source.

Vic remembers that his mother was "overshadowed" by Brute, but that she was clever and in subtle ways could manipulate her husband. "She was very good at stroking his ego," Vic says. Amy knew that when Brute walked in the door, he would sample whatever she was cooking and tell her how it could be made better. He would suggest salt or pepper, and she would say, "Oh, you are so smart. What would I do without you?"

At age sixteen, Vic went to Phillips Exeter Academy in New Hampshire. The admissions director there was Hamilton "Hammy" Bissel, the former coxswain of the Harvard rowing crew whom Brute had met as a midshipman. Bissel arranged a scholarship for Vic at what many considered the finest prep school in America. But Vic was not impressed, primarily because he had no vote in whether he would attend Exeter. Brute simply said, "You are going." On Vic's first trip home, he found that his old room had been turned into a guest room and he had to sleep in the pantry. He felt as if he had been excluded from the family. "I was a guest," he remembers.

Krulak would later send Bill to Exeter because it was "the best," and like Vic, Bill would have no say in the matter. Chuck says that he went voluntarily because he wanted a better education than he would have received at Quantico.

On the matter of Exeter, Brute was operating with a mind-set not unlike that of his own father. Brute wanted his boys to attend the school seen as the prep school of America's gentry, a place that would give his sons social connections that would benefit them all their lives. At Exeter, Vic attended classes with Jay Rockefeller, John Heinz, and John Negroponte. Chuck was a classmate and wrestling teammate of John Irving.

Just as he had no vote about going to Exeter, Vic says he had no vote about college. It was a given that he would attend the Naval Academy. When Bill said that he favored Dartmouth, his father said, "Fine. But who is going to pay for it?" So he, too, went to the Naval Academy. After Exeter, Chuck was accepted at Princeton but chose the Naval Academy instead. The three boys were going into the family business, the Marine Corps, and Annapolis was the best place to begin their careers.

During the years on Dittmar Road, the Krulak boys became interested in their family history. They knew all there was to know about their mother's ancestors, as the Chandlers were quite proud of their family. But they knew almost nothing about their father's side. Brute never talked about Denver or Cheyenne or about his parents, and he would entertain few questions on the subject. Throughout the boys' childhood, the Krulaks were always en route somewhere else when they passed through Denver.

That Brute put Denver and Cheyenne behind him does not mean he ignored his mother. In fact, his family back in Denver says that he was extraordinarily good to her, solicitous in the extreme, with frequent phone calls and gifts. And he always made much of the kiffles she sent every Christmas.

\* \* \*

THE two most damaging and embarrassing events in the history of the Marine Corps occurred in the mid-1950s. This was a time when the Corps lost much of its luster in the eyes of the American public. It was also a time that would deeply affect Krulak and cause him to realize that if the Marine Corps was going to keep its place in Americans' hearts and keep its friends in Congress, great changes had to be made.

The first disastrous event was known as the Schwable case, and it happened in 1954. (The second event occurred in 1956 and is discussed in chapter 12.) Frank Schwable was an Annapolis graduate and a Marine colonel who had been chief of staff of the 1st Marine Air Wing in Korea. Shot down in July 1952 over No Name Valley, he was captured and subjected to the psychological torture that would come to be known as brainwashing. Schwable was a highly visible and symbolic figure in that he was the senior Marine POW in Korea and the second most senior of all American POWs.

Before he went to Korea, Schwable worked for the Joint Chiefs of Staff, where he was privy to some of the most highly classified material of the U.S. military: his job involved the distribution of America's nuclear weapons and target assignments within the Soviet Union. As a POW, Schwable, afraid that he might break and reveal his top-secret knowledge, "confessed" to his captors that the United States was engaged in germ warfare against North Korea. While demonstrably untrue, Schwable's statement made headlines around the world. Never in history had the Marine Corps been so embarrassed by the behavior of a senior officer.

When Schwable was repatriated, there was a movement in the Marine Corps to court-martial him. That idea quickly died out, however, because a court-martial would mean that Schwable's work as a nuclear targeting expert might become part of the trial, and it would be hard to find officers with both the security clearances and the "need to know" such testimony.

The Marines did convene a court of inquiry, and President Eisenhower even commented on the Schwable case during a White House press conference, but Schwable was exonerated and restored to active duty. Shepherd ordered a letter written to Schwable advising him that he would never again command Marines; he would control only a desk for the remainder of his career. Krulak wrote the letter.

But the incident has far more direct relevance to Krulak. After Schwable was assigned to desk duty, the American military realized that many of the enlisted POWs—and, by extension, many enlisted members of the military—did not know the history of their country or of their respective branches of the service. They had such a poor grounding in these subjects that under the pressures of interrogation, they lost their moorings and became psychologically adrift, only to be "rescued" by Communist doctrine, which many of them subsequently espoused.

President Eisenhower directed that a new code of conduct for American military personnel be written and that every member of the military not only memorize the code but carry a copy on his person for reference. To Krulak, this was not enough. That Marines could be brainwashed because they did not know or understand their history disturbed him deeply, and the time was approaching when he would have the rank and position to make radical changes in teaching history to Marines.

In March 1955, Krulak received a FitRep saying, "His capabilities excel those of any officer I have ever served with in any rank." In August came another saying that Krulak was "by far the best qualified Marine officer I have ever served with in any rank" and so superior that he could not be compared with other Marines. Both FitReps were signed by General Randolph M. Pate, the Commandant, who strongly urged that Krulak be promoted to general.

In June, Krulak was ordered to Hawaii to become chief of staff for General William O. Brice, CGFMFPac. En route, Krulak stopped in San Francisco to attend a reception for General Shepherd. As he passed through the receiving line, Shepherd leaned close and whispered, "You can be expecting to hear some good news."

Such whispered confidences from a superior officer could only mean a promotion. That was confirmed several days later when Krulak walked into his office, a remodeled World War II barracks at the Pearl Harbor Naval Shipyard, and the man he was replacing bluntly greeted him with, "The selection board choices for brigadier general have been announced, and you were selected. I think there are at least fifty people who were just as deserving as you."

Krulak was a rare "deep selection" for general—that is, the selection board passed over dozens of colonels who were senior to Krulak to choose him. At age forty-two, he was one of the youngest generals in the history of the Marine Corps and the first member of his Annapolis class to reach flag rank. Only a few graduates of each class at any of the service academies ever become generals or admirals, and among those few, it is a mark of great distinction to be first. Given that Krulak had been commissioned only because of a most serendipitous chain of events, the fact that he was first in his class to wear a star was not without irony.

Some half-dozen colonels put in their retirement papers upon hearing of Krulak's selection. Not all were members of the ROAD Gang; some believed in their hearts they were better qualified, that they had far more command time, than Krulak. They considered him a "horse holder" who, because of his closeness to Shepherd, had been chosen over them.

None of this mattered to Krulak. He took comfort in the knowledge that given his relative youth, he had a better chance than any one-star general in the Marine Corps of becoming Commandant. It would depend on his performance over the next few years.

# 12

## Back to the Pacific

A few weeks after Brute went to Hawaii, Vic entered the U.S. Naval Academy as the recipient of a highly competitive presidential nomination. Plebes who were the sons of active-duty officers—and there were many of these at Annapolis—were referred to as "juniors," but Vic was the only junior bearing the name of the man who had just been selected to become one of the youngest generals in the history of the Marine Corps. Vic was now in the family business, and the burden was great.

Part of the orientation for plebes was a visit to the rifle range, which was supervised by Marine sergeants—crisp, no-nonsense men who carried swagger sticks as a symbol of their authority. Vic was a singularly bad shot and did not qualify with the rifle. The prodding he received with the swagger stick was usually accompanied by the disgusted voice of a sergeant saying, "What would your father think of you?"

By the time the midshipmen (upperclassmen) returned to campus in September, Vic was not doing well. While at the rifle range or while marching, he would suddenly faint and lie unconscious for ten or fifteen seconds. Again and again, he was reminded that he was a pale shadow of the officer now known as "the Brute," who, everyone agreed, was one squared-away Marine.

On September 15, Vic was admitted to the hospital at Annapolis and then transferred to Bethesda Naval Hospital, where he stayed until October 18. Naval doctors could find no reason for his fainting spells, and he returned to the Academy. On November 1, he was again admitted to Bethesda, where he stayed until November 15. His medical record shows "DU (Fainting Dizzying)." "DU" usually means "diagnosis undetermined."

Midshipmen are given assignments to write papers on Navy or Marine battles, and when one of those midshipmen came to Vic and asked, "What can you tell me about your father's raid on Choiseul?" Vic could only shake his head and say, "I never heard of Choiseul."

Vic is not to be faulted here. Marines rarely talk about the battles in which they receive medals or decorations, and asking about the details of those engagements is simply not done. But the simple fact that Vic remembers such a trivial incident reveals that this was one more time when he felt he did not measure up.

Vic is vague about his time at Annapolis, saying, "I did not like the Academy." He alludes only tangentially to his fainting spells, and concludes, "It was not a marriage made in heaven." Many plebes find the discipline and rigor of the Academy too much and return, voluntarily or involuntarily, to the civilian world. Usually it is of little note when a plebe resigns. But when Victor Harold Krulak Jr. announced his intention to resign, the superintendent of the Academy called Brute to let him know. "He flew from Hawaii to Annapolis to square my ass away," Vic says. He laughs. "It didn't work."

When Vic resigned, his symptoms disappeared. Covered with ignominy, he went to Hawaii to live with his family ("because they told me to") and enrolled at the University of Hawaii. He was there for one year before entering William & Mary in Virginia, where he paid his own way, studied history, and pondered his future. If he could not find approval from his father, perhaps he could find it in his life's work. But what would that work be?

Vic's brief experience at the Academy became one of those shadowy and mildly embarrassing events that cause family members to relate the story in a vague fashion. Bill says that Vic "had a serious infection that put him in the hospital for several months, and afterward he simply was not strong enough to continue." Chuck speaks vaguely of psychosomatic disorders that forced his older brother to resign. Whatever the explanation, Brute was angry and disappointed. In the small world of the Marine Corps, it would soon become known that his namesake couldn't hack it at the Academy. Those who did not like Brute would experience no small amount of schadenfreude over this. And because of his rapid advancement, his intimidating intellect, and his friendship with the most powerful officers in the Marine Corps, those who did not like the Brute were legion.

BRUTE threw himself into several new projects in Hawaii. He learned that the Navy had declared as excess property a 220.5-acre site atop Halawa Heights. The property was several miles from Pearl Harbor, but the elevation was some six hundred feet higher and afforded a splendid view of the harbor, Honolulu, and the Pacific. The Aiea Naval Hospital, deactivated in 1949, was the most prominent building on the property, but it and the surrounding buildings had deteriorated: windows were broken, birds were nesting indoors, and kiawe bushes had grown ten feet high. Krulak saw a place of great possibility and proposed to General Brice that the property become a Marine Corps base and the new location for Fleet Marine Force, Pacific (FMFPac) headquarters. Brice instantly agreed. But the cutoff date for stating a need for the property was only a few days away, and the Commandant would want to know the costs of rehabilitating the building.

Krulak pulled a number out of the air—$500,000—and said, "We can refine that later."

The Commandant approved the proposal, and as no other government agency had any interest in the run-down property, it was turned over to the Marine Corps on October 15. Krulak ordered that the top floor, which during World War II had been a ward for wounded or sick officers, become the new offices of the commanding general.

The renovations were completed by late October, and Brice and Krulak moved into their new quarters. Krulak recommended that the facility be named Camp H. M. Smith. The Commandant agreed and set the official dedication for January.

Krulak also rehabilitated the officers' club and turned a large, unused area on the side of a hill into an athletic field. Rough and covered with thick bushes, the hillside had a magnificent view of Pearl Harbor. At the time, intramural sports played a significant role in the military, and within a few months Bordelon Field, named for a Marine who had been posthumously awarded the Medal of Honor for his bravery at Tarawa, was open for business.

AMY's vivacious and independent nature came into full flower in Hawaii. She took hula lessons and became good enough that she often glided onto the dance floor at parties and performed a spontaneous version of Hawaii's traditional dance. Brute watched indulgently as his wife performed, often to her favorite tune, "To You Sweetheart, Aloha."

HEADS of state, other officeholders, and senior military officials from around the world often visited Hawaii when they were making a final grand tour before retirement. If these public figures wished to receive honors from the Marines, the Marines were happy to oblige. For these parades, the parking lot in front of FMFPac headquarters became what Marines call the parade deck.

It was tight and thus called for great skill by the marching units, but the drill team at Camp Smith was one of the most squared-away drill teams in the Marine Corps and could cope with the cramped conditions.

On January 31, 1956, Camp H. M. Smith was officially dedicated. General Smith was ill and unable to attend, but his wife unveiled a bronze plaque at the main entrance to the headquarters building. The words engraved on the plaque were written by Krulak himself:

*Camp H. M. Smith*
*Named in honor of*
*General*
*Holland McTyeire Smith*
*United States Marine Corps*
*Through whose vision and resourcefulness the concept*
*Fleet Marine Force, Pacific became a reality and under*
*whose aggressive leadership that unit distinguished itself*
*in the Pacific campaigns of the Second World War.*
*31 January 1956*

General Brice also was ill at the time, and it fell to Krulak to escort Admiral Felix Stump, Commander in Chief, Pacific (CINCPac), on a tour of the new facility. During the tour, Krulak overheard the admiral say to his aide, "This is a fine building. Why the hell didn't we take it over?"

That conversation gave Krulak an idea: why not invite the large CINCPac staff to relocate from Pearl Harbor to Camp Smith? Their presence would help defray maintenance costs on the building. The Navy accepted, and the CINCPac moved in one floor below the CGFMFPac.

In February, General Brice wrote a FitRep for Krulak saying, "This officer is truly outstanding in every respect. The esteem in which I hold him is this: after being promoted in June to brigadier general, I recommend accelerated promotion to major general. There is no assignment that he cannot fill with distinction."

By now Krulak's second son, Bill, was showing the independence and initiative often found in military dependents. In the summer of 1956, when he was fifteen, he climbed aboard a commercial airliner in Hawaii and flew to San Francisco, where he made it across town to a bus station and caught a bus to Denver. There he spent a few days with his grandmother Bess, whom the Krulak boys called "Gommy." She bought him an airline ticket to Washington, where he stayed with his maternal grandmother for a few days before catching a train to Phillips Exeter.

Bill would graduate from Exeter with an average grade of C, good enough to gain him admission to almost any university in America. But he would go to Annapolis and then into the family business.

The Marine Corps has two places where recruits are turned into Marines: the Parris Island Marine Corps Recruit Depot at Beaufort, South Carolina, which is called simply Parris Island or PI, and the San Diego Marine Corps Recruit Depot, usually called MCRD. In the 1950s, at both Parris Island and MCRD, drill instructors (DIs) were known for their brutality toward recruits. Collectively, DIs were a vicious group representing the dark side of the Marine Corps.

Not atypical was the experience of Chuck Cummins, who went through MCRD in 1955 and would later work directly with Krulak. Cummins had four front teeth knocked out by a DI wielding a rifle butt. He also saw DIs crush recruits' testicles and clap their hands over recruits' ears and rupture their eardrums. He considered himself lucky that he was not among the many recruits washed out of training because the injuries they had sustained at the hands of DIs precluded their being accepted into the Marine Corps.

In 1956, this institutionalized brutality came to a head in the second, and by far the most damaging, of the two traumatic body blows to the Marine Corps during the 1950s. This one would have a more direct effect on Krulak than did the Schwable case, and his reaction to it would cause significant changes in the way the Marine Corps trained its recruits. Overcoming Marine Corps culture would be difficult, and it would be several more decades before the last vestiges of brutality were erased. But the efforts to do so would begin in earnest with the man whose nickname in this case had a sharp ring of irony.

At 8:15 p.m. on Sunday, April 8, Staff Sergeant Matthew McKeon, a DI at Parris Island, stumbled into a recruit barracks and ordered the seventy-five young men of Platoon 71 to fall out for a night march. He led his recruits into Ribbon Creek, a tidal creek that wends through the marsh, where six recruits drowned. McKeon did not stay to find the bodies; instead he formed up the remaining recruits and marched them back to the barracks.

McKeon had been drinking, the night march had not been authorized, and he had committed the cardinal sin of leaving dead Marines in the field. The incident went beyond hazing and beyond a training accident; this was murder. The media turned on the Marine Corps as they had never done before, and Ribbon Creek became the single most embarrassing incident in Marine Corps history.

In the days after Ribbon Creek, the Marine Corps tried to manage the media, a serious mistake that caused media coverage to become even more scathing. Ribbon Creek became a "death march," and *Time* magazine published article after article about the brutality of the Marine Corps. An institutional firestorm swept over the Corps, becoming so serious that a congressional investigation began. McKeon's subsequent court-martial included testimony by the Commandant, as well as by General Lewis "Chesty" Puller, the most decorated Marine in history.

Ribbon Creek fragmented the Corps like no other event in Marine Corps history. Americans wanted assurance that Marine recruits would not be subjected to such callous brutality. Across the creek, as it were, retired officers such as Puller spoke up for rigorous training and night marches and said that tough training was necessary if Marines were to survive in combat. To retired Marines who were proud of their recruit experiences, Ribbon Creek was an unfortunate training accident. But many, if not all, active-duty officers saw that reform was necessary.

McKeon spent three months in the brig, was reduced in rank to private, and returned to active duty. The Marine Corps began monitoring and retraining DIs and restructuring the recruit training programs at Parris Island and MCRD. DIs began wearing the Marines' distinctive campaign hat as a sign of their new professionalism. But the recruit training programs, like battleships, could not be easily turned around. The men who were DIs had been brutalized themselves as recruits and believed it had made them better Marines.

As a result of the Schwable case, Krulak realized the need for better educated Marines, both officers and enlisted men. As a result of Ribbon Creek, he realized that a drastic reform of recruit training was necessary if the Marine Corps was to maintain its place in the hearts of Americans. Very soon he would have the opportunity to put both lessons into practice.

NOT long after Brute became a general, he said to Amy, "The trouble with being a general is that everyone lies to you." He said it in such a way that it was clear he believed he could detect such deception.

After a brief assignment in Japan, Krulak went to Okinawa and was soon appointed commanding general of the 3rd Marine Division. By then a nuanced portrait of Krulak was beginning to emerge, the central point of which was his stature.

A general makes many speeches, and it was understood in the officer ranks that whoever was at the podium before Brute had to lower the microphone; Krulak would get livid if he had to do this himself. It was also known that when Krulak inspected Marines, they should keep their eyes straight ahead; Krulak would explode if a six-foot-plus Marine looked down at him.

When Krulak inspected his Marines, he missed nothing. His hard eyes could rake a Marine from his "cover" (his hat) to his shoes in half a second and take in every detail. Was the cover at the wrong angle? Was there a smudge on it? Was the Marine's collar frayed? Was every button, including those on the sleeve placket, buttoned? Did the trousers fit properly, and were they the proper length? Krulak was fanatical about shoes, believing, as do many military men, that a man's shoes reveal all there is to know about his character. Did the laces show signs of wear? Was there a mirror surface? Were the shoes "run over" on the sides or—most heinous of all—were the corners of the heels worn off?

During one inspection, Krulak's eyes lingered on a sergeant's shoes. He looked down at his own shoes, then back at the sergeant's. He walked behind the sergeant for further study, then motioned for the sergeant's commanding officer to come over and said, "Give this man a seventy-two-hour liberty. His shoes are shinier than mine."

That said, Krulak was often tolerant of mistakes made by junior officers. After all, he had lost the anchor of the *Arizona*, destroyed a jeep, sunk several vessels while testing them, and come up with a cockamamy idea that cost taxpayers a fortune. But Krulak believed that by the time a Marine became a colonel, he should not make *any* mistakes. From colonels he expected perfection, and when he did not get it, he berated them in words that lashed and humiliated, then he scornfully dismissed them from his presence. Later

241

in his career, colonels would retire rather than serve under the Brute.

SHORTLY after arriving on Okinawa, Krulak encountered a situation that, had he handled it differently, could have wrecked his career.

On September 5, 1956, Typhoon Emma formed in the Marianas and began churning toward Okinawa. Already a high surf had formed on the eastern side of Okinawa, where a battalion of Marines engaged in a field exercise decided they wanted a bath. The battalion commander was concerned about the surf and allowed only one squad at a time in the water. He did not know that along with the high surf, vicious undercurrents had formed, and he watched as eleven Marines in water barely waist-deep lost their footing and were swept away. Some of the bodies would wash up on the beach over the next ten days, but not all were recovered.

Barely six months after Ribbon Creek, Krulak had lost eleven Marines in another training accident. How he handled the incident is an example of the public relations axiom, "Tell the truth. Tell it all. And tell it quickly."

Krulak sent immediate messages to the CGFMFPac and the Commandant telling them what happened. He ordered that a press release be written omitting no details. He ordered land and sea searches for the bodies. He contacted his subcommanders and told them that when reporters called, they should answer every question truthfully and completely. He even contacted reporters in Japan and at major American newspapers and invited them to fly out to see him, and he provided helicopters to take local reporters to the scene.

Perhaps because these deaths were purely accidental and not caused by any malfeasance, not one reporter elected to take a helicopter ride to the scene. In fact, few newspapers bothered to cover the story at all. The *Los Angeles Times* and *New York Times* printed articles, but that was the end of it. Krulak handled eleven deaths on Okinawa better than the Marine Corps handled six deaths on Parris Island.

It may be said that divine intervention was the real reason the story disappeared. Three days after the Marines drowned, Emma, now in the super typhoon category, struck Okinawa with winds measuring 156 miles per hour before the wind indicators broke. Emma snapped utility poles, ripped up runways, and destroyed hangars. She dropped more than twenty-two inches of rain and left seventy-seven people dead. But there is no doubt that Brute handled the potential crisis not only with remarkable judgment but also with remarkable ethics.

In 1957, President Dwight Eisenhower climbed aboard a Marine helicopter and became the first president to use a military helicopter on a regular basis. The Air Force had wanted the job, but its helicopters were too slow and too small. Eisenhower naturally wanted the Army to transport him, so the Army and Marines shared the job. Several times over the next two decades, the Army "dropped a lift"—the phrase used when the White House wants a helicopter and none is available—and in 1976 President Gerald Ford gave the mission exclusively to the Marine Corps. Marine "white tops" flying in to and out of the South Lawn of the White House are the most photographed helicopters in the world. And every Army general who sees Marine One lifting off the lawn probably grits his teeth, knowing it could have been Army One.

In 1957, following his belief in rigorous and realistic training, Krulak led the 3rd Marine Division in one of the largest amphibious landings since Inchon. Called Operation Beacon Hill, the landing took place at Dingalan Bay, northeast of Manila.

Private First Class Chuck Cummins, the recruit who had had

his front teeth knocked out by a DI, was Krulak's personal radio operator during the operation. He tells two revealing anecdotes about the general, the first of which speaks to Krulak's empathy for enlisted troops.

Cummins says that part of the operation called for an element of Marines to march inland in a simulated pincer movement with the landing force. The men marched for seven days through the hot, steamy jungle, unable to take a bath and daily growing more discontented with the incessant itching, the stench of old sweat, and the dirty clothes. Morale was low when the Marines reached a river and thought that at last they would be able to bathe. But a Navy doctor traveling with them tested the water and said that the troops could not go into the river because the danger of ear fungus was too great. Morale sank to a new low.

Cummins says, "I looked up and saw this little skinny shit in green boxer shorts and flip-flops. It was General Krulak. He said he was going to bathe and for the Marines to follow him." Krulak sensed the mood of his Marines, weighed sagging morale against the chances of contracting ear fungus, and, as Cummins says, "led us into the river."

Cummins is telling this story more than fifty years later, but his voice trembles. "He was concerned about us. We would have followed him to hell."

The second story reveals both Krulak's concern for his men and his propensity to show up at the most unexpected places.

One evening toward the end of Operation Beacon Hill, several dozen Marines were jammed into a large tent, shooting the breeze and listening to older sergeants talk about the 'Canal, Iwo, Pusan, and the Frozen Chosin. Cummins, because he was a PFC, was sitting on the ground in the rear of the tent when suddenly the bottom of the tent lifted up, and there was the general crawling under the canvas. Cummins opened his mouth to call the tent to attention, but Krulak restrained him. For a half hour, the PFC and the general sat side by side listening to stories of World War II and Korea, then the general lifted the canvas and was gone. He had come to determine the mood of his men and was satisfied to have found them sharing tales of valorous Marines and keeping alive the combat history of the Corps.

In July 1957, Krulak returned to Quantico, where he became director of the Marine Corps Education Center. He was responsible for directing the writing of new texts, modernizing the curriculum, and teaching international relations and how to integrate Marine air and ground units in combat. His boss was Bill Twining.

As usual, Krulak was everywhere. He would slip into the back row of a class at The Basic School to observe the instructor and monitor how well the new lieutenants were absorbing the material. The instructors were told not to call the class to attention when Krulak visited, and often the students did not know he was there.

Lieutenant Colonel John Love was supervising a live firing exercise one day when he looked up to see Krulak and members of his staff. When Krulak motioned for Love to join him, Love turned to a lieutenant and said, "You're in charge," then walked over to where Krulak was standing. "Aren't you afraid of leaving a lieutenant in charge of a live-fire exercise?" asked a member of Krulak's staff.

"No, he's one of *my* students."

Krulak smiled in approval.

Some fifty years later, Love said of Krulak, "He was always complimentary with people who did something right. If you knew your job and you did your job, you could not have a better friend in the Corps than General Krulak."

\* \* \*

Not long after arriving at Quantico, Krulak had a reception at his home so that the young officers could meet him in a relaxed social environment. Brute's young cousin from Denver Ronnie Zall and his wife, Marilyn, arrived for a visit while the reception was under way. After a quick greeting, Ronnie and Marilyn were escorted to Krulak's study, where they sat alone until the officers had gone home. Although Ronnie was the most adulatory of Krulak's Denver cousins, he says that he felt as if he and Marilyn were being hidden away. He understood that two civilians might have been out of place at the reception, but it was a party, and he was part of the family. However, Brute could not take the risk that they might out him and his Jewish background.

The waves from Ribbon Creek were still washing over the Marine Corps in October 1957. Perhaps because General Randolph Pate knew that his Commandancy would forever be tainted by the incident, or perhaps because he sensed that he would be judged as one of the least effective Commandants in the history of the Marine Corps, he sent a note to Krulak asking, "Why does the U.S. need a Marine Corps?"

A few days later, Krulak wrote back that the United States did not *need* the Marine Corps; the Army and Air Force could do anything the Marines could. The Marine Corps flourished, he said, because of what "the grassroots of our country *believes* we are and *believes* we can do." He said that America had three beliefs about the Marine Corps. First, when troubles come, the Marines will take care of them and do so at once. Second, Americans had an "almost mystical" belief that when the Marines go to war, their performance will be "dramatically and decisively successful—not most of the time, but always." And third, Americans saw the Marines as masters of an "unfailing alchemy" that converts "unoriented youths into proud, self-reliant, stable citizens into whose hands the nation's affairs may safely be entrusted."

He ended by saying that although America did not *need* the Marines, it *wanted* them. But, he warned, if Marines ever lost the ability to meet the high, almost spiritual standards of the American people, "the Marine Corps will then quickly disappear."

In 1959, Bill Twining and David Shoup were competing to be the next Commandant of the Marine Corps. Although the Commandant is nominated by the president, the incumbent Commandant at that time had a say regarding his successor.

Krulak believed that loyalty was a cardinal virtue and publicly supported his longtime mentor, Twining. But Shoup received the appointment, the news of which caused Krulak's mother-in-law to say, "Well, I see old foot-on-the-sofa made Commandant."

Krulak said that Shoup "chided me" about supporting Twining. Given Krulak's paradoxical propensity for understatement and Shoup's famously acerbic nature, it is possible that "chiding" was not a strong enough word.

About the same time Shoup was named Commandant, Krulak received his second star. Shoup had no control over Krulak's promotion, but he did have control over assignments. He sent Brute to MCRD, in San Diego. It is axiomatic in the military that the closer an officer is to the "flagpole"—that is, to headquarters— the better his chances for promotion. Krulak had been sitting at the foot of the flagpole for years, and now, from his perspective, he had been banished to the West Coast to a "twilight assignment." Talk in the Marine Corps was that the Brute's career was over and that he would be retired after the San Diego tour.

# 13

## Krulak Standards

With Twining's retirement, the last of Krulak's mentors was gone from the Marine Corps, and for the first time since his Academy days, when he came under the tutelage of Holland Smith, the Brute was on his own, with a Commandant who did not like him.

At MCRD, there was considerable trepidation about the incoming commanding general, both because of his reputation as a hard-edged perfectionist and because he was on the Commandant's list of bad boys. Sam Moyer was a sergeant at MCRD, a former DI now in charge of a special drill platoon that performed at Fort Rosecrans National Cemetery, at flag raisings, and at parades. His platoon could, with a single command, perform almost twenty minutes of silent drills, including rifle tosses, separation into squares, the Queen Anne Salute, and a dramatic movement called "to the winds." As behooves a sergeant who represents the Marine Corps at public functions, he was a squared-away, recruiting-poster sort of Marine. Moyer would be one of the first at MCRD to directly experience Krulak's intensity.

In late 1959, Moyer was ordered to report to the chief of staff, and his first thought was, *What have I done?*—a not unusual reaction among DIs and former DIs in the late 1950s when summoned by a high-ranking officer. Moyer put on a newly pressed uniform, dusted his already mirror-like shoes, and reported to the chief of staff, who said, "The incoming CG needs a driver, and you have been identified as a volunteer."

Moyer plugged into the Marine Corps sergeants' network and found out that the new CG was considered a nitpicking, hands-on hard-ass. A few days later, Moyer marched into Krulak's office, reported for duty, and was told to brush up on the protocol of dealing with senior officers and civilian officials, to wash Krulak's car every day, and to "pick me up at 0500 tomorrow."

That first day set the template for Krulak's tour of duty at MCRD. Krulak bounded out of the front door carrying a field jacket and a swagger stick. "I never saw anyone so constantly in motion, so full of energy, always, under all circumstances and under all conditions," Moyer remembered.

"Let's start at the mess hall," Krulak began. In the rearview mirror, Moyer saw Krulak slip on a field jacket, which he noticed had no insignia of rank.

At the mess hall, Krulak stepped into the chow line, picked up a tray, and held it out to be served. When he leaned forward, his field jacket opened enough that a mess sergeant saw the two stars gleaming on each side of Krulak's collar and knew in an instant this was the new CG. He prayed to whatever God he worshipped that the food had been well prepared. Krulak and Moyer then sat at a table with young Marines, whom Krulak questioned in detail about whether the food selections and quality were good and about what items might be added to the menu.

The next stop was the "grinder," the mile-long area formally known as the parade deck, which is famed throughout the Marine Corps as a place both where recruits learn to march and where elaborate and ceremonial parades are held. The grinder is such an iconic place that no one wearing civilian clothes can walk across it, forcing long detours both for Marines not in uniform and for all civilians.

Krulak could have picked no more symbolic place to demonstrate the beginning of his reforms. The grinder was where DIs most often showed their virtual omnipotence over recruits. Although fallout from Ribbon Creek had resulted in token reforms of the recruit training program, old ways died hard, and at MCRD in December 1959, DIs still answered only to God.

That is, until a higher authority showed up in the form of Brute Krulak.

When Krulak emerged from the car, field jacket off, swagger stick in hand, looking across the heart of his new command, he inspired a tense, collective gulp. His thinning reddish hair was neatly trimmed and combed just so, the sharp creases in his shirt aligned precisely with the equally sharp creases in his trousers, and his shoes gleamed. His Paramarine wings sat atop the Navy Cross and several rows of ribbons, and on each side of his collar gleamed two sterling silver stars. The DIs saw those stars from fifty yards away, stopped what they were doing, and rendered perfect salutes.

Krulak's mere presence at these early-morning formations sent a message to every DI that the new commanding general was watching the details of recruit training, that the DIs were no longer masters of their domain. Within the next few weeks, he ended the careers of several DIs, and he made their punishment public and as quick as a beheading.

Krulak would later say in his oral history that Ribbon Creek "shook me up right to my bootstraps. I was terrified that the Marine Corps could do this." He remembered the training exercise on Okinawa where one lax moment had resulted in the deaths of eleven Marines, and he was determined that at MCRD there would be no Ribbon Creek and no time when DIs were not under the closest supervision and held to the highest standards. Once

Krulak and his son Bill, now a midshipman at the Academy, were riding around the base when Krulak saw a DI standing in front of a row of bleachers filled with recruits. The DI called one of the recruits forward and slapped him. Krulak slammed on the brakes, jumped out of the car, and strode up to the DI, who was now at rigid attention. "Take off your cover and throw it on the ground," Krulak snapped. The DI removed his campaign hat, his symbol of professionalism, and tossed it aside. "You are fired," Krulak thundered. "Go to your quarters and stay there until I send for you." Within hours, Krulak had given the DI a summary court-martial, reduced him in rank, and transferred him.

At MCRD, Krulak became known as "the little man," who could show up at any hour of the day or night to inspect any phase of the operation and ask the most probing questions imaginable. Junior officers began comparing sightings of Krulak. "I was at an 0400 reveille for recruits, and I looked over my shoulder and there was the little man," one would say. To which another would say, "I was in the recruit chow hall at 0500 and saw the little man going into the bakery."

Perhaps his surprise inspection of living quarters for the Marine band raised the most eyebrows. If Krulak inspected the band's quarters, he could be anywhere. Bartholomew LaRocca was in charge of the band, and his quarters were so squared away that Krulak turned an accusatory stare on him and said, "You knew I was coming."

"No, sir. I did not. During duty hours, this is the way my quarters look."

Afterward, whenever dignitaries came to MCRD and Krulak wanted to show them how his Marines lived, he took them to LaRocca's quarters.

Before long, LaRocca composed the "General Krulak March" and introduced it at a parade, causing Amy to say, "I think we are going to hear that march rather often."

Not only was there no place on base where Krulak did not show up, but no detail was too small to escape his attention. A big part of Krulak's reputation for spotting small details was in what Marines call "facilities maintenance"—the eye appeal of MCRD. Krulak believed that the mother of all oxymorons was "deferred maintenance," and he instituted what came to be called "Krulak standards." He would not tolerate a single weed, untrimmed grass along a sidewalk, faded paint, or the smallest piece of paper on the ground.

Lieutenant David Rilling, who had known Krulak back at Quantico, was then at Camp Matthews, a facility north of San Diego where recruits lived in an enormous tent village during weapons training. In the middle of the camp was an abandoned telephone exchange building. Rilling hoped to refurbish the building and make it into a place for DIs to gather after they put the recruits to bed at night. He wanted ceiling tiles, carpeting, desks, lamps, a television, and furniture. He called Krulak's aide and asked if the general could stop by on his next visit to Camp Matthews.

A few days later, Rilling looked up from his desk to see Krulak striding through the door. "Good morning, Rilling," Krulak said. "What can I do for you?"

Rilling stood at attention, then said, "Sir, I wanted you to take a look at a building and tell me if we can convert it into a DI lounge."

Inside the abandoned building, Krulak looked around. He had converted the old naval hospital in Hawaii to a headquarters building, and such projects were dear to him. "Rilling, this is a disgrace," he said. "This place needs an enema." He turned to his aide. "Tell the depot maintenance officer I want this place made into a suitable DI lounge by the end of next week. See Rilling for all the details, and let me know next Friday that it has been done."

"Thank you very much, sir."

"Good initiative, Rilling. Anything else you need?"

"No, sir."

The next morning, trucks filled with supplies and dozens of Marines showed up at Camp Matthews. The Marines worked day and night for a week, finishing about 4 p.m. the following Friday. At 4:30 p.m., Rilling's phone rang and Krulak said, "Give me a status report on that DI lounge."

"Sir, the job was completed thirty minutes ago, and the place is secure."

"Are you satisfied with the work?"

"Yes, sir."

The story spread around the base and then, as men were transferred, to other Marine bases around the world. Thereafter, whenever a project needed a massive injection of ideas, energy, and commitment, it was said that a "Krulak enema" was called for.

In 1959, Chuck Krulak was nominated by a California congressman to attend the U.S. Naval Academy. He entered as a plebe during the summer of 1960.

Commandant David Shoup was an acerbic and sarcastic man, and sometimes these traits crept into the numerous memos he rocketed throughout the Marine Corps. He sent out one notice saying that some Marines were defensive toward other branches of the military and had the "philosophy of a minority group," adding, "Let us unshackle our mind from the stifling psychology inherent in the slogan 'They're sniping at us.'" Given Krulak's role in the Chowder Society and in the revisions to the National Security Act, there was little doubt about whom Shoup had in mind. He also decreed that the swagger stick was an "optional item," adding, "If you feel the need of it, carry it," an observation most interpreted to mean that the Commandant preferred that his officers not be seen sporting such accoutrements.

Krulak immediately issued a lengthy response to his Marines at MCRD in which he recognized the Commandant's ideas but made it clear he did not agree that Marines should ignore attempted predations by the Army. And he probably was the only senior officer in the Marine Corps who continued to carry his swagger stick. In fact, when he was photographed, which was often, he usually displayed it prominently, poking his finger in Shoup's eye.

PERHAPS Krulak's most important training reforms, for both officers and enlisted personnel, were the educational programs he instituted. These programs still exist today, particularly those regarding how DIs are selected and taught, how slow learners among recruits are nurtured, and the importance of strong and lengthy instruction in patriotism and history.

For recruits at MCRD, Krulak ordered the curriculum to be revised to include hours of instruction on Marine Corps and American history. A two-hour tour of the base museum became part of recruit training, and during the tour docents—retired Marines—delivered lectures on the Marines' performance at Belleau Wood, in the Pacific theater during World War II, in Korea, and later in Vietnam, Iraq, and Afghanistan.

Krulak passed out dozens of copies of *A Message to Garcia* to his officers, and staff meetings became dreaded events in which he quizzed his commanders on American history. Brute believed that Marines were put on earth to protect the American way of life, and that way of life included knowing about things such as the Magna Carta, English common law, and the U.S. Constitution.

A junior officer once incurred Krulak's displeasure by being late for a staff meeting. As the young officer tried to slip into his seat,

Krulak said, "Captain, tell me about the Plymouth Compact." The wide-eyed officer looked at Krulak in bewilderment. "Sir, do you mean the Valiant?" Even Krulak laughed. But afterward Brute was careful to say "Mayflower Compact."

The Mayflower Compact, the anniversary of the fall of the Alamo, and John Adams's unwavering commitment to freeing his country from Britain may seem to have little relevance to Marine officers at a recruit training depot, but these things reminded them that the Marine Corps had a heritage to maintain and reinforced the responsibility of citizenship in a republic. Finally, such knowledge reminded them that there is often a threat somewhere in the world that is contrary to ideals set forth in America's founding documents. Today, in large part because of Krulak, the Marine Corps teaches more history to recruits than does any other branch of the U.S. military.

About five minutes after arriving at a recruit depot, many recruits come to the conclusion that joining the Marine Corps was the biggest mistake of their young lives. When Krulak arrived at MCRD, an average of thirty-six recruits were absent without leave (AWOL) at any given time. Krulak started a program called They All Come Back, the point of which was that AWOL recruits would have to come back to MCRD to face their punishment—whether it was of their own free will, because the FBI brought them back in handcuffs, or they were turned in. Within a short time, the average number of AWOL recruits dropped to six.

During Krulak's time at MCRD, his Birthday Balls became legendary events of such pageantry and showmanship that they would have pleased even Lemuel Shepherd. Krulak moved the ball to the Hotel del Coronado, the grand old matron of San Diego hotels, and the carefully orchestrated program for those events included Marines in period dress, beginning with the Continental Marines of 1775 and continuing to the present. Martial music played in the background as a Marine wearing, say, the puttees and campaign hat of the "banana wars," stepped into the spotlight and a sonorous voice recounted details of each victory.

In addition, Krulak's Mess Nights, social functions second only to the Birthday Balls, set the standards for decorum and protocol, as well as the customs and traditions upon which Mess Nights are still based. Much looser were Krulak's own birthday parties, at which San Diego politicians and businessmen, along with Marines from the East Coast, Hawaii, and Okinawa, became acquainted with Fish House Punch. Usually more than two hundred people attended these parties.

IT is part of a commanding general's job to meet local officials, but no CG in the history of MCRD has had a closer connection to the San Diego community than Krulak. He sent out word that he was available to speak anywhere, anytime, and he became a virtual speech-making machine. His speeches, of course, celebrated the role of the Marine Corps in American history, and during his two years at MCRD, he became one of the best-known figures in San Diego, often appearing on the front page of the local newspaper, on the radio, and on television.

Once a month, LaRocca's band gave a concert on base. Historically, a few civilians, usually family members or girlfriends of Marines, attended. Krulak not only was present at every concert, but he also invited dozens of business leaders, along with city and county officials, to join him on the reviewing stand. He came to know all of them but was particularly close to James Copley, publisher of the *San Diego Union*.

LaRocca always played the "General Krulak March" during the concerts, and each time Krulak would point out to his guests that the piece of music they were listening to was a "very soldierly work," which of course provided the opening for someone to ask,

"What is the name of it?"—a question Krulak was delighted to answer. He was equally delighted to talk about the U.S. senator from Massachusetts who was running for president and to tell how they had met in the Pacific.

Two stories illustrate that while Krulak had a flinty reputation, there was another side to his personality.

Parades and parties were two of Brute's favorite events, and the first story involves both. The parade was held on one of those glorious Southern California days, when the air is cool and officers delight in wearing their white uniforms. As Marines passed in review in front of Krulak, a major leading a formation rendered the sword salute and knocked off his cover, which several hundred Marines then trampled. Krulak had Moyer retrieve the hat.

The major was humiliated and did not attend the party that followed the parade. Krulak slipped into a side room of his house, wrote a note, and summoned Moyer. He gave his aide the major's hat and the note, saying, "The major who dropped this hat is not here. Please find out where he lives and deliver these to him."

Moyer drove to the major's house some thirty minutes away and rang the bell. A woman answered the door, stared for a moment at the sergeant in his crisp uniform, and then turned away and softly called a name. The major, still in his whites, came to the door. His collar was unbuttoned, his eyes were distressed, and it was clear that he had been drinking.

"Yes, Sergeant."

Moyer gave him the hat and the note. "With General Krulak's compliments, sir." He paused. "Sir, I will wait and see if you have a reply."

The major slowly opened the envelope and read the note. Moyer saw the tension drain from the major's face, and his lips began to tremble. "Sergeant, have you seen this note?"

"No, sir."

The major handed him the note, and Moyer read, "Dear Major _____. In 1934 a young Marine second lieutenant knocked off his cover when passing in review in front of President Roosevelt. I don't think it seriously affected my career. Semper Fidelis, VHK."

THE other incident also involved a party at Krulak's house. Brute and Amy entertained often, and when a young officer attended, he was expected to be accompanied by a female companion. On this particular evening, Lieutenant Rilling found himself without a date, so he hastened to the officers' club, where the bar was often patronized by San Diego's discerning young women. He met a woman and said, "I need someone to go with me to the general's reception. Would you like to go?"

She agreed, and as Rilling and the woman went through the receiving line, Krulak, who enjoyed the small talk of parties, quickly discovered that she was from Alabama. Then he asked, "What do you do here in San Diego?"

Rilling was surprised to hear her say, "Well, I'm a schoolteacher, and I would like to be teaching. But I got out here too late, so I'm looking for a job."

"What grade do you teach?"

"Elementary school, first to third grade."

"It is so good to meet you. I will see what I can do."

Krulak then turned to Rilling and said, "Lieutenant, give me this young lady's name, phone number, and address."

Rilling found a napkin, wrote down the information, and passed it to Krulak's aide.

Two weeks later, Rilling was in the officers' club, and in walked the woman from Alabama. She thanked him for taking her to the reception and said, "Tell that general I said thank you. The day after I met him, I got a phone call about teaching at an elementary school around the corner from my apartment. I walk to work."

259

\*   \*   \*

KRULAK's last Birthday Ball at MCRD was in November 1961, and the birthday message he sent to his Marines reminded them that the Marine Corps was born eight months before the Liberty Bell rang out a message of freedom. Marines not only were the first ones called upon when America was in extremis, but when they came home, they brought victory with them.

IT is the quintessential Brute Krulak story that he went from being in the Commandant's doghouse to having one of the most visible and important military jobs in America, and that his orders came not from Headquarters Marine Corps, but from the White House.

Over the years, there would be many stories about how Krulak went from San Diego back to Washington. The true story is that JFK read General Maxwell Taylor's *The Uncertain Trumpet*, which convinced him to move away from Eisenhower's nuclear doctrine of massive retaliation and instead to embrace the concept of smaller wars. Kennedy urged the military to place far more emphasis on counterinsurgency as a way to handle what was becoming a growing problem in Vietnam and in other locations around the world. The Army, Navy, and Air Force liked big set-piece battles with lots of firepower and considered Kennedy's ideas nonsense. And because the Marine Corps thought it knew all there was to know about small wars, having fought them in the Caribbean and Central America in the early part of the twentieth century, Shoup and the Corps were equally skeptical and would slow-walk whatever newfangled ideas Kennedy came up with.

To sidetrack Kennedy's ideas—not to implement them—the Joint Chiefs of Staff came up with a new job, special assistant for counterinsurgency and special activities (SACSA). The general officer who became SACSA would report directly to Secretary of Defense Robert McNamara and be among those who met regularly with the president. It was a position in which a single misstep could wreck a career, a job no one wanted. Each branch of the service said it had no general officer with the qualifications to become SACSA.

Then an Army general recommended Krulak to McNamara and told him how the president had rescued Krulak's men on Choiseul. McNamara brought up Krulak's name with JFK, who, based largely on the Pacific connection, approved. About the same time, Admiral Ulysses S. Grant Sharp recommended Krulak for the job.

Given the lingering Army animosity toward Krulak over the unification fight, there would almost certainly have been Army officers who wished for his failure. Given the reluctant respect of Navy and Air Force leadership for what they saw as Krulak's Machiavellian political maneuvering, there would have been those who hoped Krulak would find himself out of his depth and self-destruct. Shoup's beliefs are well-known: he did not like Krulak and did not like the idea behind SACSA. Thus Krulak's own branch of the service would offer him no safety net.

But the Brute had no reservations. The new job put him on a stage worthy of his talents. He would be operating at the highest levels of government—at the nexus of military and civilian power—and reporting to people who, if they listened to him, would do the right thing for America. Kennedy had rescued his Paramarines during World War II, and now he would come to the aid of the president and assist him with the growing problem of Vietnam.

It was with great alacrity, then, that on February 16, 1962, he reported for duty in Washington.

# 14

# JFK and the Brute Confront Vietnam

KRULAK loved to tell the story of how in 1962, he showed up at the White House and announced, "I want to see the president," explaining, "Back then a general could go to the White House without an appointment and see the president." Krulak said that he arrived bearing the bottle of Three Feathers he had promised JFK back on Vella Lavella some nineteen years earlier and that Kennedy remembered the promise and said, "Why don't we have a drink of this stuff?" Krulak claimed that he responded, "It isn't very good, Mr. President," but that he and Kennedy had a ritual drink and talked about the old days in the Pacific—about Choiseul and the young Marine who died in Kennedy's bunk aboard the PT boat.

It is true that the Kennedy White House was notoriously lax about unscheduled visits, but even so, it is doubtful that a two-star general could have shown up unannounced and been received by the president.

ALTHOUGH it is impossible to verify this story, from the time Krulak arrived back in Washington, he did participate in White House meetings with McNamara and Kennedy. Most of those sessions concerned Vietnam and the inexorable escalation of American military personnel. (The number of U.S. advisers jumped from 1,400 in mid-1961 to 11,300 toward the end of 1962.)

During these meetings, Krulak was dual-hatted. As the special assistant for counterinsurgency, he was the government's top expert on counterinsurgency matters. As the special assistant for special activities, he held one of the most sensitive jobs in the U.S. government: liaison between the military and the CIA. This was the blackest of the black holes and involved some of the most highly classified matters of national defense. It meant that in Vietnam, Krulak was in charge of psychological warfare and covert activities against the enemy, a job that in a few years would be turned over to a much larger group with the innocuous name Studies and Observation Group (SOG).

As had been true since his days in China, Krulak's influence was far out of proportion with his rank. As a two-star general, he was subordinate to almost everyone with whom he came into official contact. But that was a technicality. He reported to the secretary of defense and met regularly with the secretary of state, the director of the CIA, and Ambassador-at-Large Averell Harriman. As a result, he had as much influence as any four-star general in Washington and more than most—heady business for any military officer but sheer nirvana for Krulak. Barring a serious mistake, he could receive a third star. As the Marine Corps had fewer than a half-dozen three-star generals, the promotion would automatically make him a candidate for Commandant and the accompanying fourth star.

Few military officers in Washington had a brighter future than Brute Krulak. He was confident enough that when White House staffers suggested he follow the protocol of military officers working in the White House and wear civilian clothes, he refused, saying he was a serving officer and "it would diminish the impact of the military for me to wear civilian clothes." In White House pictures of the time, Krulak is always in uniform.

THE Krulaks' social life was as busy as ever, but now there was a difference. In Washington, everything is about proximity—about who is close to the president and who has power. It was common knowledge that JFK's time in the Pacific had been the defining moment of his life; he and his closest aides wore tie pins of a miniature *PT-109*. But going behind enemy lines in the middle of the night to rescue Krulak's Marines had been Kennedy's last big mission in the Pacific, and having been the commanding officer of those Marines gave Krulak a unique cachet. Plus, Krulak was the point man, the acknowledged expert, in an area of the highest importance in the Kennedy administration: counterinsurgency.

THE cold war was heating up, and JFK would have to deal with a standoff in Berlin, the Cuban Missile Crisis, and troubles in the Congo, Laos, Angola, South Korea, the Dominican Republic, Tunisia, Brazil, and, of course, Vietnam. He wanted a military capable of what he called a "flexible response" to such incidents. Kennedy sent out the word that further promotion of high-ranking military officers would depend on the degree to which they supported counterinsurgency.

REDUCED to basics, Krulak's job was to develop America's techniques for fighting a counterinsurgency war in Vietnam and to develop programs that would enable JFK to measure America's progress and the progress of South Vietnam as an ally. To do this, Krulak had to push not only the reluctant American military and the slow-moving State Department but also the American people to undergo a radical shift in their thinking about the war. This war was not about taking the hill; it was, to use the phrase of the time, about "winning the hearts and minds" of people. "Protection is the most important thing you can bring" to the people of South Vietnam, Krulak said. "After that comes health. And after that, many things—land, prosperity, education, and privacy to name a few."

Krulak often lectured to senior State Department officials on this new-old form of war. He addressed Army leaders and students at the National War College, audiences that simply did not understand what he was teaching. The cold war military policy of the time still anticipated a Soviet invasion of Europe and massive set-piece battles with hundreds of tanks slugging it out in the Fulda Gap. Attrition warfare was the tried-and-true method of conducting war, safe and based on proven doctrine. If things went wrong—and in war they always did—generals could say that they had followed the book. But Vietnam called for leaders who would throw out the book.

Some have written that as SACSA, Krulak was a strong proponent of traditional military doctrine, that he actively supported Kennedy's escalation in Vietnam. This is true, but at the same time Krulak pushed his own ideas about a new form of war—usually without success. Indeed, in the counterinsurgency part of his White House job, Krulak was an abject failure. He never got across to the American military or the American people what a war of national liberation was all about, what the Vietnam War meant to the United States, and why America had a stake in Southeast Asia. One reason he failed was that the government itself did not understand these issues.

Even though many American generals had read Bernard Fall's *Street Without Joy*, the seminal work documenting French mistakes in Vietnam a decade earlier, they seemed hell-bent on repeating the errors. Kennedy, McNamara, and the top generals confused counterguerrilla with counterinsurgency. That is, they focused on military measures—JFK's beloved Special Forces and small-unit tactics—to the exclusion of social, economic, and political measures. To the Army, counterinsurgency meant widespread use of helicopters and the new doctrine of "air mobility."

Neither McNamara nor JFK knew how complex, how frustrating, and how nationally enervating a counterinsurgency war could be. They grossly underestimated the resolve and determination of the North Vietnamese. They also failed to realize how long a counterinsurgency war would take. No factor is more critical in war than time, and the Kennedy administration—like most administrations—knew that the American people do not like long wars. McNamara would give Krulak everything he needed except the one thing he needed above all else: time. There was *no* time; everything had to be done *now*.

"We never learned there is no substitute for time," Krulak said. "You don't change people's minds overnight. Time is very disruptive of all factors in wartime. The exigencies of war never allow enough time."

If Vietnam was a place where good ideas went to die, no better example can be found than counterinsurgency.

IN 1962, Krulak was at the heart of one of the most famous Vietnam stories of the Kennedy administration. As he tells it, a report came in to the White House that members of the South Vietnamese army were defecting in great numbers to join the North Vietnamese army. It was urgent that a top U.S. military officer go to South Vietnam and determine whether the story was true.

At the White House meeting on this matter, JFK turned to McNamara and asked, "Who will you send?"

"General Krulak," McNamara replied.

Whereupon the president turned to Krulak and asked, "How soon can you go?"

"I can go now."

JFK turned back to McNamara, looked at his watch—it was almost noon—and said, "Have an aircraft ready to go to Saigon at one p.m."

Averell Harriman did not like the idea of a Marine general nosing around Vietnam on his own and said, "I'd like to send someone with him." Harriman had a valid point in that an insurgency is only about 20 percent military; much larger parts of the equation have to do with economic, diplomatic, political, mental, and sociological factors, areas usually attended to by the State Department. But, in fact, Harriman simply wanted to send someone to protect State Department turf.

JFK nodded his assent.

When Krulak arrived at Andrews Air Force Base, Joseph A. Mendenhall of the State Department was already aboard the aircraft.

Krulak and Mendenhall took an instant disliking to each other and barely spoke during the long flight. (When Krulak told the story of the trip, he manifested a trait for which he became famous during the last decades of his life: if he did not like someone, he "forgot" the person's name. After 1962, Krulak could not remember "Mendenhall," only that on the trip to Vietnam, he was accompanied by "some mid-level State Department person.") Once in Vietnam, Mendenhall visited Saigon, Hue City, and Qui Nhon. Krulak commandeered two aircraft, one for his use and the other as backup, and away he went, hopscotching all over South Vietnam, being met at various military installations and then traveling by helicopter to remote parts of the country to talk with American advisers and aviation units. (American forces were not yet "officially" fighting in Vietnam.) For the next twenty-four hours, Krulak was a whirling dervish, asking the same crucial question again and again: is the South Vietnamese army on the verge of mutiny, revolution, or going over to the enemy?

In Saigon, he had Marine aides and a host of stenographers transcribe the results of every meeting, notarize the results, and compile everything in a briefing book. Then he rushed to the airport for the return flight to Washington. On the flight, he and Mendenhall talked "damn little" and certainly did not divulge their findings.

Krulak radioed ahead, and when the aircraft landed early in the morning, Marines were standing by to make copies of his briefing book and to provide him with a fresh uniform. Krulak and Mendenhall appeared at the daily 11 a.m. meeting of the National Security Council, where Krulak passed out his document and delivered a briefing, the essence of which was that there had been no defections, that the South Vietnamese were willing to fight, and that they were patriotic and could be relied on as staunch allies.

In stark opposition, Mendenhall said that the South Vietnamese military was deeply immersed in politics and about to turn tail and go over to the enemy. He said that there had been defections, there would be many more, and the South Vietnamese could not be relied on as allies.

For a long moment, there was silence. Government leaders are strong-willed people and rarely averse to making their opinions known, but in this instance they could not formulate a response. Then JFK asked the question that became a metaphor for the war: "Have you two gentlemen been to the same country?"

Published accounts of the incident usually end at this point, but Krulak recalled that he broke another long silence by saying, "I believe I know the answer to that question, Mr. President. This war is a rural war, and the military is in the countryside. That is where I went. This fellow confined his visits to three cities and has given you the metropolitan viewpoint."

Krulak said that JFK stood up and asked him to come into the Oval Office, where, in the presence of the chairman of the Joint Chiefs of Staff, he said, "I understand what you said, and I believe you." (In 2008, Krulak told this story and finished with, "Of course, I was right. There hasn't been a revolution or defection in the Vietnamese army yet.")

ON Monday, June 4, 1962, Krulak spoke at the Naval War College in Newport, Rhode Island, on the topic "Tactics and Techniques of Insurgency and Counterinsurgency." The speech was primarily a historical look at insurgencies around the world, but Krulak, in speaking of Vietnam, said that America's "terrifying array of military strength...has no real identification with the counterinsurgency battle." He said that the battle in Vietnam was not found "on some classic area of tactical terrain selected by one of the antagonists, but in nameless villages and hamlets, and the objective to be gained is not a hill or a city, but the hearts and minds of thousands of little people, without whose support there can be no victory."

The importance of this speech is that as early as 1962, some three years before America entered Vietnam in great numbers, Krulak was preaching the counterinsurgency gospel. But much of what he said was ignored and would continue to be ignored by the military's senior leadership, by McNamara, and by the White House. McNamara and Kennedy talked the talk, but they did not walk the walk.

In 1962, the South Vietnamese government and the U.S. government became alarmed that the National Liberation Front (NLF)—the political arm of North Vietnamese forces—was making major progress in gathering support in South Vietnam. To stop those advances, the two governments introduced the Strategic Hamlet Program, the idea of which was to move South Vietnamese farmers into new villages that were surrounded by walls and patrolled by the military. Meanwhile, Krulak wrote a paper titled "Joint Counterinsurgency Concept and Doctrinal Guidance," the purpose of which was to give American military and civilian leaders a better understanding of counterinsurgency. It was read and tossed aside.

EVEN though the military had little interest in counterinsurgency, the president had considerable interest in the subject. In October, to give the appearance that the military supported JFK's ideas, Army general Lyman L. Lemnitzer, chairman of the Joint Chiefs of Staff, wrote a letter to the Commandant of the Marine Corps in which he commended Krulak for developing and implementing a program to concentrate the power of the U.S. military in meeting insurgencies around the world. (It is important to note that Krulak's work embraced national needs rather than those of the individual military services.) Lemnitzer reported that Krulak had written a paper that had become the basis for America's national counterinsurgency doctrine and had provided the focus for twenty-three training publications and ten training films.

The scope of Krulak's work and his outpouring of position papers led to a recommendation in one of his FitReps that he be jumped over his contemporaries for promotion to three-star rank, and he was being talked of as a sure bet to become Commandant.

THE arcane, secretive, and highly sensitive practice of "disinformation" was Krulak's responsibility during the Cuban Missile Crisis of October 1962. Even today, it is difficult to sort out what was real and what was a ruse during those days when the world came close to nuclear war. And despite a host of books about the crisis, the CIA, and clandestine operations, it is difficult to know exactly which of the black arts Krulak was practicing. That he was involved is made clear in several books. But doing what? Was he behind the rumors sweeping Miami's Cuban community? Did the warplanes being moved to Georgia and Florida herald an attack on Cuba, or were they a diversion? Was there really a host of

American submarines in Cuban waters, or was that a rumor designed to pull the Cuban navy offshore?

Bill Krulak and his wife visited Brute and Amy during these hectic days, and Bill's wife was impressed with the fact that Brute had a White House telephone. The phone rang often, Brute engaged in whispered conversations, and then he returned to his family with a heavy countenance. Brute kept his secrets.

THE January 1963 issue of the *Marine Corps Gazette* published a special issue on counterinsurgency that included a piece by Krulak titled "Counterinsurgency: Fighting the Abstract War." Echoing his 1962 speech at the Naval War College, he wrote that America was fighting a land war in Southeast Asia, whereas throughout the past century, it had fought primarily on the high seas or on the land of an invaded ally. Furthermore, the battlefield was not a geographic area but a psychological one; the capture or liberation of territory was subordinate to winning the support of the local people. Krulak also believed that for the first time in history, America's military was fighting under "stultifying restraints." America was granting sanctuary to the enemy—places that, for fear of offending the Chinese or the Russians, the U.S. military could not attack—which was preventing the Americans from winning on the battlefield.

Even as the Vietnam War continued to gather momentum, Krulak wrote of possible defeat when he said that World War II had enjoyed widespread support from almost everyone in America, but that Vietnam, although it was a "total war" calling for every source of national strength, did not. Counterinsurgency, he said, involved not just soldiers but also politicians, propagandists, economists, and educators, and America was not organized to fight such a war.

By 1963, the Krulak boys had become young men. Vic had graduated from William & Mary and the Church Divinity School of the Pacific, an Episcopalian seminary in Berkeley, California. He was now an ordained minister working at a mission on Oahu. His burdens were his name, his painful memories of the Naval Academy, and the fact that he was not in the family business, a burden that had grown heavier since Bill had graduated from the Academy and was a Marine officer. For his part, Chuck was in his third year at the Academy. There was little doubt that both Bill and Chuck would be going to Vietnam.

KRULAK knew of Mao's book *On Guerrilla Warfare* and General Vo Nguyen Giap's recently published *People's War, People's Army*. He also was aware of Ramón Magsaysay's campaign against the Hukbalahap rebellion in the Philippines during the 1950s. Perhaps he knew a bit about the Soviet revolutionary strategy from Lenin. And he knew of the *Small Wars Manual* published by the Marine Corps in 1940, a book that even today remains a seminal work on counterinsurgency. Almost certainly, he read about U.S.-backed partisan activities in Europe during World War II. From all these sources and his own firsthand knowledge, he wrote America's counterinsurgency doctrine and at every opportunity talked with McNamara about how America should conduct this new-old form of war. He continued to attend many group meetings at the White House. According to White House visitor logs, his first one-on-one meeting with Kennedy came on August 21, 1963. Between then and November 1, he had ten private meetings with the president, which lasted anywhere from twenty minutes to more than two hours. The subject of most of those meetings is listed simply as "Vietnam." No topic is listed for others.

IN August 1963, Krulak began what would become a longtime adversarial relationship with David Halberstam, a young reporter for the *New York Times* assigned to Saigon. It was a curious battle, the origins of which are best understood by fast-forwarding to a

2007 article by George Packer in *The New Yorker*. After Halberstam was killed in a car accident that year, Packer wrote that the famous writer had been a Jewish kid from the Bronx "clawing his way" into the "elite culture." He quoted Neil Sheehan, author of *A Bright Shining Lie*, who said of Halberstam, "His insecurity showed...in his compulsion to be recognized and in his need to test himself." Both Packer and Sheehan could have been writing about Krulak. But there were two obvious differences. First, Krulak was nearing the top of his game when Halberstam was only beginning his career. Second, the elite culture in which Krulak had gained recognition, the U.S. Marine Corps, was a true elite.

The battle between the two men began with an August 15, 1963, story by Halberstam titled "Vietnamese Reds Gain in Key Area." The point of the article was that Communist forces were making strategic advances in the Mekong Delta south of Saigon. The sources Halberstam listed in the article were an "American adviser," "military men," "one expert source," a "highly placed American," "observers," "long-time observers," "highly reliable sources," a "high official," and "one civilian." Not one named source was quoted, a not unusual but still questionable journalistic practice, especially when, in this instance, the story was about a highly sensitive issue of national security and ran on the front page of what was arguably the most influential newspaper in America.

During his tenure as SACSA, Krulak made five trips to Vietnam. He had more time on the ground in Vietnam than anyone else in the White House. He wrote a classified nineteen-page deconstruction of Halberstam's article, pointing out that certain salient points underlay all military activity in South Vietnam and that a writer who could not grasp these basics could not write an accurate story. He said that in the Mekong Delta, war was seasonal, that combat in the monsoon season was far different from war at other times. He pointed out that this was a guerrilla war and that even after an area was essentially tranquil, the Vietcong could still manage limited offensives. Finally, he explained that U.S. strategy was to destroy hard-core enemy troops, stop enemy attacks on rural populations, and compress the enemy into the Delta.

On September 15, the *New York Times* published another Halberstam article titled "Rift with Vietnam on War Tactics Underlined by 2 Red Attacks." The story said that a serious schism existed between U.S. military advisers and the South Vietnamese— a schism of such consequence that it could threaten the Strategic Hamlet Program and create military apathy, even defeat. Halberstam claimed that the United States was withholding funds from the South Vietnamese military.

Even though Krulak had no connection with the Strategic Hamlet Program, he wrote another classified White House paper saying that Halberstam was wrong: no rift existed, and no funds had been withheld. The Strategic Hamlet Program did fail later that year, but not for the reasons put forth by Halberstam. Rather, the program had changed the rhythms of a centuries-old rural lifestyle and thus alienated the very people it was intended to benefit.

The chasm between Krulak, who had access to highly classified military documents, and Halberstam, who was on the scene in Saigon, is illustrative of those historical differences that continue to exist in regard to Vietnam. Because Krulak's battles with the media would continue over the next five years, and because the media versus military battle was of such huge dimensions during the war, the Krulak-Halberstam differences must be put into perspective.

Of crucial importance is that Halberstam, and most other correspondents, covered the Vietnam War the same way Joseph Mendenhall had—from an urban viewpoint. Except for quick helicopter trips or an occasional foray into the countryside, reporters spent their time in Saigon, where their offices and Tele-type machines were located.

Along with fellow print reporters Neil Sheehan, Stanley Kar-now, and Peter Arnett, as well as television reporters such as Mor-ley Safer, Halberstam would make his bones in Vietnam. Halberstam was twenty-nine in 1963 and would win the Pulitzer Prize the next year for his reporting on Vietnam. The war was the foundation for the blazing careers of all these men. In Vietnam, they were recognized by their peers as reporters who "stood up" to the U.S. military in their pursuit of truth, and they became pop icons. They also became advocacy journalists with an agenda, and reduced to basics, that agenda was built on the belief that the war was wrongheaded and unjust and that America had no busi-ness in Vietnam. Because they had an agenda, these reporters—Halberstam and Sheehan in particular—were easily manipulated by maverick U.S. Army adviser John Paul Vann. Both Halberstam and Sheehan had considerable influence over Henry Cabot Lodge Jr., America's ambassador to South Vietnam. The antimilitary stance of Halberstam and Sheehan was so clear that a 1963 con-gressional mission described them and other American journalists in Saigon as "arrogant, emotional, un-objective, and ill-informed." Later, prominent academics, some of whom were antiwar protest-ers in the 1960s, would solidify the media version of the Vietnam War until it became the generally accepted truth.

The great gulf between the story told by the young reporters and the story that military people knew as their truth may be the reason that, almost a half century later, the Vietnam War remains the source of a cultural rift in America. Today a small but growing group of writers is looking back and finding a different story than the one told by many reporters of the day.

Halberstam's 1972 book about the origins of the Vietnam War is titled *The Best and the Brightest*. The book relies heavily on hear-say, is guilty of great leaps in logic, does not identify many sources, and includes an anemic bibliography. Though iconic, it has little credibility among most historians. Even those without a Ph.D. could see through the fog. Mary McCarthy, a liberal writer and social critic who bitterly opposed the Vietnam War, became one of the first to pillory Halberstam, pointing out numerous factual errors in his book and saying it read like historical fiction.

Marguerite "Maggie" Higgins, who reported on World War II and won a Pulitzer Prize for her coverage of the Korean War, traveled extensively in South Vietnam in the early 1960s and interviewed hundreds of military and political leaders for her book *Our Vietnam Nightmare*. It is a sobering experience to read the books of Halberstam and Sheehan and then read hers. Upon finishing, one might well ask the same question that JFK asked Krulak and Mendenhall: were they in the same country? Halberstam and Sheehan were better writers than Higgins, but she was by far the better reporter. She says that when Americans went to Vietnam, "they brought everything but understanding," and she also says that Krulak's assessment of the war was correct.

More recent writers such as Lewis Sorley and Mark Moyar offer a revisionist version of the Vietnam War. Sorley and Moyar contend that many Vietnam-era reporters, but especially Halberstam, Karnow, and Sheehan, not only were wrong in virtually everything they wrote but also had no desire to correct their errors, because their careers were based on their early work. The revisionists believe that these men perpetrated a massive fraud on the American people.

Shortly before he died, Krulak said, "Halberstam's book is full of lies. Full of lies. But he didn't think they were lies. He believed them. And so did the people around him. Because it was comfortable to believe them." Krulak said that reporters in the 1960s were predisposed to think ill of South Vietnamese leaders, even though, compared to other Asian leaders, they were men of relative probity. He said that reporters looked on the South Vietnamese military as inept and incompetent, when in fact young South Vietnamese soldiers went to war when they were fourteen or fifteen and fought for a decade. When those soldiers went home for a few weeks to visit their families, Halberstam called them deserters, not knowing that they would inevitably return.

Halberstam's book says that through much of 1963, Krulak was guilty of "serious misrepresentations to the President" and that he attempted "to destroy any civilian pessimism about the war and to challenge the civilian right to ever discuss military progress, or lack thereof." One thing Halberstam appears to have gotten right is that among JFK's Vietnam advisers, Krulak "was the most important figure. He was the military's most skilled bureaucratic player in Washington at the time, a figure of immense import in the constant struggle over Vietnam."

In August 1963, Admiral Herbert Riley, director of the Joint Chiefs of Staff, wrote a letter for Krulak's personnel file saying that Krulak continued "to add to his illustrious service reputation and his stature as one of the key military figures in Washington, many of which exceed his rank and current assignment by a wide margin." The letter noted that Krulak was fully qualified to become Commandant and recommended him for the job.

In November 1963, Kennedy was assassinated. In the preceding months, he had grown more "dovish" (to use the phrase of the day) and had issued orders to withdraw one thousand troops from South Vietnam. Another body of revisionist history about Vietnam contends that had JFK lived and been reelected in 1964, he would have withdrawn American forces entirely. We will never know whether that is true, but when Lyndon Johnson assumed the presidency, he countermanded Kennedy's withdrawal orders, authorized covert military operations against North Vietnam, and paved the way for full-scale U.S. military intervention.

Johnson was a tough-talking Texan who believed, with most of his generals, that he could hammer the North Vietnamese into submission. LBJ was not fond of "Kennedy people," particularly the little Marine general who was said to have known Kennedy in the Pacific and who was too smart for his own good. And given that Krulak's friends out in San Diego were mostly Republicans, Johnson couldn't understand how Brute had risen to such prominence in a Democratic administration. Krulak, in turn, had little respect for LBJ and in the next few years would grow to have even less. He told his old friend Wallace Greene, who would become the new Commandant in January, that he would welcome a new assignment.

KRULAK received his third star in late 1963. With that star, he became commanding general of the largest field command in the Marine Corps, FMFPac. If the Vietnam War continued to escalate, Marines would be ordered into battle, and Greene wanted them ready. No Marine general had a better record in training combat troops than Brute Krulak. He was ordered to report to Hawaii as soon as possible after the first of the year.

Krulak resolved that when his Marines were sent to Vietnam, they would understand the doctrine of counterinsurgency and would be ready to fight that kind of war.

# 15

## Hope and Glory

IN the weeks leading up to March 1, 1964—the date Brute Krulak reported for duty in Hawaii—some half-dozen members of the ROAD Gang at Camp Smith took early retirement. The departees did not have left in them the commitment Krulak required, and had some of the younger and more ambitious officers known what they were in for, they might have followed.

The change-of-command ceremony at the three-star level involves much pomp and ceremony, in this instance two fifteen-gun salutes: one for the outgoing general, the other for the incoming general. The *Landing Party Manual*, the book that then dictated procedures for every possible situation a Marine might encounter, said that these salutes must be slow and majestic, with a five-second pause between shots. And so it was with the salute to the outgoing commander.

Then came the salute for Krulak: *BoomBoomBoom...Boom... BoomBoom.* Not only was the salute ragged, but the gun crew fired twenty-one times. The proceedings would have been an embarrassment for a group of Boy Scouts; for the Marines, it was mortifying.

David Rilling, who had served under Krulak at MCRD, was

now in Hawaii as commanding officer of Headquarters Battalion, and the saluting battery came under his command. He expected to be relieved of duty, but Krulak had more important things to tend to. The day after the ceremony, Brute was in his office before 6 a.m., wanting to see his intelligence officer for a briefing on Vietnam. The officer was not yet at work. Later that morning, Krulak assembled his staff and told them that a new era was beginning. Henceforth, when he arrived at work, he expected his staff to be there, and there they would remain until after he left the building, which, as they soon found out, would be some fourteen hours later. The Marines would soon be called to war, and nothing short of a maximum effort by all hands would be tolerated.

To prepare for Krulak's daily morning briefing, his staff had to be at work by 3 a.m. They could not complain because they knew that at the end of the day, when Krulak left the office, with him went not one but three bulging briefcases. And when Krulak returned the next morning, opened those briefcases, and started throwing papers and reports and studies across his desk to various officers, there would be work to keep much of the staff busy for days.

"Marines don't take elevators to go three floors," he told his panting aide as he strode briskly up three flights of stairs to his office, taking the steps two at a time. Upon arrival, he threw open his office door so hard that a pad had to be installed on the wall to keep the doorknob from pushing through. On the wall behind his desk, a place that all could see, he placed a sign that read, "The Harder I Work, the Luckier I Get." Also on the wall was a large photograph of Lemuel Shepherd.

Staff officers quickly learned that when they briefed the general, they had best be prepared. If they were not, he peremptorily and scornfully dismissed them from his presence. More than one colonel was told, "Get out of here and do your homework."

A month after assuming command, Krulak summoned Rilling

and said, "I want you to know I have not forgotten the saluting battery performance. Have you any thoughts on that matter?"

Rilling, at rigid attention, said, "Yes, sir. But the explanation would take up too much of the general's time."

"I am all ears, and time is not a consideration. Please proceed."

Rilling explained that to recognize the general's high-energy reputation, he had changed the five-second interval between shots to two seconds. And though his gun crews were high in motivation, they were lacking in calmness. "I am responsible," he finished.

Krulak thought for a long moment, nodded, and said, "That will be all."

Rilling spun on his heel and was halfway out the door when Krulak's voice rang out. "Rilling, there *is* one more thing. The troops do not seem to be polishing the backs of their shoes as well as they do the fronts. Could you do something about that?"

"Aye, aye, sir."


VIC, now assistant pastor of a small Episcopal church in Honolulu, loved to tell a story of what happened during his father's initial round of parties to meet local officials. When Brute was introduced to one woman, her eyes lit up when she heard his name. "Oh, I know who you are," she said. "You are Father Krulak's father."

Brute was taken aback. Never had he been identified in the context of one of his sons, and he had no idea that one of them might be better known in some circles than he was. Brute became fixated on the story and told it for months.

A few months before this incident, Ronnie and Marilyn Zall had come out from Denver to visit Hawaii. They looked up young Vic, who, church proud, took them to visit his church. In the middle of his tour, Marilyn turned and asked, "What is a Jewish boy doing in this place?"

Ronnie Zall says that Vic reeled as if he had been struck a heavy blow. In Vic's eyes, Zall saw a thousand details coming together for the first time, and he realized that Vic *did not know about his Jewish background*.

By May 1964, Krulak, lacquered bamboo swagger stick in hand, had inspected every outfit under his command—bases from California to Okinawa. He asked questions of both privates and generals that had never been asked before ("What is the cost of the equipment you are carrying?") and noticed things that had rarely been noticed (lights burning during the day, dripping showerheads, trucks moving about with only the driver aboard). Krulak saw entirely too many overweight Marines, and during his inspections he began suggesting that they to do less eating and more exercising.

Perhaps because his father had once told him that he would be short and bald but he did not have to be fat, Krulak was fanatical about staying trim. In one of the rare personal comments he ever made to an aide, Krulak pointed to an overweight Marine and said, "That's what I would look like if I didn't watch my diet."

One weight-blessed gunnery sergeant figured out a way to avoid both dieting and Krulak's ire. When the gunny heard that Krulak was about to conduct an inspection, he bought a uniform several sizes too large. When Krulak commented on the baggy uniform, the gunny said, "Yes, sir. But I've been losing weight so fast I haven't had time to tailor it." Krulak nodded in approval and moved on.

In August 1964, Admiral Thomas H. Moorer, the Navy's CINC-Pac, wrote a FitRep for Krulak in which he recommended that Krulak be the next Commandant.

Krulak's job was to train, equip, and supply the thousands of Marines under his command. He was certain his Marines would be going to Vietnam, and he was determined that they would be ready.

From the moment Krulak assumed command, counterinsurgency was the order of the day. As a result, the fundamental nature of training changed. His Marines had to think of the political-military nexus and understand that people were the battlefield, that winning hearts and minds was more important than winning set-piece battles. "You cannot defeat an idea with a bullet," he was fond of saying. "You can defeat an idea only with a better idea."

Krulak believed that fighting a counterinsurgency war would be a long, hard slog with no guarantee of success. But, he believed, search and destroy, the fundamental principle of the Army in war, was guaranteed to fail.

He was perhaps the only American general who held such beliefs. Both William Westmoreland, who as head of the Military Assistance Command, Vietnam (MACV), was the top American commander in Vietnam, and his operations officer, William DePuy, were of a cold war mind-set, trained for massive land battles on the plains of Europe. When they thought of war, they thought of apocalyptic clashes involving hordes of soldiers and countless tanks. Not only would these two top Army generals vehemently disagree with Krulak's ideas about what was called "pacification," but they also were suspicious of him, knowing of his remarkable skill in navigating the bureaucratic maze. They knew of Belleau Wood and Guadalcanal and the Pusan Perimeter, and they knew that in every war, Marines emerged trailing clouds of blood and glory. But this time, Westmoreland would keep the Marines in check; Vietnam would be an Army war fought the Army way.

Krulak knew that Westmoreland would not be a problem until the American presence in Vietnam was much greater, so he put the Marines on Okinawa on a war footing, began asking for more helicopters, and changed the way Marine pilots trained to prepare them for this different war he saw just over the horizon. At the same time, he prepared for the interservice battles to come.

In November, Krulak redefined the standard for the Birthday Balls in Hawaii by moving them to the Royal Hawaiian Hotel on Waikiki. As guest of honor he flew in long-retired General Holland M. "Howlin' Mad" Smith. For young Marines, it was as if a history book had opened up and a legendary figure had stepped from the pages. That night, even though the protocol for Birthday Balls proscribes emotion, Marines wept.

In late 1964, American commanders realized that the airstrip at Da Nang, South Vietnam, was overcrowded and growing more so. A new field was needed, and although logistical constraints meant that construction could not begin for almost a year, it was essential to choose a location quickly. At a meeting of top military leaders in the Pacific, the Air Force said that once a site was picked, building a proper runway would take a year, maybe fourteen months. Heads snapped up in amazement when Krulak stood up and declared, "We can have a field operational twenty-eight days after we begin."

Krulak was given the go-ahead to locate a site and, when spring came, to begin construction. After the meeting, Admiral Ulysses S. Grant Sharp, Krulak's close friend, pulled him aside and said, "Brute, your head is stuck out a mile on this one."

To Krulak this was a high-hearted and glorious adventure, a chance for Marines to show what they could do. He studied maps of the area around Da Nang, climbed aboard a helicopter, and begin flying over the countryside. Fifty-six miles southeast of Da Nang, where the Truong River dumps into the South China Sea, he found an open plain, ordered his pilot to land, took a look around, waved his swagger stick, and proclaimed, "This is the place." An aide realized that there was no village within miles and wondered what the name of this place was or if it even had a name.

From his Shanghai days, Krulak remembered the first thing he had learned in his Chinese language class. "Chu Lai," he said. "That is the name."

KRULAK was flying high. But there were some who wanted to bring him down, some who were still questioning whether he deserved the Purple Heart he was awarded after the Choiseul raid. In early October 1964, Krulak was forced to write a statement noting that on October 30, 1943, he had been wounded in the arm by Japanese rifle fire and later wounded in the jaw and forehead by high-explosive fragments. He followed up the next day with another written statement saying that he had been treated at a hospital on Guadalcanal and then hospitalized for ten days at Bethesda Naval Hospital. He did not explain that the ten-day hospital stay was for an operation to relieve sciatic pain. Three weeks later, an eyewitness account from Choiseul was added to the record. The account said that Krulak had indeed received wounds in his jaw and forehead.

The episode ended with Krulak keeping his Purple Heart, but the experience was humiliating to a three-star general, and the timing could not have been worse. He was in the middle of Operation Silver Lance, a three-week exercise at Camp Pendleton that was the culmination of the Marines' counterinsurgency training.

Krulak liked a big room for his productions, and this exercise called for some 45,000 sailors and Marines; an armada of 60 ships, including 3 aircraft carriers; and 520 Marine and Navy aircraft. The four-inch-thick script called for the Marines to land at a place called Lancelot, the capital of which was given the name Camelot.

Krulak had some Marines assume the role of infiltrators, indigenous people, State Department personnel, the U.S. ambassador, even clergymen, in an effort to portray a counterinsurgency scenario. He had almost as many Marines representing the native population as were involved in the fighting—a wrinkle, Krulak noted, that was "very unpalatable to most of the participants."

The scenario asserted that the sovereignty of Lancelot was threatened by guerrilla bands from a country called Merlin and that the Marines were coming to the rescue. When the Marines landed, guerrillas shouted anti-American slogans, threatened them, and threw sand in their faces. A Marine general landed in a helicopter and was met by a somewhat clueless U.S. ambassador. When threatening mobs rushed them, they had to flee. The operation was conducted at a rapid tempo, with guerrillas pouring into Lancelot, sending out propaganda, capturing villages, and even kidnapping the American ambassador.

The 1st Marine Brigade from Hawaii had a major role in Operation Silver Lance. After the operation ended, the brigade shouldered their combat packs and boarded Navy vessels, weary to the bone and relieved that they were sailing back to Hawaii. About the time the brigade was making plans to disembark, however, members were informed that plans had changed: America was about to make its presence known in a big way in Vietnam, and as always, the Marines would lead the way.

About 9 a.m. on March 8, 1965, Krulak's Marines went ashore at Da Nang, the first significant use of ground troops in Vietnam. Even long after he retired, Marines would come up to Krulak and said, "General, Silver Lance was really Vietnam, wasn't it?"

As Krulak's story begins to merge with the Vietnam War, we move onto a stage with no foundations and few physical limits; a stage with shadowy backdrops and overwhelming characters of every stripe. The war, with its vague beginnings and disputed ending, is a graveyard for slogans and clichés and simplistic beliefs; almost everything ever said about the war can be disproved. Decades have passed since the war ended, but not enough time to heal what remains a painful national wound. Although hundreds of books have been written and are still being written about Vietnam, there is no undisputed and widely accepted history of that war.

The intent here is not to add to the body of Vietnam War history, but rather to tighten the focus so that Krulak remains at the center of the frame. Paradoxically, to do that means that we must zoom back to the widest of shots, as Krulak's ideas went to the very heart of how America would fight the war.

When America goes to war, finding troops with brave hearts is not a problem. The problem is finding the right men to lead them. Great commanders are the link between national strategy and what Eric Larrabee has called the "low, bloody business of carrying it out."

Already a wide and growing gulf existed between the Army and the Marines over how the war should be prosecuted. Westmoreland and DePuy believed in continuing proven techniques of the past and to this end attempted to force the Marines into the Army style of fighting. But Krulak believed that most of Vietnam had no strategic significance, that the great majority of Vietnamese lived near the coast and the rice fields. From the Red River in the north to the Mekong Delta in the south, Vietnam was a rice culture. Krulak wanted to "oil spot" the war—that is, to spread security outward from where people lived and grew rice. One of his battalion commanders had come up with the Combined Action Program, also called the Combined Action Platoons (CAP), in which a small group of Marines, along with South Vietnamese troops, moved into hamlets to protect the local population from the Vietcong. Krulak endorsed the program, the priority of which was not fighting big battles, but rather protecting the Vietnamese people and helping them move toward economic and political self-sufficiency. Throughout the war, CAP would be called by many names: pacification, the other war, the Peace Corps with Rifles, and, of course, winning hearts and minds.

Westmoreland sensed that he should keep an eye on the Marines, or they would interfere with his tactical operations. Krulak, in an effort to reassure him, said that any orders Krulak issued to the Marines would go through Westmoreland's staff. Of Westmoreland, Krulak said, "I think he always had an apprehension that I didn't like the way he was doing things and what he was doing. In this respect, he was often correct."

One story crystallizes the difference between the Marines and the Army in Vietnam. Around Da Nang, the Marines found that numerous Vietnamese suffered from rashes and sores that in many instances could be cured simply by keeping the infected areas clean. The Marines ordered tons of soap to pass out locally as part of CAP. About the same time this was going on, when Westmoreland was asked how he planned to win the war, he responded, "Firepower."

COUNTERINSURGENCY made Westmoreland nervous; it did not pile up the body count that he and LBJ craved. When a general does not know what to do, he does what he knows. America was winning every major battle but clearly not winning the war, so Westmoreland began blaming the Marines, saying that they were afraid to fight. He became increasingly angry toward them, particularly Krulak. It was easy to be angry at Brute: he was abrupt and impatient, he had the certitude of the intellectually arrogant, and his "advice" bordered on insubordination. On one occasion when Krulak was preaching about CAP and counterinsurgency, Westmoreland exploded and said, "Your way will take too long." Not missing a beat, Krulak fired back, "Your way will take forever."

That the Army, at both the strategic and the operational levels, could not grasp the fundamental concepts of counterinsurgency is best proved by how it reacted to the idea of winning the hearts and minds of the Vietnamese people. An Army officer came up with what became that branch's unofficial slogan for the war:

"When you grab them by the balls, their hearts and minds will follow."

WHILE counterinsurgency doctrine would be the foundation of Krulak's tenure, his job dictated that he be involved in all three levels of warfare: strategic, operational, and tactical. Because the news media could not appreciate, or even know of, these levels, there would be numerous apparent conflicts in how Krulak would be viewed in the coming years. In fact, reading about Krulak in Vietnam War literature causes one to wonder how one man could espouse so many contradictory beliefs. Some understanding comes by making a distinction between the three levels of warfare.

As CGFMFPac, Krulak was concerned about the strategic side of the war being directed from Washington. He favored stopping the flow of supplies from North Vietnam to South Vietnam because this would aid in implementing his ideas about counter-insurgency. Thus he was in favor of both mining the harbor at Haiphong and bombing the north. Such actions were external to his theater of operations but would have a direct impact on his ideas.

The next-lowest level of war is the operational level, where Krulak's ideas about counterinsurgency were most important.

The third level is tactical. This is about individual battles. Tactical Marine operations such as Starlite and Harvest Moon were notable battlefield successes in 1965. Although Krulak did not agree with the Army's ideas of search-and-destroy missions and aggressive taking-the-war-to-the-enemy tactics, he could understand the need for such tactics.

IN March, Krulak received word that Lord Louis Mountbatten, former first sea lord of the British navy and now chief of the British Defense Staff, would inspect the Marines at Camp Smith.

Mountbatten was a tall, imperious man whose dour countenance gave away his Germanic birth. He expected and enjoyed the perks that went with being both a member of the royal family—the queen was his cousin—and the highest-ranking military figure in Britain.

Krulak knew that impressing Lord Mountbatten would not be easy, but he was determined to do so. He ordered Rilling and the camp maintenance officer to meet him at Bordelon Field, the extra-large, extra-green athletic field Krulak had constructed back in 1955. When Brute arrived, he walked up to them, returned their salutes, and with no preamble said, "I do not want any more honors ceremonies in the parking lot in front of headquarters building. I intend for this to be a parade deck first and an athletic field secondarily. Now listen carefully. We will perform honors for Lord Mountbatten here on this field two weeks from today. Here is what I want to see happen between now and then." It was clear that Krulak had thought everything through to the last detail. He turned and began pointing with his swagger stick. "The entry will be there, the turnaround there, the reviewing stand there, troops in formation there, saluting battery there, and a line of mature palm trees there. Questions?"

Rilling had experienced a "Krulak enema" before and said, "No, sir." But the warrant officer was wide-eyed. The road work alone was staggering, not to mention that thousands of cubic yards of gravel had to be spread and dozens of mature palm trees planted. And when finished, it had to look smooth and elegant and settled. The warrant officer followed Rilling's lead, however, and said, "No, sir."

"That's all," Krulak said. Rilling and the warrant officer saluted, and Krulak was gone. Then the two officers looked around and absorbed Krulak's vision. Making Bordelon Field the new parade deck was an inspired idea. But how to do it in two weeks?

Marines say that the difference between a Marine general and

God is that God doesn't think he is a general. If Krulak decreed that a new world would be created in two weeks, his will would be done. And it was.

Mountbatten arrived. The saluting battery performed perfectly. Mountbatten took in the lush green grass of Bordelon Field and the majestic prospect of Pearl Harbor and the Pacific, felt the soft Hawaiian breeze wafting across his face, and nodded in approval. Then he trooped the line, moved to the front of the reviewing stand, and watched as Krulak's Marines passed in review.

Rilling had trained them to perfection. Their long-sleeved khaki shirts and dress blue trousers were crisp, and their white gloves were bright in the sun. The backs of their shoes were as shiny as the toes. They carried M1s, the perfect marching rifle, and they were confident as they passed in review. They were clean-shaven, their backs were straight, and their faces were stern. The Drum & Bugle Corps was led by a gunnery sergeant who favored Sousa marches—perfect music for the day. Bright flags swirled in the breeze—a sight to bring a tear to the eye of any man with a military bent. After the ceremony, Mountbatten's aide commented on how good the "soldiers" looked, to which Mountbatten gruffly responded, "Of course they look good. They are Marines."

For Krulak, that was enough.

DURING the next three years, Krulak would make fifty-four "inspection" trips to Vietnam. Because of his meddling in Army and Marine operational matters, these trips were often contentious. His relationship with Marine general Lewis Walt was particularly prickly. Walt was a big, lumbering, avuncular bear of a man who was loved by his Marines. Though junior in rank to Krulak, he was operational leader of the Marines in Vietnam and as such reported to Westmoreland. Walt had two nicknames. One was "Silent Lew," which he liked; the other was "Big Dumb Lew," which he did not know about. One day Vic walked into his father's home office to hear Brute shouting into the telephone, "Goddammit, Lew, don't *ask* them. *Tell* them." It was pretty clear which of the nicknames Krulak preferred.

The military chain of command in Vietnam was complicated and confusing even to those involved. A simple version is that while Walt reported to Westmoreland, Krulak reported to both Admiral Sharp and the Commandant. But the Joint Chiefs of Staff in Washington often ignored the chain of command and went straight to Westmoreland. Stirring this devil's brew was Krulak's penchant for ignoring the chain of command and going directly to his old friend Secretary of Defense McNamara to advance his counterinsurgency ideas. And Krulak would be a constant thorn in the side of Walt, always coming to the battlefield, always making "suggestions," always offering "advice" on tactics and operational matters.

Westmoreland seethed with anger toward Krulak, who was constantly making speeches to anyone who would listen, both in Hawaii and back on the mainland. Almost always they were about how America and the Army were taking the war in the wrong direction. CAP was the key to winning, and if Westmoreland was smart, he would embrace the Marine model.

In late April 1965, right on schedule, Navy ships entered the mouth of the river at Chu Lai and began off-loading hundreds of two-by-twelve-foot pieces of aluminum matting, each weighing 144 pounds, for what was called a short airfield for tactical support, or SATS. This was the first SATS to be built in a combat zone in the history of the Marine Corps. Small A-4 jets could take off with the help of jet-assisted takeoff (JATO) bottles attached to the fuselage, and they could land with the help of arresting gear—the same sort of cable system used aboard aircraft carriers.

Twenty-five days after Navy construction crews began working, four thousand feet of the aluminum matting was in place. On May 28, the first aircraft took off from the bare-bones "expeditionary" field, and Krulak sent a message to McNamara: "Chu Lai operational this date."

To the anger of the Air Force and the disgust of the Army, the Marines had done what Krulak said they could do. The airstrip had both short- and long-term significance. First, it proved that the Marine Corps was agile and innovative and could make things happen fast. Second, it became another exemplar for the expeditionary capability of the Marine Corps. And finally, its presence gave the Marines an additional toehold in the eastern part of South Vietnam.

Chu Lai became one of the legendary American bases of the Vietnam War. But one thing that is not widely known about Chu Lai is that military leaders could not find it on any map of Vietnam. Bases are often named for the nearest village, making them easy to find on a map. But when military planners measured fifty-six miles southeast of Da Nang, right there on the coast where the Truong River empties into the South China Sea, they found no village named Chu Lai. Only a few Marines knew that Krulak had given the site his Chinese name.

When one considers the origins of this expeditionary airfield, the hoopla surrounding it, its initial success, and the ultimate outcome, no better metaphor for Krulak's — or America's — Vietnam experience can be found. Because in the end, Chu Lai was a failure. Krulak had ignored engineering reports that the soil substratum was not sufficient for frequent and prolonged military aircraft operations. After about three years, the Marines left and turned the now sprawling base over to the Army.

IN ever-increasing numbers, aircraft carrying wounded Marines were landing in Hawaii for refueling, usually around 2 a.m. When Sergeant Major O. B. Joyner was notified that an aircraft carrying wounded Marines was inbound, he in turn notified Krulak, whose standard response was, "I'll be right there." He walked through each aircraft accompanied only by a nurse, shaking the hand of every conscious Marine. Of course, the Marines knew who he was: the three stars on his collar, the Navy Cross and Paramarine wings on his chest, and the bamboo swagger stick all signified that the legendary general known as the Brute was aboard.

To honor these wounded and dead Marines, Krulak ordered that a sixty-five-foot-tall cross be erected at Bordelon Field. The cross, which was lighted at night, could be seen for miles and over the next few years became a beloved landmark to the people of Honolulu.

In 1965, the war became personal for Krulak. Two of his sons, Bill and Chuck, were in-country and in combat. On one of Brute's inspection tours, he arranged to visit Chuck. When Brute stepped out of the helicopter, his utilities were well starched. So was he.

Brute arrived only a few hours after Chuck had emerged from a battle in which he was almost killed by friendly fire. Chuck and his men had been caught out in the open (oddly enough, in a cemetery) as they approached a tree line hiding a strong enemy force. A jet flying close air support dropped napalm that landed short, and the fireball rolled across the ground toward Chuck and his platoon. He jumped into a hole as napalm rolled overhead, sucking out the oxygen and burning and killing his men.

Brute's arrival—with all of his requisite cerebral talk about war on a strategic level, about Washington not letting the military bomb Haiphong harbor, and about politically imposed limits on the U.S. military crossing into North Vietnam—could not have been more ill timed. For the first time in his life, Chuck exploded in anger toward his father. "What the fuck are you talking about?" he snapped. "We are getting our asses handed to us. These guys are good. They are well equipped, well armed, and well trained. We have serious problems here."

Brute's eyebrows rose. A Marine first lieutenant does not raise his voice to a general, and a Krulak son did not raise his voice to his father. Brute waited a moment, then asked, "What happened?"

Chuck still had his wind up. "I know you went through Choiseul. But I went through this. You want to talk fighting, we can talk fighting."

They did, the longest conversation Chuck had ever had with his father, and the news he passed to the general was not good.

CHUCK was not the only Krulak son who barely escaped death. During his first tour in Vietnam, Bill was leading his platoon on a patrol when he stepped in a hole and heard the telltale clicking of a mine. He thought he was a goner. Usually mines exploded instantaneously, but this one sputtered for a couple of seconds, enough time for Bill to shout "Mine!" and dive to the side before the explosion force was directed straight up out of the hole. No one was hurt. Bill assembled his men and pressed on. By all rights, he should have been dead or, at the very least, have lost several limbs. The incident would haunt Bill for years, ever growing in his consciousness.

VIC, now Father Krulak, was living a quiet life in idyllic Hawaii, where he had the respect and affection of his congregation, but there were always military aircraft passing through, coming from and going to Vietnam. His two younger brothers were there, he had the same name as the senior Marine in the Pacific, and yet he was sitting out the war as a civilian. It felt all wrong, and then it came to him: he could join the Navy as a chaplain and ask to be assigned to Marine Corps units. He would not be a real Marine, but he could be with Marines.

When Vic called his father to announce that he would be commissioned in the Navy, Brute said, "Oh," and hung up. Nevertheless, on September 30, 1965, Vic was commissioned, in Brute's office.

YOUNG reporters, like old generals, make their reputations in war, and by now the American press corps in Vietnam was in full bay, consumed by a bloodlust greater than that of frontline combat troops. Krulak's troubles with the media reached crisis proportions when, on August 3, Morley Safer of CBS joined up with a group of Marines about to attack the hamlet of Cam Ne. Because Safer arrived as the Marines were boarding their vehicles, there was no time to brief him on the operation. Cam Ne had been controlled by the Vietcong for years. In recent days, four Marines had been killed there and twenty-seven wounded. Cam Ne was a "hot area," and the Marines were on a search-and-destroy mission with orders that if they were fired upon, they were to return fire.

Safer, then thirty-three, had been with CBS for about a year, and a few months earlier he had opened the CBS bureau in Saigon. Now he was with Marines who were taking fire and returning it, as Marines do, in overwhelming fashion. Safer hunkered down in a rice paddy.

There is no middle ground between what Safer reported and what Krulak later said happened at Cam Ne. Safer did a piece for CBS Radio, followed on August 5—when his film arrived in America—by a piece on the *CBS Evening News*. He talked of burned huts and fires set by tracers and flamethrowers, reporting that the Vietcong were "long gone" when the Marines arrived and that the Marines used Zippo cigarette lighters to burn down as many as 150 huts. Safer claimed that the Marines had orders "to burn the hamlet to the ground if they received so much as one round." He also said that they killed a baby, wounded three women, and got only four "old men" as prisoners. Safer ended his piece as the camera panned over crying women and children and he said, "This is what the war in Vietnam is all about."

The story shocked America. The *Washington Post* picked up the story, as did other newspapers. Antiwar groups read these articles and compared the Marine Corps to the Nazis. Norman Cousins, then editor of the *Saturday Review*, used the magazine to raise money for Vietnamese families at Cam Ne. All across America, there were demonstrations against the Marine Corps. The image of a young Marine torching a house with a Zippo would become one of the enduring photographs of the war.

If one story could be singled out for launching the brilliant career of Morley Safer, it would be Cam Ne. He received the 1965 Overseas Press Club Award and later the Sigma Delta Chi Award, which talked of his "independence and refusal to submit to U.S. government restrictions on TV coverage of the war." Today the CBS Web site says that Safer's story about Cam Ne was one of television's finest hours and that it "changed war reporting forever."

Before getting into the Marine version of what happened, it is worth noting that Keyes Beech of the *Chicago Daily News* was on the raid and filed an altogether different story than Safer. Beech was a combat veteran of World War II, and he wrote that heavy small-arms and automatic-weapons fire greeted the Marines at Cam Ne and that at least one hundred Vietcong were in the village. But Beech's assessment was lost in the more shocking and sensational treatment by CBS.

BRUTE Krulak and the Marine Corps were bitterly angry about Safer's pieces and the subsequent fallout. Krulak ordered that every Marine involved in the operation be interviewed and asked detailed questions about Cam Ne and that the transcripts of the interviews be sent to him. After receiving the transcripts and the official after action reports, he wrote a scathing internal paper about Safer, saying the reporter absolutely knew that Vietcong were in Cam Ne; that he knew of the sniper and automatic-weapons fire received, because he was "ducking and hiding"; and that he had altered, disguised, and misrepresented facts at the expense of the Marine Corps. Krulak said that 51 huts, not 150, had been burned and that every hut burned either had an enemy inside or was linked to a tunnel or bunker. He said that at one point after the battle, when Safer was interviewing a group of Marines, he asked them all to nod their heads "yes" and then shake their heads "no"; later he matched the nodding and shaking with questions that were never asked. He said that Marines showed Safer the extensive system of trenches and booby traps in Cam Ne, but Safer was concerned only with getting pictures of a Marine with a Zippo. Nevertheless, CBS would not back down on the story.

Only a few weeks after Cam Ne, newspaper columnist Jimmy Breslin wrote a piece saying that in Vietnam, wire was used to secure the hands and close the mouths of the prisoners. The story left the impression that such behavior was an institutional practice, when in fact, as in every war, a few renegades had crossed the line. Peter Arnett, a wire service reporter who was critical of the military, wrote an article titled "Paratroops Go Where the Action Isn't." More than thirty years later, in 1999, Arnett would be reprimanded by CNN in connection with a report that the U.S. military had used sarin gas to kill American defectors in Laos during Operation Tailwind. CNN retracted the story. Afterward, Arnett's contract was not renewed.

Whether Krulak liked it or not, and whether Safer was correct or not, it was Safer's version that prevailed among Americans. More than forty years later, however, in 2007, a four-day symposium at Hillsdale College titled "The Vietnam War: History and Enduring Significance" came to the conclusion that what people thought they knew about the Vietnam War caused a rupture in American society that continues to the present day—a rupture that threatened American success in Iraq and beyond. Those at the symposium were largely the "new historians" of the Vietnam War, who have challenged the orthodox view of the war that continues to dominate American universities, media, and popular culture. Mark Moyar, author of *Triumph Forsaken: The Vietnam War, 1954–1965*, led off by defining the accepted view of the war as an unwarranted American intervention in a civil war in support of a corrupt ally. Moyar argued that this conventional wisdom came largely from David Halberstam, Neil Sheehan, and Stanley Karnow, who, he said, did more than anyone else to promulgate an untrue and negative view of America's role in Vietnam. Those at the symposium heard that it was not idealism that motivated the antiwar movement of the 1960s, but rather the military draft and the desire of many to avoid serving in Vietnam. As proof, one speaker pointed out that after Nixon ended the draft in 1973, the antiwar movement almost disappeared.

AN obvious exception to Krulak's disapproval of the media's war coverage was Don Moser's profile of him in the April 30, 1965, issue of *Life* magazine. The article described Krulak as a "wispy, hyperactive" man of fifty-two, with "a long foxy nose, eyes that spark with Machiavellian intelligence and a tic in his right cheek that twitches when he gets angry." Moser said that Krulak looked more "like an aging Boy Scout than a three-star Marine general," but that he was as "tolerant of mistakes as a well-oiled rat trap" and he was such a "relentless, hard-driving perfectionist that even senior officers quiver when they hear he is coming." The article described Krulak chewing out his driver for being thirty-five seconds late and said that he walked so fast that even six-foot staff officers had to race to keep up with him. Moser said that guests came from several thousand miles away to attend his birthday parties; that he collected fine watches; that he spoke eloquently of the compatibility of religion and the military life, saying, "You can't go into this disciplined life, giving up so many things, without spiritual support"; and that he attended church regularly. But Krulak's strongest characteristic, according to Moser, was his self-assurance. According to the article, Krulak knew more about cars than his driver and more about cooking than his cook. "He knows more about anything than all those around him."

Scott Chandler, Amy's nephew, said the Chandler family was impressed with the article and with the famous Marine Amy had married. Several of the nephews thought it clever to send Krulak Brut cologne at Christmas.

"Uncle Brute was a serious and calculating man, very conscious of who he was," Chandler said. "We all got the impression that he believed he was the smartest guy in the room." But the one thing Krulak never talked about was his childhood. "About all he ever told us was that his father was a watchmaker."

When Vic saw that the issue of *Life* magazine with the article about his father had a fetus on the cover, he said that the article about Brute was the cover story.

By December 1965, the Marines in Vietnam had used their Korean War–era helicopters for several major air-ground operations and further developed the concept of vertical envelopment. New CH-46 twin-rotor helicopters were arriving, and with them the speed, cargo-carrying capability, range, and application in war were catching up to Krulak's ideas about helicopters of almost two decades earlier. The Army would bring in massive numbers of light utility helicopters called Hueys and publicize its "air mobility" concept, in which battalions were moved onto the battlefield via helicopters. The media publicized this concept as a radical innovation in warfare. The Marines knew better.

# 16

## Dust and Despair

For Brute Krulak, the pain of Vietnam began in 1966.

Congress had grown restive and wanted to know why Westmoreland was not making more progress. Westmoreland had grown impatient and wanted to know why the Marines were hung up on the CAP business. LBJ had grown imperious and wanted to prove he was a better man than Ho Chi Minh. Undeterred and perhaps even oblivious, Krulak continued to preach the gospel of CAP, to talk of "oil spots," and to suggest that the Army follow the "more innovative tactics" of the Marine Corps. He fought constantly to prevent the Air Force from taking control of Marine aviation, and he continued to ignore the chain of command and to write letters to the undersecretary of the Navy and Defense Secretary McNamara suggesting that America change its policies to be more in line with his ideas. On trips to Washington, Krulak had long conversations with McNamara. He later said that McNamara agreed with 90 percent of his ideas and that he "fought to gain the other ten percent." But Congress and LBJ wanted results *now*. They knew that the American psyche and political system were not geared for a long war.

In 1966, an internal Army study, sensing defeat if the military continued on its present course, concluded that this year was the last chance to win the war. But to do so, the Army had to shift away from search-and-destroy missions—which almost always killed civilians, whose support the Army needed—and move more toward the pacification model. The study was suppressed by the Army chief of staff and ignored by Westmoreland.

Krulak continued to disagree publicly with Westmoreland and LBJ. In July 1966, he wrote, "You cannot win militarily. You have to win totally, or you are not winning at all." He added, "It is our conviction that if we can destroy the guerrilla fabric among the people, we will automatically deny the larger units the food and intelligence and the taxes, and the other things that support what they need. At the same time, if the big units want to sortie out of the mountains and come down to where they can be cut up by our supporting arms, the Marines are glad to take them on, but the real war is among the people and not among the mountains."

CAP was a small part of the war, and as thousands of additional military personnel poured into Vietnam, it lessened in importance even as Krulak's frustration grew. By criticizing his government's Vietnam policy, he was treading a very fine line. To protect himself from the media, which he saw as ever more critical, he began recording every speech.

Although he seemed self-possessed and a man whose iron facade could not be cracked, there were signs that he felt besieged. One example is how he dealt with the combat heroism of his son Chuck.

Chuck Krulak was recommended three times for the Silver Star, an award recognizing extraordinary bravery and second only to the Navy Cross, but each time Brute downgraded the award to a Bronze Star. A fourth recommendation for the Silver Star came after Chuck was wounded in action, refused to be evacuated, and moved his men seven thousand meters through the jungle to safety. "It was like Dad on Choiseul," he said later. Again Brute downgraded the recommendation to a Bronze Star, and it was only when another Marine general interceded that Chuck received the Silver Star. Chuck never asked his father for an explanation, saying, "My father is a hard man. I knew why."

In 1966, Chuck finished his first combat tour in Vietnam and was at the airport in Da Nang awaiting a ride to Hawaii. His wife, Zandra (Zandi), had been staying with Brute and Amy as she waited for her husband's return. Chuck had spent an extra month in combat, a total of fourteen months, and was anxious to get home, but he arrived in Da Nang about the same time a typhoon grounded civilian and military aircraft for two weeks. As he was about to leave, a typhoon struck Okinawa, a refueling stop for Marine aircraft, delaying him another week.

About that time, Brute arrived in Da Nang aboard his personal C-130, conducted a whirlwind inspection tour, and had his aide announce to homeward-bound Marines waiting at the airport that he could carry thirty of them as far as Hawaii. Chuck was number fifteen in the queue. He gathered his bags and was about to board when his father's aide pulled him out of the line, put an arm around his shoulders, and said, "Chuck, you are not going on the plane."

"What do you mean?"

"Your dad won't take his own son back. It wouldn't look right."

"I've been in-country fourteen months. I've been sitting here at the airport for weeks. I'm on the manifest."

"Your father says you are not going on his aircraft."

It was another week before Chuck caught a flight to Hawaii, and when he saw his father, he did not mention the airport ordeal. More than forty years later, as he told this story, he said ruefully, "That is my dad."

Brute Krulak knew that perceptions are reality. And given the fight he was engaged in with Westmoreland and LBJ, as well as his strong desire to become Commandant, he could not afford to have anyone think he was showing favoritism toward his son. He could have no weak spots. He was the Brute.

HERE is a good time to look at Brute at the very top of his career. On the surface, he could be charming and, despite his actions toward Chuck, generous. But he had an inner chill, a remoteness; he was unwilling—or, more likely, unable—to express emotion and warmth. He was not one to hug his sons or to show affection toward them. Amy often told him, "Brute, I love you so much," and each time Brute replied, "That's nice." His sons never heard their father tell their mother that he loved her, nor did he ever say "I love you" to his sons.

It is not unusual for an aide to become almost a surrogate son to his general, much as Brute had been to Holland Smith. But Brute rarely revealed anything personal to his aides. Throughout his Marine Corps career, he was close to only one person, Robert Hogaboom, and that was more of an intellectual connection than one of personal warmth.

At the bottom of Krulak's icy self-control was the memory of Cheyenne, of his first undisclosed marriage, of the misrepresentations he had made on his Naval Academy application papers—official government documents—and his knowledge that were it not for the Marine Corps, he would be an obscure little Jewish boy working in the family jewelry business in Denver. The Marine Corps did for Brute Krulak what it has done for untold thousands of wayward young men: it made him a proud contributor to America. The Marine Corps was Krulak's only world, and in that world he had to dominate and control. If he could become Commandant of the Marine Corps, he could leave a lasting mark, he could bring about changes that would give him a place in Marine Corps history, and no one would ever know or care about Cheyenne.

In June 1966, the new fleet commander, Admiral Roy Johnson, wrote a FitRep for Krulak saying that he was "a very forceful per-

sonality who uses to excellent advantage his very broad understanding of political/operational matters" and that he was
"qualified in all respects" to be Commandant. But just as Krulak
was finding that he had little control over the war, he would find
that he had little control over who would be promoted and who
would not.

In July, Vic arrived in Vietnam as a Navy chaplain assigned to a
Marine battalion. He was greeted by the battalion commander,
who said, "For months I have been asking for an Episcopal priest.
Now I get one, and he is a fucking general's son."

Vic went beyond what chaplains are expected to do, in that he
was often with Marines engaged in firefights, moving about the
battlefield, comforting the wounded and dying, and exposing himself to great risks. He could have done this for any of a number of
reasons: theological beliefs, sense of duty, the desire to impress his
father, the knowledge that his younger brothers had gone to war
before he did and both were decorated officers. But when asked
about his actions, he said, "I never thought I was doing anything
out of the ordinary. It was just what I thought was my job."

After one battle in which the Marines suffered heavy casualties,
Navy corpsmen hastily separated the living from the dead, sending the living for medical treatment and lining up the dead for
body bags. Vic recognized one of the "dead" Marines, Captain
Henry "Hank" Stackpole, detected faint signs of life, and insisted
that Stackpole be treated. The corpsman confirmed that Stackpole was indeed alive, though barely, and rendered treatment.
Stackpole recovered and became a three-star general. He never
forgot that it was Father Krulak who saved his life.

When word came down that Brute was visiting Vic's battalion,
various officers came to Vic and asked what they could do to
impress the general. "Just tell him the truth," Vic said.

So when Brute stopped and asked a gunnery sergeant what he thought of his South Vietnamese allies, the gunny looked at him and said, "General, I don't trust the little fuckers." And a lieutenant briefing the general painted something other than the rosy picture that Brute wanted to see.

Afterward, Brute pulled his son aside and said, "What is wrong with your battalion? Everywhere else that I go, I get a different story."

"Did it ever occur to you the others might be lying to you?" Vic asked.

It was clear from Brute's stunned silence that such a thought had never crossed his mind. He had forgotten the first thing he had learned upon becoming a general: subordinates told him what they thought he wanted to hear.

Great events were swirling about Krulak, great forces were in play, and sometimes it seemed to Brute he was only a spectator. But some things he could control. Vic had lost a considerable amount of weight, a fact that Brute brought up to the regimental commander. After Brute departed, the commander summoned Vic and ordered, "You will gain weight." For months afterward, Vic weighed himself weekly, and the infrequent announcement of an additional pound brought significant satisfaction to his boss.

Almost a year later, a chaplain in Vic's regiment, Father Vincent Capodanno, known as "the Grunt Padre," was killed in a firefight. His bravery in that instance was so exemplary that he was posthumously awarded the Medal of Honor and years later would be recognized as a "servant of God," the first step in the beatification and canonization process of the Catholic Church. Even though Capodanno was a Navy officer, he was assigned to a Marine unit, and the Marines considered him one of their own. Today's Marines think it no small matter that a brother Marine is being considered for sainthood.

After Father Capodanno was killed, the division chaplain convinced the chief of staff to enjoin the chaplains in the 1st Marine Division from leaving their battalion command posts; that is, they were to stay off the battlefield. Vic's battalion commander took a different approach. He summoned Vic and said, in effect, do what you think is best. But then he urged prudence and rhetorically asked, "What would happen if you were killed?" Vic, demonstrating the same sense of humor as his father, said, "I would be in heaven, and your career would be over."

Vic left Vietnam wearing a Bronze Star with the combat "V" and a Navy Commendation Medal, also with the combat "V." He is remembered by Vietnam War–era Marines as a chaplain who often exposed himself to enemy fire and who was always with his Marines in the thick of battle. They still have great respect for the man they know as "Father Krulak."

Several high-ranking Marines had sons in combat in Vietnam. Brute Krulak, however, was the only officer with three sons in combat, and Amy was the only Marine wife who experienced the anguish of having three sons and a husband in combat.

Dal Neitzel was an eighteen-year-old private first class stationed at Kaneohe Bay, Hawaii, as a cameraman/photographer in April 1967, when he was instructed to report to the CGFMFPac. His first sergeant told him, "Whatever the general says to you, say 'Yes, sir.' And when you get out, report everything he says to me."

Neitzel reported to Krulak, who, for at least thirty seconds, kept writing and did not look up. Suddenly, Krulak stood up, stood on his chair, and then stood on his desk, hands on hips, looking down at Neitzel.

"Do you see how tall I am right now, Marine?"

"Yes, sir."

Neitzel's enthusiasm was not what Krulak wanted. He repeated the question, and this time Neitzel shouted, "YES, SIR."

"That is how tall I am going to be in every picture you take of me."

"YES, SIR."

After Neitzel relayed the events to his first sergeant, the sergeant paused and asked, "Do you know what that means?"

"It means I should crouch down to take pictures of the general?"

"No. It means you dig a hole and get in it before you take a picture of the general."

And that is why, in many pictures taken of Krulak at the time, he appears to be an almost lofty figure.

In May 1967, Westmoreland asked Brute to come to his office in Saigon. Exactly what Westmoreland said is unknown, but after the meeting Krulak wrote a memorandum for the record in which he said that Army antipathy toward the Marine Corps was clear, that Westmoreland thought the Marines were not sending their best troops to Vietnam, and that the Army did not like the Marine method of fighting the war. "What he said made it clear the Army still harbors deep resentment toward the Marine Corps," Krulak wrote.

In July, Krulak picked Captain John Grinalds to be his new junior aide. A three-star general of Marines is entitled to two aides—a senior aide, who is usually a major, and a junior aide, who is usually a captain. Grinalds had just served a tour in Vietnam and was en route to Quantico when Krulak saw his personnel records. "I picked him because of his mind," Krulak said, which is easy to believe given that Grinalds went to West Point, was a Rhodes scholar, and, in a conversation about the importance of persistence, could casually point out that Flaubert rewrote *Madame Bovary* forty-three times before he deemed it acceptable.

Grinalds was the only aide Krulak ever had who was his intellectual equal, and Grinalds would long remain friends with Brute and his family, even flying from South Carolina to California for Brute's funeral in 2009.

Asked what he remembers most about Krulak, Grinalds replied, "He was the most controlled man I ever saw." Krulak played golf once a week, and the general's goal was not to improve his score, Grinalds recalled, but to play this round faster than the previous one. A good military campaign is a fast-moving campaign, and golf was a game that presented eighteen holes for Brute to conquer.

Each afternoon, as Krulak prepared to leave for the day, Grinalds went to the third-floor lobby, summoned the elevator, and locked the door open so that Krulak would not have to wait. When Krulak was ready, he pressed a button, and two junior officers picked up three bulging briefcases to put in his car. Krulak emerged from his office, moving fast, and expected to walk directly into the elevator without waiting. Sometimes this led to conflict with the CINCPac, one floor below, whose aides wanted their boss to have the same perk. Brute didn't care.

Grinalds also remembers the aircraft that stopped in Hawaii en route from Vietnam to America—aircraft filled with wounded and dead Marines. These planes were arriving with increasing frequency, landing day and night, causing Krulak to think that his Marines were suffering far too many casualties. Brute walked through each aircraft, talking with the wounded, then returned to his car, where Grinalds was waiting. Usually the car was an extension of Krulak's office—a place where he read reports and wrote memos. But after these airport visits, he was somber, staring out the window and not speaking, and his briefcases remained closed.

EVERY month, Krulak wrote a compendium of all that had happened in Vietnam the month before and sent it to Marine headquarters. He wanted a historical record of his time as CGFMFPac and of the Marines in Vietnam, and he wrote and edited the reports himself. These reports were so optimistic, however, that when they arrived at the Marine historical office, they were dismissed as "Krulak's fables."

In the late summer of 1967, Krulak leaned into a situation that leaned back. Appalled at Marine casualties and how "White House functionaries were invading the prerogatives of the military and telling us how to do our business," he flew to Washington to air his complaints with Commandant Wallace Greene. "He listened to my story and was sympathetic. He told me I should talk about this with my old boss McNamara," Krulak said.

Most Commandants would have wondered why a three-star general whom everyone was talking about as the next Commandant would start rocking the boat, going up the chain of command to complain about civilian leadership and government policy that was tying the hands of combat leaders. But Greene had known Krulak since the two were in China together and was not surprised. It was Brute Krulak's nature to tell his superiors how they could do their jobs better.

The next morning, Krulak told the secretary of defense that no-fly zones and enemy "sanctuaries" in North Vietnam—places that could not be bombed—were hindering the military. Krulak wanted to bomb the harbor at Haiphong, enemy airfields, and the big electric power plant on the outskirts of Hanoi.

"Why don't you talk to Governor Harriman?" McNamara said, a suggestion showing that Averell Harriman had retained his unique position as a power broker inside the LBJ administration.

Brute did so, and Harriman reacted by saying, "General, do you want to start a war with China or with Russia?"

Brute's next stop was the White House. When Brute walked into the Oval Office, the first words out of LBJ's mouth were, "Well, General, how are things out there in Vietnam?"

"Not very good, sir. We are suffering lots of casualties. Unnecessary casualties."

Krulak said that his comment "electrified" the president, who asked, "What do you mean?"

"I told him the blame for the excessive casualties and the meddling went to the top of the government, 'including you, Mr. President,'" Brute said. "And I told him if he did not change, he would lose the war and he would lose the next election."

It was a shocking thing to say, but Brute did so without compunction.

Johnson had had enough. "He got to his feet," Krulak recalled, "walked around, and put his hand on my shoulder — not to console me or to say he was in agreement, but to propel me to the door. He did not say a word. He just ushered me out."

Lending credence to Krulak's story is a picture of the meeting taken by a White House photographer. It should be remembered that LBJ was often called "the Great Intimidator." In a famous triptych, the first picture shows LBJ talking with a congressman who is standing several feet away, the second shot shows LBJ standing close to the congressman, and in the third shot LBJ is bending forward, leaning over the congressman, who in turn is leaning backward over a piece of furniture. In the picture taken during Brute's visit, a stern-faced Krulak is pointing at the president, who is leaning back in his rocking chair as if to get as far away as possible from the accusatory finger. LBJ's face is not filled with his usual predatory glee, but his eyes are hooded and his body language defensive.

Here it must be emphasized that although the idea of a general presenting unvarnished facts to his commander in chief represents the highest duty of a military officer, in practice such candor, especially to an overbearing president such as LBJ, was rare in the 1960s. Military officers, from the time they are lieutenants, are used to overbearing senior officers and know how to tread lightly around them. Krulak had done the right thing, but there is often a price to pay for doing the right thing. Krulak fully expected to be punished; in fact, from the White House meeting, he went to the Pentagon and told McNamara, "I will be fired tomorrow."

He wasn't. In fact, his name was mentioned even more prominently as the leading contender to become the next Commandant. He was the choice of Wallace Greene, of the secretary of the Navy, and of the secretary of defense. He seemed a shoo-in. Greene even sent Brute a note saying that within forty-eight hours, the White House would announce that he had been named as the next Commandant. Brute notified old comrades and told them to prepare for staff duty at headquarters. He began planning how he would reassign Marine Corps generals and how he would take an even more active role in influencing the war in Vietnam. As being promoted to Commandant meant an automatic promotion to four-star rank, Amy bought a set of four-star insignia for the president to pin on Brute at the White House promotion ceremony.

But forty-eight hours came and went, and then seventy-two hours, and still no announcement. Greene told Krulak the process had slowed, but it was still a done deal. Later, Greene said, "The Commandant's job is up for grabs." The tenor of news stories about the selection began to change. The Associated Press (AP) ran a story saying that Krulak was the favorite to win what was now a three-way contest between Krulak, Lew Walt, and a dark horse, Leonard Chapman Jr. The AP said that although there was much behind-the-scenes antagonism toward Krulak, he was smooth, had considerable experience at the highest levels of government, was a close friend of McNamara, and had a reputation for moving decisively where others tended to hold back and let headquarters make the decisions. The tall, wide-shouldered, blue-eyed Walt presented a movie-star image of the Commandant, but his ability lay in the field rather than at the staff and planning levels. The article said that former Commandant David Shoup favored Chapman.

In an unprecedented breach of protocol, Westmoreland wrote a letter saying that he favored Walt. Generals from one branch of the service normally do not become involved in the promotion process of officers in another branch, but Westmoreland had had enough of Krulak

On December 15, *Time* magazine predicted that Chapman would be the compromise choice between the "popular, barrel-chested" Walt and the "acerbic, shrimp-sized" Krulak.

*Time* was correct. A few days later, LBJ selected Chapman. Rather than firing Krulak, he had responded in a way that hurt Krulak far more.

DURING the Iraq War beginning in 2003, it was common to read of retired generals criticizing the president for his prosecution of the war. These generals were more often than not portrayed as bold and courageous men, but what is overlooked in such a portrayal is the operative word "retired." The pension of a retired general is secure, and he has no need to worry about future assignments or promotion. It takes no courage to second-guess the commander in chief when there is no price of admission.

In Vietnam, it was the job of active-duty senior officers to present unvarnished advice to the president, but those generals, in every branch of the service, were silent and servile. At the end of the day, they were men of little integrity, and there is a school of thought that says every one of them should have resigned in protest of LBJ's policies. Their actions, or lack thereof, did not reflect well on them, on their respective branches of the service, or on the fundamental character of American military leadership.

Krulak, as far as can be determined, was the only senior general who confronted LBJ. Other generals may be quick to point out that Krulak was pushed aside and may ask what is the point of doing the right thing if you are no longer in a leadership role. But that is the response of a careerist. Krulak knew he would pay a price, and he still did the right thing. At a time when he had everything to lose, he was the only general in the American military whose sense of duty and love of country were greater than his careerism.

IN December, Brute had his annual physical, which said he had blue eyes, was slender, weighed 134 pounds, had 20/20 vision, and was "physically qualified to perform all duties of his rank at sea and in the field." Physically, he was at the top of his form a few weeks later when his birthday rolled around. But there was an air of desperation about his birthday party in January 1968, almost as if he sensed this would be his last as an active-duty officer. He continued to besiege McNamara with notes asking why LBJ had not fired him. McNamara finally told him, "The president said you were not important enough to fire."

Krulak's ideas about CAP were being ignored, and Westmoreland had marginalized him, but for the president to minimize his importance was the unkindest cut of all. Thus Krulak's birthday party, which was one thing he could control, assumed an even greater significance. He became immersed in every detail of the intricate preparation, particularly in the ritualized selection of what was known at Camp Smith as the "general's pig," the roast suckling pig that would be the centerpiece of his fifty-fifth birthday party.

Guests from Oahu, California, even as far away as Quantico came to the party on January 13, 1968. They pulled back the skin on the pig; devoured small, moist pieces of pork; and oohed and aahed over how tender and tasty it was. Grinalds and a few other junior officers walked about with a pitcher of Fish House Punch in each hand, making sure that no glass was empty. After several hours, their arms trembled with fatigue.

Krulak had one drink, a brandy and soda, and then drank only soda. He sat in a large chair, his guests before him and an aide on either side, to open his presents. There was nothing slow or easy about opening the packages. He jerked the ribbons and ripped the paper, tossing the scraps aside, where aides grabbed them before they reached the floor. All the time, he laughed, made jokes, and read poems and birthday wishes sent to him with the presents. He went through the presents so fast that an aide, whose job was to write down a description of each gift and the person who sent it, could barely keep up.

Then, filled with Fish House Punch and roast pig, the guests disappeared into the soft Hawaiian night.

SEVERAL days after the party, Krulak left for Vietnam. During his tour as CGFMFPac, he would spend 210 days in Vietnam and fly 1,500 helicopter sorties. This time, he flew up to the northwestern part of the country, to a mountaintop airfield called Khe Sanh, where his Marines were engaged in a mighty battle and the news was not good. Westmoreland wanted to show the North Vietnamese a thing or two about set-piece battles, and he was using the Marines to prove his point. Khe Sanh was under siege, bringing up inevitable comparisons with the French debacle at Dien Bien Phu fourteen years earlier, and LBJ was quoted as saying, "I don't want any damn Din Bin Phoo."

The seventy-seven-day siege at Khe Sanh captured world attention. A small group of Marines was holding off two divisions of North Vietnamese regulars, and the fight was about to become another battle of wills, another piece of barren soil soaked by Marine blood, fertilized by Marine grief, and consecrated by Marine valor. And to Krulak, it was all folly, sheer folly. Khe Sanh had no strategic value, and Marines were not made for defensive work.

Krulak landed at Khe Sanh, jumped out of a moving aircraft,

317

and ran as fast as he could for the safety of a trench. Then he moved about, talking to his Marines, standing close to each one so he could be heard over the noise of the rockets and artillery, gripping their arms, and questioning them closely about what they needed to win. When they looked at him, their thoughts were in their eyes: *What is a three-star doing on this goddamn hill?* Grinalds followed Krulak, getting the name of each man so that afterward the general could send the Marine a personal note. As Krulak walked away from a six-foot-five gunnery sergeant, the gunny looked after him in awe and said to Grinalds, "That is the biggest little man I have ever seen."

In late January, the North Vietnamese launched attacks all across the country in what history remembers as the Tet Offensive. The Americans won every battle and broke the back of the North Vietnamese attack, but the American media described Tet as a great victory for North Vietnam. Back home, the president, the Congress, and the American people wanted more than ever for the war to end.

By now Krulak's comrades were commiserating with him about not becoming Commandant. They knew that he was approaching the end of his career. But Krulak put on a brave face and on January 17 wrote to a friend, "The CMC business gave me no irreparable pain." He added, "I am wholly tranquil about the entire affair."

This was not true, because on February 24, Krulak wrote a "Dear Chappy" letter to the new Commandant saying that "something might be lost" if he relinquished command at such a crucial time in the war. He wanted to defer his retirement.

On March 7, Chapman responded, saying, "Some slippage is always inevitable at any level of command when change occurs," a nice way of telling Brute it was time for him to go. But he ended by saying that the timing for Krulak's retirement was a decision that Brute must make himself.

On March 21, Krulak wrote Chapman and said that because of the Tet Offensive and the seizure by North Korea of the *Pueblo*, a Navy intelligence-gathering ship, he had been forced to "reappraise" his situation and had decided to postpone his retirement. He ended by "asking frankly if there is any other job which you might wish me to do for the USMC."

Krulak must have realized his efforts were futile, because on March 25 he wrote the Commandant, "Upon completing 34 years of active commissioned service, it is requested that I be transferred to the retired list of officers of the Marine Corps, effective 1 June 1968"—thirty-four years to the day after he had been commissioned at Annapolis.

THE fighting at Khe Sanh continued until early April. Of course, in the end the Marines prevailed; they held the hill. And then, when the battle was over, Westmoreland ordered the Marines to abandon the hill. Such was Vietnam.

DESPITE his March 25 letter, behind the scenes Krulak was frantically lobbying McNamara. On April 27, an article in *Stars and Stripes*, a military newspaper, said that Krulak was the leading contender for two jobs: CINCPac and deputy to Creighton Abrams, who was about to relieve Westmoreland. Both were four-star billets. General Earle Wheeler, chairman of the Joint Chiefs of Staff, sent a note to Abrams asking if he would accept Krulak as his deputy upon the latter's promotion to four-star rank. Abrams said, "I am confident that I can work effectively with most associates I may have." Regarding Krulak, however, he wrote, "In my judgment, no Marine has the full professional military qualifications to satisfactorily discharge the military responsibilities of the office." Abrams let it be known that if his bosses overrode his wishes, he would go public in opposing Krulak. McNamara, about to retire, was tired of all the squabbling and gave in to the Navy. Admiral John S. McCain Jr. took over as CINCPac.

Krulak had run out of options. But it was important to him that people think he was retiring voluntarily and not being pushed aside. He wrote a letter saying that he would retire because "it does the Marines no favor to stay around and impede the promotion of some deserving man."

Amy put away the four-star insignia.

But Brute was not yet ready to go over the side. On May 13, the *New York Times*, in a front-page story, reported on what it called Krulak's "secret valedictory" speech at Quantico to ranking officers and the students of all the Marine schools. Krulak gave one of his finest performances. There is some evidence that Chapman knew in advance what Krulak would say and was not enamored of the idea, but rarely will a Commandant deny a retiring three-star general his last wish. Without benefit of notes, Krulak told some four hundred Marines, sprinkled with a few Army officers, to stand up to Army critics and extol the proud Marine record of Vietnam. The *Times* described Krulak as "one of the military's leading strategic planners and counterinsurgency experts," who was being forced into retirement. Krulak warned the Marines that when the war in Vietnam was over, the Marine Corps might once again be forced to fight for its survival, and "our postwar survival may well turn on our ability to articulate our contribution." He told the audience that he had sent to Quantico some 1,080 reports, some 20,000 pages of history, about the Marines in Vietnam, and it was all there for the Marines to study. He spoke for more than an hour in what the *Times* called "unusually candid terms about interservice struggles."

The Marines in attendance knew that Brute had confronted LBJ and had been denied the job of Commandant. They knew that this was the last active-duty appearance of this legendary general of Marines, and the applause was thunderous and prolonged.

The *New York Times* followed up with a piece on May 19, saying that Krulak, who was "widely regarded as the Marines' 'thinking general,'" was warning that the Marines were in another fight for their survival, that the Army was criticizing the Marines' performance and capabilities in Vietnam and the Air Force was still seeking to take over command of Marine air wings.

ON May 28, Chapman wrote a notice to all Marines: "This week the active list of the U.S. Marines loses one of its very finest."

A few days later, Krulak received his last FitRep. Signed by Admiral John Hyland, Brute's Naval Academy classmate, the FitRep was exemplary in all categories including personal appearance and military presence. It said that Krulak was "the single most accomplished and capable Marine" Hyland had ever known.

Krulak had a retirement ceremony at Kaneohe Bay and later an elaborate parade at Camp Pendleton. At the latter, for the first time in history, all of the major Marine Corps commands on the West Coast joined together for a retirement parade. It was a grand pageant for a storied general.

CREIGHTON Abrams had decided even before he took over from Westmoreland that he would change the military direction in Vietnam. Rather than a search-and-destroy policy throughout the country, he would conduct what he called a "seize-and-hold" policy along the littoral. It was a modified version of CAP, although he did not call it that. But, then, it is the historical pattern of the Army that when it jumps on a Marine lily pad, it always changes the name of the pad.

Brute Krulak had been right all along.

# Epilogue

AFTER a military man retires, there is often little of significance to add to his story. Grandchildren and hobbies, that's about it.

But Brute Krulak was a proud man who would not be denied his place in history; he would "not go gentle into that good night." He had left his mark on the Marine Corps, and in the forty years he lived after retirement, he would leave his mark as a father, a writer, and a leader in civic affairs.

When a career military man retires, home is wherever he wants it to be, often a town with a large military presence. For Brute Krulak, home became his beloved San Diego. The retirement pay of a three-star general enables a couple to live comfortably, and in a few more years, Amy would inherit a not inconsiderable amount of money from her family. Nevertheless, Brute went to work for his old friend James Copley as president of Copley News Service — the man in charge of Copley's news bureaus around the world.

Copley News Service was a most curious business: a collecting pot — some at the *San Diego Union* said "dumping ground" — for Copley's reporter friends (the old, tired, and alcoholic), and a surprising number of former military people, mostly in foreign bureaus. The news service lost money for years, but it was a pet project of Copley's and he owned the business, so that was that.

Krulak wrote columns under his own name and, when he wanted to distance himself from the topic, as John J. O'Malley. The charade was unnecessary, as he told everyone he was O'Malley, an example of how Krulak's desire for recognition was still a driving imperative in his life.

Five women were in Copley's executive secretarial pool. The youngest was Judy Moore, a wife and mother going to school at night to learn shorthand. She knew nothing of Krulak's background, only that he walked the halls with purpose and determination. She was more than a little intimidated by his unsmiling face, and the first time Krulak called her in to take a letter, she confessed that her skills were minimal.

"I'll dictate short letters," he said. And he did, building her skills and confidence, until she became proficient. Thus began a relationship that would last forty years. Judy became Brute's secretary and later, after he retired from Copley, his personal assistant, aide, confidante, and friend. For Judy, who had never known her own father, Brute became a father figure.

Brute and Amy bought a home in Point Loma, high on a hill and with a splendid view of the Pacific. They entertained often and lavishly, and at Brute's birthday parties, the Fish House Punch still left attendees reeling.

Brute's mother had remarried — to an Episcopalian — and had left Denver for Phoenix without saying goodbye to her relatives. After her second husband died, she settled in an upscale retirement home in La Jolla, California, and fussed over Brute as if he were still a boy. They were so close that when Bess called Brute at work, the two talked for hours. She still made kiffles for him every Christmas.

Krulak joined the boards of the San Diego County Council of

Boy Scouts and the San Diego Zoo. As with every organization he joined, he became the leader of both. He told various newspaper reporters that he considered San Diego home; after all, his family had lived in San Diego when he was in elementary school.

For her part, Amy joined the board of the San Diego Civic Light Opera, twice serving as president, and became an effective fund-raiser for the Combined Arts and Education Council of San Diego County and the San Diego Symphony. She taught the hula and rarely missed an opportunity to dance in public, getting up from the table, bending her knees, telling the story with her hands, smiling and swaying in that most alluring of dances, as Brute looked on, smiling indulgently.

At one of Brute's parties, Amy was wearing a fashionable pant-suit, the tunic of which fell midway between her hips and knees. When her favorite Hawaiian song, "To You Sweetheart, Aloha," began playing, she began a solo version of the hula. When her long pants became too restrictive, she took them off. Krulak watched in forced amusement, but were it not for the loud music, those in attendance might have heard the grinding of his molars.

In the years after his retirement, a number of writers came to Krulak, drawn by the rich fabric of his life, wanting to write his biography. He turned them all away with the same comment: "I don't like these womb-to-tomb biographies."

Krulak was invited to join San Francisco's Bohemian Club, a group originally founded by artists and writers, but later an organization before which the highest officials in state and national government gave off-the-record speeches. The club was divided into various "camps," which met occasionally for elaborate dinners. Brute was in the Owl's Nest, where one of his camp mates was Ronald Reagan. The two men were soon on a first-name basis.

\* \* \*

In 1976, Brute's mother died and left him a generous inheritance. He put it thusly: "All my life, I worked hard, and then my mother died and left me a million dollars."

In 1977, a story appeared in a national magazine saying that Copley News Service was a virtual subsidiary of the CIA and the agency planted stories with Copley, knowing other news services would pick them up. Further, the CIA gave Copley major stories, one of which earned the reporter a Pulitzer Prize. Krulak, according to the article, was the spymaster of this group.

Krulak had resigned from Copley about a month before the article was published. He said there was no connection between the story and his retirement, and he continued to write columns for Copley. He was prolific and conservative, receiving numerous Freedom Foundation awards for his writing.

The Army, Air Force, and Navy could not hold back the tide forever, and in 1979 General Louis H. Wilson became the first Commandant of the Marine Corps to have an authorized seat on the Joint Chiefs of Staff. In no small degree, it was Brute Krulak's postwar work that had laid the foundation for the Commandant to become a full member of the Joint Chiefs.

In the early 1980s, Krulak began writing *First to Fight*, a combination memoir and history of the Marine Corps. For more than a year, he worked out of an office at MCRD only a few steps down the hall from the office of the commanding general. Judy Moore arrived at the office every morning to take dictation. She typed the manuscript, Brute edited it, she retyped it, Brute reedited it... The process seemed endless to Judy. But the book was published in 1984 and, within the Marine Corps, was considered an instant classic. The combination of Brute being present at so many important events during the tumultuous middle years of the twentieth century and a felicitous writing style made the book a compelling read. As is the nature of such sharply focused military books, sales were modest but consistent, and those who read the book never forgot it.

Krulak next attempted to write a book he called "Tidewater Warrior," a biography of his old mentor Lemuel Shepherd. He sent the manuscript to Marine Corps historian Allan Millett, who said, in effect, that the effort was too much of a hagiography to be published. In an effort to discover a few minor vices that would humanize Shepherd, Krulak wrote to Shepherd's son for help. The son replied that his father had two serious vices: he used the word "nigger" frequently, and he was loyal to an extreme.

Few had benefited from Shepherd's loyalty more than Krulak, and he was too loyal to write of Shepherd's first vice. The project was dropped.

By the late 1980s, Brute's birthday parties had moved from his garden to the officers' club at MCRD, then, because many people their age could not drive at night, the Krulaks began having the parties at noon. The Fish House Punch was not as stout as in the old days, and people drank far less.

By now Brute's sons were middle-aged men.

In 1990, Vic retired from the Navy as a commander, a Navy rank equivalent to lieutenant colonel in the Marine Corps. It had not helped his career that he had spent most of his assignments—twenty-one of twenty-five years—with Marine units. He bought a small condominium in Point Loma, only a few blocks from his parents. He never married, saying that he had spent his career as a chaplain and when he retired, there were no women of a certain age who were available.

Vic became an assistant pastor for several Episcopal churches and often was called upon to officiate at the funerals of Marines. A talented Marine Corps historian, he began sending out occasional e-mails on matters of interest to Marines. Chuck and Bill say that Vic is "the best Marine in the family."

Vic remembers well the admonitions he received as a boy. Any gift or favor to him quickly resulted in a thank-you note, always on off-white paper and always written in black ink. And because Vic could never please his father, few people can please Vic, in either his work or personal life, and he can be harsh in his criticism. Although he went his own way, he is still and forever Brute's son.

BILL would have stayed in the family business, but he resigned from the Marine Corps after fifteen years at the request of his wife. He then joined the reserves and rose to the rank of colonel. He has a son named after him and a daughter named after his mother.

Brute's second son continued to be haunted by his experience in Vietnam — by the fact that he had survived the war only because of a mine with a faulty fuse. Why had his life been spared? The question became almost an obsession.

Bill went into real estate development, made a fortune, lost it, and found himself heavily in debt to the Internal Revenue Service. He asked his father for a loan, but Brute refused, saying that he and Amy had no more money coming in, that the money on hand was all the money there was, and that "I have to save that for your mother." Bill had some resentment toward his father about this, saying, "At the time, he was worth about five million dollars" (a combination of Amy's inheritance, the money from Bess, and wise investments).

When Bill emerged from his financial difficulties, still thinking about the mine in Vietnam, he decided that God had a special plan for him: he wanted Bill to be an Episcopalian priest. So in 1988, when he was forty-seven years old, Bill entered divinity school. He worked his way through school, making ten dollars an hour as a gardener, was ordained in 1991, and moved to his first church near Charlottesville, Virginia.

Vic thought of his younger brother as an interloper in the God business, but Bill had finally found what he'd been looking for.

Chuck, the youngest son, was, in both looks and style, most like his father. He stayed in the Marine Corps and in the summer of 1989 pinned on his first star. When he was introduced at a meeting of the Marine Corps Association as "General Krulak," a crusty retiree stood up and shouted, "He ain't the *real* General Krulak."

Chuck's story deserves elaboration because of the track his career was about to take. In the summer of 1991, he returned from Operation Desert Storm with a reputation as a logistical wizard. That reputation flowed in part from what was called the "miracle in the desert."

When the U.S. Marine Corps decided to attack Kuwait on two axes, Krulak moved the Marines' major supply base from Kirbrit to Khanjar. The division needed 100,000 gallons of water per day, and it was Krulak's job to find it—a difficult task, as even the oil company, Saudi Aramco, knew of no wells in the area. Local maps, nomadic tribes, and historical documents all indicated that there was no water near Khanjar.

Two days before the Marines launched their attack, Chuck was summoned from church and driven to a place on the road to the Kuwait border, a place he and hundreds of other Marines had passed numerous times in recent days. Out in plain sight, newly painted, was what he describes as a "cross-shaped pipe" towering above the ground. At the base of the pipe was a pump, a diesel engine to run the pump, and a 500-gallon container of diesel fuel. Chuck pressed the switch on the engine, and the pump began spewing out water...at the rate of 100,000 gallons per day.

Chuck says that there is no "official" explanation for the well. The maps could have been wrong. Aramco may have installed the well and forgotten about it. But why did the nomadic tribes not know of the well? And who painted it? And why didn't the Marines see it when they constructed the nearby road and drove up and down that road for several weeks?

"There is only one real explanation, but it requires faith," Chuck says.

In the fall of 1991, and in keeping with an executive order issued by President George H. W. Bush, the military services were directed to cut their manpower levels—the Marine Corps from 177,000 to 159,100. If followed, the order would mean that most Marines would be withdrawn from Hawaii and the western Pacific, and shipboard deployments, the heart of the Marine Corps, would be cut back.

The Marine Corps, as it had done back in the 1940s with President Truman, went over Bush's head and appealed to Congress. Chuck Krulak was the point man for this effort. He told Congress that the Marine Corps needed to stay at 177,000 in order to be "ready, relevant, and capable" to meet national military needs. Krulak and the young lieutenant colonels who worked for him— some called them the Chowder Society II—were successful in maintaining their manpower even as every other branch of the military was forced to cut its strength. Congress once again came to the aid of the Marine Corps.

That winter, Chuck Krulak was selected to become a two-star general, a promotion that would not take effect for several months. In the spring of 1992, before he received his first paycheck as a two-star, he was nominated for his third star. For the first time in the history of the Marine Corps, a father and son were both three-star generals. The three stars Chuck pinned on belonged to his father. Later, Chuck became CGFMFPac, again the first time in Marine Corps history that a father and son had held the same major command. In Hawaii, Chuck relieved Lieutenant General

# Epilogue

Henry "Hank" Stackpole, whose life Chaplain Vic Krulak had saved in Vietnam.

SOMETIME in the 1990s, Bill became interested in genealogy and wanted to learn more about his father's family. On a trip to California, he brought up the subject with his father, who looked him in the eye and with a voice of absolute assurance said, "We are Moravians. The Krulaks were all Moravians."

As a theologian, Bill knew that the Moravian Church—or, to use its formal name, the Unitas Fratrum—had been formed in what is now the Czech Republic in 1457 and was one of the first Protestant denominations. But there was nothing in Bill's genealogical research about this obscure Christian sect, and he was so astonished that he could only look at his father in amazement and say, "Dad! The Moravians?"

The Brute was adamant: until he became an Episcopalian, the Krulaks had all been Moravians.

IN 1995, Chuck became the thirty-first Commandant of the Marine Corps. At a ceremony in the Oval Office, President Bill Clinton, about to pin the new four-star rank on Chuck, looked around the room and asked who had the general's new set of stars. Chuck's wife, Zandra, stepped forward and said, "I do."

Then Amy moved in front of Zandra and said, "No, I do," and handed Clinton the set of stars she had bought for Brute almost thirty years earlier.

This was a moment of great emotion for Amy. She was standing in the same office from which her husband had been physically ejected by an angry president, and now she was here with her son, who had been personally congratulated by Clinton. It was in the Oval Office that Brute had effectively ended his career. Now, in that office, Chuck was about to assume a rank and a job that meant he had reached the highest peak of his profession.

Not long afterward, Norwood Grinalds, wife of John Grinalds, who had been Krulak's aide in Hawaii, visited Brute and Amy. Norwood ventured that if Amy had a choice as to whether her son or her husband became Commandant, it was good that her son had been chosen.

"No, it should have been Brute," Amy said, and she said it with such passion that Norwood stepped away.

Brute became his son's most trusted adviser. He and Chuck talked almost daily, and Chuck says that the best advice his father gave him was to make whatever big changes he envisioned during his first year of his Commandancy, because he would need the remaining three years of his term to institutionalize those changes.

In 1999, at the end of his term as Commandant, Chuck retired, and for the first time in sixty-five years, there was no Krulak in the Marine Corps. Chuck is, of course, sensitive to how history views his four years in office. But the only assessment of those years that really matters to him is that of his father, who wrote to him, "The greatest contribution you have made, the best and the most valuable by far, is not even visible. Call it what you will—honesty, truthfulness, character, morality, reliability, integrity, dependability. Any one will do. In each and every case, it creates respect, and not just for you, but for the entire Marine Corps. That is one hell of a legacy to leave."

Today, more than a decade later, Chuck's contributions to the Marine Corps are considered both significant and lasting. He developed the "three-block war," the idea that in the space of three urban blocks, a Marine might be involved in full-scale military operations, peacekeeping, and humanitarian efforts. Another legacy of his is the "strategic corporal," the enlisted man whose decisions in combat could affect America at a strategic level.

At a time when the other services were relaxing their recruiting standards, Chuck not only toughened those in the Marine Corps but also instituted "the Crucible," the most radical and significant innovation in recruit training in a century. Coming at the end of the training cycle, the Crucible is fifty-four hours of food and sleep deprivation and is built on the idea that Marines do not succeed without teamwork.

Another part of Chuck Krulak's legacy draws mixed reviews among Marines. In 1977, he was "born again" and left the Episcopal Church "for a church that feeds me and my wife." He says that he favors sermons that come directly from the Bible rather than from the Book of Common Prayer. He and Zandi have attended a variety of churches, including Calvary Chapel, which believes in "the inerrancy of the Bible," and the Church of the Nazarene, a fundamentalist church. As Commandant, Chuck had a sign on his desk that said INTEGRITY, which no one quarreled with. But a number of officers did quarrel with his idea of having a chaplain lead a daily 7:15 a.m. "devotional" in his office. Even though the devotional was voluntary, some Marines felt that because it was held in Chuck's office, attendance was mandatory.

During his Commandancy, Chuck called three generals into his office, said it was known that they were having affairs with their secretaries, and gave them the choice of early retirement or court-martial. They elected to retire. Some officers also contend that Chuck "demonized alcohol" and destroyed the traditional camaraderie of happy hour at officers' clubs.

All this causes some Marine officers to see Chuck as narrow, prudish, and judgmental, a verdict that tends to upset his equanimity.

As the decade of the 1990s drew to a close, it was clear that Amy and Brute were aging. They were no longer able to maintain the grounds of their home at Point Loma and did not seem to care whether anyone else did. Amy ruined a beautiful desk that had belonged to her grandfather by leaving flowerpots atop it, and she began showing signs of what would later be diagnosed as Alzheimer's disease.

Often at a party, she would smile and greet people warmly, then turn to Brute and ask, "Who was that?" She also would drive off on errands and get lost in the town she had known for decades.

In the fall of 2000, Brute and Amy sold the Point Loma house for $750,000 (making a substantial profit) and moved into a $6,000 per month one-bedroom cottage at Wesley Palms, an assisted-living facility that their son Bill had found for them. The cottage sat atop a high ridge, had a magnificent view of the Pacific, and was only ten minutes east of downtown San Diego.

The last years at Point Loma and the first months at Wesley Palms were not happy ones for Brute. But counterbalancing this unhappiness was the satisfaction of seeing some of his ideas, particularly those about the Vietnam War, become more widely held. Lieutenant Colonel Michael Norton, an Army infantry officer and a student at the National War College, wrote a paper titled "Operational Leadership in Vietnam: General William Depuy vs. Lieutenant General Krulak, or Attrition vice Pacification." Norton showed that he was not hobbled by institutional bias when he concluded that "Krulak's methods offer a higher probability of success." Norton said that operational leaders must recognize the kind of fight they are in and must see the road to victory. "Krulak's vision was clearer than Depuy's in these two functions," he wrote.

In 1998, Krulak was inducted into the Navy's Acquisition Hall of Fame for his work in developing landing boats during World War II. A few years later, he was recognized as a "distinguished alumnus" of the Naval Academy. But the Marine Corps never officially recognized Krulak. Other officers have statues, awards, writing contests, buildings, parade decks, or other honors in their names, but there is nothing for Brute Krulak.

By 2003, the once vivacious and independent Amy Krulak was showing more signs of Alzheimer's disease. She would lock her keys inside her car with the engine running. She could not remember whether she had fed the family dachshund and thus overfed the dog, causing it to die of obesity. Day after day, she wore the same red jacket, causing Vic to say to his father, "She looks like a bag lady." Vic was so critical of his mother that eventually she would not let him drive her on errands.

Brute was bewildered by Amy's behavior. "She went through her whole life doing exactly as I asked her to do," he said. "In her final years, it was the reverse. If I asked her to do A, she would do B." But it was Vic, not Brute, who made all the decisions regarding Amy's care. On the evening of January 9, 2004, the director at the hospice where Amy was a patient called Vic to tell him that his mother had died. "Do you and your father want to come out and see her one more time?" the director asked. Vic called his father, who said yes, but when Vic arrived, Brute had changed his mind. "I don't want to go out there and see her dead," he said. "I want to remember her alive."

Vic conducted his mother's funeral. At the service, Brute stood up and recited "To You Sweetheart, Aloha," the last two lines of which are:

We two will meet again
Until then, sweetheart, aloha

A few days later, Brute and Vic were talking about Amy's last days, about how Vic had spent long hours with his mother at the hospice facility and been strong enough to conduct his mother's funeral. Brute said, "I could not do what you did. I admire you."

It was the only time in Vic's life that he remembers his father saying such a flattering thing to him.

BECAUSE the Krulak name is forever linked to the Marine Corps, we must take a look at how the Marines are doing today. In 2004,

335

the Marines were ordered to the most dangerous place in Iraq: Anbar Province. During the assault on Fallujah, Marine commanders intercepted an enemy radio conversation and heard an insurgent say, "We are fighting, but the Marines keep coming. We are shooting, but the Marines won't stop."

Lieutenant Donovan Campbell was a platoon leader in Iraq. His platoon fought long and bitter firefights in Anbar Province, a place written off as lost until the Marines tamed it. In his book *Joker One*, Campbell tells how after the platoon's first prolonged engagement, one of his Marines came up to him and said, "Sir, do you think we fought well today, sir? I mean, that was our first big fight. Would the Marines who fought at Iwo Jima and Okinawa, you know, be proud of us?"

Campbell had to turn away and compose himself before he answered that the Marines had indeed acquitted themselves well. And as time passes, the battle for Fallujah, some of the bloodiest door-to-door fighting in history, will rank among the great battles of the Marine Corps.

Michael Yon, a former special forces soldier who runs a highly respected blog from Iraq and Afghanistan, has pointed out that when the Army went into Afghanistan in 2001, it first sent in those who could build protective barriers and infrastructure. When the soldiers arrived, they settled into a place of relative comfort. But the Marines simply arrived at some remote place and set up camp. The infrastructure came later, sometimes much later. When Yon asked a young Marine what it was like to live three months in squalor and without having a shower, the man responded, "Living the dream, sir. Living the dream."

Amy's death marked the beginning of Brute's rapid decline. He would be driving his gray Mercedes and pause, or even stop in the middle of the road, to get his bearings. He did not understand the gestures being made by other drivers until Vic said to him, "Those people are not telling you that you are number one."

Brute relied heavily on Vic, but he still treated his firstborn son in a peremptory fashion. One day he called Vic and, as was his fashion, said, "I need to see you."

"What about?" Vic asked.

"I'll tell you when you get here," Brute said as he hung up.

When Vic arrived, his father pointed to a box of candy on the bookshelf and said, "I want you to take that box of candy down to the front desk and have them pass it out." Vic later called Chuck and said, "Today, you almost became an orphan."

Another time, Vic was driving his father to dinner when Brute reached out to turn down the air conditioner. "Leave it alone," Vic said, slapping his father's hand. Brute slapped back and continued to adjust the controls. Down the expressway they went, slapping each other's hands like young boys.

In 2005, General Peter Pace became the first Marine general to serve as chairman of the Joint Chiefs of Staff. It was Brute Krulak's efforts in the mid-1940s that led to this grand moment, a time when the Marine Corps stepped out from the shadow of the other services.

In 2006, Brute began polling family members to determine what items from his house they might want. All Vic wanted was his father's Annapolis ring.

"Well, you're not getting it until I'm dead."

A few days later, Brute called Vic and said, "I need to see you."

Vic knew better than to ask "What about?" and drove to his father's cottage, where Brute said to him, "I don't want some hospital orderly giving you my ring. Or losing it." He pulled the ring from his finger and handed it to his son. The ring had been smoothed by years of wear, and Brute, in banging it on his desk, had long since shattered the onyx. For a while, the setting had been sealing wax, then a melted toothbrush. But that did not matter to Vic.

"Thank you very much," Vic said as he slipped the ring on his finger. Vic had the ring resized and wore it proudly, his fingers often caressing it and turning it so the setting faced downward.

For some seventy years, Brute had twisted that ring around his own finger as a reminder of things he wanted to do, and two years after giving the ring to Vic, he called Chuck and asked if he could buy a new one. Chuck contacted Annapolis, had a special one-off duplicate made, and gave the ring to his father. But Brute did not like the new ring and called Vic to say he wanted the original one back. Vic had the ring resized again and gave it to his father. Brute said the ring no longer fit and blamed Vic for not having it resized properly. "Another example of my many shortcomings," Vic says.

In 2006, Commandant James T. Conway directed that every Marine read and discuss *First to Fight*, and in the next two years the book sold more than twenty thousand copies. Sales continue to be brisk today, according to retired Major General Thomas Wilkerson, the chief executive officer of the Naval Institute Press. Few people know that all royalties from the book go to the Marine Corps University Foundation.

Brute had been diagnosed in 2004 with normal pressure hydrocephalus (NPH), for which the classic triad of symptoms is failing memory, difficulty walking, and incontinence. In 2006, he began a physical decline. A shunt had been placed in his head to drain an overproduction of spinal fluid, but he continued to suffer from vertigo so severe that his doctor said he should not leave the house unless he used a walker or, better yet, sat in a wheelchair. "He's just a goddamned doctor," Brute said. But he did consent to use a walking stick.

The Brute's increasing frailty, combined with what his three sons had recently learned about his childhood, caused Vic and Bill to wonder whether he had ever been baptized. As Episcopalian priests, they were disturbed that their father might enter the here-after without benefit of baptism and agreed that Vic should con-duct a "conditional baptism" for Brute. A conditional baptism holds that if the person was never baptized, now he is. But if he was baptized, this one doesn't count.

Brute refused the offer, saying that he had already been bap-tized. But he did not know any of details, not even the time or place, and Vic became even more concerned about his father's spiritual welfare.

RARELY are those who live in retirement homes known as sharp dressers. But in his slacks, sports coats, and jaunty Irish driving cap, the Brute was the best-dressed man at Wesley Palms. Though stooped and frail, he was a very dapper old man, whose eyes were as bright as the morning and who retained not only his famous brilliance but also his impressive ability for extemporaneous and eloquent speech.

Millie, Brute's thirteenth dachshund, was his daily joy. Brute fed the dog every morning but would not walk her, which meant that Millie ("I named her Millie because she is one in a million") urinated and defecated on the carpet. Brute knew that Judy would arrive midmorning and clean up, but the cottage reeked of urine and feces.

Brute's home was filled with furniture from China and Oki-nawa, along with rare porcelain vases, silver, and at each end of the sofa a glass-topped case containing watches. Brute had col-lected a total of sixty watches over the years, all of them stopped and never rewound. Because the blinds stayed drawn, the bright

California sunshine and the view of the Pacific were not visible; the house was in perpetual twilight.

Each morning after breakfast, Brute returned to his cottage, frequently checking his watch and wondering why Judy had not arrived. Judy was not as concerned about time as he was, and once when she arrived at 10:31 a.m. instead of 10:30, he said, "This is the earliest you have ever been late."

Judy was indispensable to Brute during his last years. Not only did she handle his considerable correspondence, run his errands, and drive him to doctor's appointments, but every day she also cleaned up behind the dog.

Judy knew a side of the Brute that he revealed to few other people. Every year on her birthday, he called her very early in the morning—once at 4:30—so that he could be the first person to wish her happy birthday. She adored Brute, as did her daughters, and sometimes Brute was more considerate toward Judy than he was toward his sons.

Brute was at his best during the midmorning hours. He was rested, alert, and articulate. He looked forward to and knew he could depend on two things: telephone calls from retired General Thomas V. Draude, head of the Marine Corps University Foundation, and from his son Chuck. Even though Chuck was a board member of several large companies and traveled widely, Chuck called his father daily at 10 a.m. Pacific time, and the two men talked about the Marine Corps, world events, and politics.

On July 18, 2007, Secretary of Defense Robert Gates spoke at an annual dinner of the Marine Corps Association and devoted much of his speech to Lieutenant General Victor Krulak and his contributions to the Marine Corps.

In 2008, Linda Robinson published a book called *Tell Me How This Ends: General David Petraeus and the Search for a Way Out of*

*Iraq.* The book tells how Petraeus produced a new version of the Army's counterinsurgency manual in which the central theme was *political,* not military. Under his orders, villages, towns, and cities were cleansed of insurgents and then turned over to Iraqi government forces. Petraeus believed that understanding local citizens and being empathetic toward their needs was crucial in a counter-insurgency. A flattering review by James Traub in the *New York Times* said that Petraeus was right and that America owed him a debt of gratitude. A more nuanced review would have noted that the ideological roots of Petraeus's manual could be found in the Marine Corps during the Vietnam War.

DURING one of my last sessions with the Brute, I asked if he had any regrets about his life. It was a foolish question, because the Brute never had regrets about anything. He smiled indulgently and said, "I had a regret once." He paused. "But then it disappeared."

Then he grew pensive and surprised me. "My regret is that I did not become Commandant. I regret that I was not promoted to four stars. I knew it came from the disagreement between LBJ and me."

A few days before the 2008 Marine Corps Birthday Ball, the commanding general at MCRD held a cake-cutting ceremony. This was Brute Krulak's last public appearance. He was surrounded by his beloved Marines, and he drew strength from them, but attending the event depleted his last reserves. He went home and stayed in bed for several days.

Brute knew he was near death. His hearing aid no longer worked, and he was, for all practical purposes, deaf, a malady he found immensely frustrating. He was so wobbly that as he walked about his cottage, he put a hand on every available piece of furniture for support. He had what appeared to be a small stroke but which he described as a cold. He had a caregiver with him twenty-four hours a day and slept much of the time. When he was awake, he was still in charge, griping that Vic "is just dying to be the boss."

Bill and Chuck made what they knew would be their last visit to their father. He told them that he loved them, the first time he had ever done so. And he told them that he had decided that Vic was "not so bad."

Every day when Judy left Brute's cottage, he told her goodbye and thanked her for being his strong right hand over the past forty years. "Time is short and growing shorter," he told her. "One day I am going to jump up and die."

Even though he knew he was in his final days, Brute did not vary his morning schedule. He arose at 5 a.m. and sat in his big chair—the one he had commissioned in China in 1937; put his feet on the small circular rug with the Marine Corps emblem—also commissioned in China; and watched television for a half hour. Then he showered, shaved, and dressed before calling the front desk and saying, "I need a ride." A moment later, an attendant driving a golf cart was at his front door. Even though he walked into the dining room with the frail, stiff, wide-legged stance of the elderly and physically unstable, a cloud of dignity surrounded him. People murmured, "There's the general."

After breakfast, he returned to his big chair to wait for Judy. The phone rang occasionally; sometimes Marines he had served with in the Pacific were on the line. Marines writing books about helicopters or landing craft would occasionally call, the awe and reverence palpable in their voices. They found that the Brute remained mentally alert and had phenomenal recall about most things. His conversation was elaborate and punctuated with flourishes, but if a questioner presumed too much, his eyes would turn hard and he would snap, "I don't remember," and that was the end of that. If the questioner brought up the name of a person he did not like, Krulak would not speak the person's name and would refer to him only as "that person."

On most days, the time between breakfast and Judy's arrival was a time of reverie, and in his reverie the Brute always returned to Choiseul: he was with his Marines, surrounded by superior forces, raising hell as only Marines can do.

In October 2008, Brute's caregiver called Judy and Vic and said that he wanted to issue last-minute instructions. When Judy and Vic arrived, Brute was confused, impatient, and rambling; they called 911 to have him taken to the hospital. The EMT who arrived stuck his baby face close to Brute's and in a perky voice asked, "And what have you been doing today?"

For a split second, he was the Brute of legend. He glared at the EMT and said, "Just fucking around."

Brute returned home, but on the evening of December 29, he and Vic got into some sort of disagreement that ended when Vic said, "You are no longer in charge," and called for an ambulance to take his father to the hospital. At the hospital, Brute slipped into unconsciousness, and Vic administered a conditional baptism.

That night, nine days short of his ninety-sixth birthday, Brute Krulak died of respiratory failure.

A few days later, the *Wall Street Journal* and the *New York Times* ran half-page obituaries of the storied general.

The chapel at Marine Corps Air Station Miramar was selected for the January 8 funeral. The burial of such an important figure as Brute Krulak is no small matter and must be done in the proper fashion. The day before the funeral, a practice funeral was held. Observing was the newly arrived senior chaplain at Miramar, who asked, "Is it true that Father Krulak is conducting the service?"

Assured that this was the case, he shook his head in awe and said, "He is a legend in the chaplain corps. I worked for General Stackpole once, and he had a special place in his heart for chaplains. Something to do with Vietnam, I think."

The Marine platoon that would serve as the honor guard was practicing in front of the chapel when Chuck walked among them, called them close, and told them that on the morrow, they would be participating "in the funeral of a legend." He exhorted them to turn in a stellar performance, "not because I was Commandant," he said, but because "you are a participant in history. Do it for my father, because fifteen years from now, you'll be proud to say 'I was there.'"

Some five hundred people, many of them active-duty Marines, attended the funeral. A bus full of people from Wesley Palms was there, and the board of the San Diego Zoo was represented. Vic led the traditional Episcopalian Requiem Eucharist and controlled his emotions until the end of his homily, when he gripped the lectern tightly and said that the Marines who guard the streets of heaven "had best be squared away."

The next night, the Krulaks, the Hogabooms, and a few friends repaired to Point Loma for a last meal at Tio Carlos, Brute's favorite restaurant. During the evening, Vic stood up and, with a pleased smile, announced that he was now the patriarch of the Krulak family.

BRUTE'S estate was valued at almost $4 million. Over the years, he had amended his will to increase the amount he left to Judy, and when it reached $750,000 and included his Mercedes, his lawyer advised him to call his sons to tell them the money was for Judy's years of faithful service and that he wanted no disagreement. Each of the boys received about $1 million.

CHUCK earlier thought that his father would be buried at Arlington National Cemetery and had made plans to carry Brute's body across the country. But a few days before he died, the Brute announced that he wanted to be buried at Fort Rosecrans National Cemetery, near San Diego. "I have a civic responsibility to the people of San Diego," he said.

It was not until several days later that Ronnie Zall, now a retired lawyer and prominent figure in Denver, heard of Brute's death. He sent warm e-mails to Vic, Bill, and Chuck, saying that the family had once been close but that after Bess died, "the chain was broken." He said that he had reached out to Brute on a number of occasions, but to no avail, and he asked if the family could reunite, saying, "Cousins raised in different religions can always have a good relationship."

Bill and Chuck were gracious in their responses, and Chuck later agreed to go to the University of Denver to speak to a large crowd at an event sponsored in part by Zall. Vic said that he never received the e-mail.

In addition to a substantial amount of money, Brute Krulak also left scars on his sons that they will carry to the grave. If, as Chuck once said, his father steered by the stars, it could have been because the wake was so turbulent.

After retirement, Chuck was a bank executive in Europe and was financially comfortable. Vic and Bill were not. Now they were millionaires, in part as a result of money that had come from the Jewish side of the family, the family with which their father had severed all ties decades earlier.

When the Brute died, his sons were of late middle age and, one might reasonably think, men who could control their emotions. But a life without the monumental presence of the Brute suddenly seemed much emptier to his sons.

The passing of Bill's wife in 2007 had caused him to seek professional help. Now, less than a year later, he had an increased desire for counseling. The therapist told Bill that his entire life, and the lives of his brothers, had been about seeking affirmation from their father. Chuck had found that affirmation by becoming a general officer in, and then the Commandant of, the Marine Corps. But Bill and Vic had never received such affirmation. The counselor pointed out to Bill that an Episcopalian priest is looked up to by his flock, admired, respected, and called "father."

"Nick and I were looking for that," Bill said.

Unlike his younger brothers, Vic could not talk about his father's death. "It is too early," he said. But in some ways, he was affected at the most primal level. He believed that he had failed his father from the very beginning, that his inadequacies were legion, and that even though his brothers described him as "the best Marine in the family," he never really was a member of the family business.

At the end, we must return to the Marine Corps. No father-son in history have had more influence on the Corps than Brute and Chuck Krulak. Their influence covered much of the twentieth century, and the changes they implemented are still felt across the Corps. In addition, both foiled attempts to diminish the Corps.

Only a few Marine generals have the honor of being known as "Giants of the Corps." It does not diminish the lives of any of those generals to say that their accomplishments pale beside those of Brute Krulak, who, for one simple reason, was the most important officer in the history of the Marine Corps: Krulak's work benefited America, while the work of those other generals benefited the Marine Corps or, in some instances, the U.S. military.

Brute Krulak was a hinge of history, a hard man who could make hard decisions. And that is how he should be remembered.

In 2009, when the Quadrennial Defense Review (QDR) began, the roles and missions of the Marine Corps once again became the target of budget cutters. The Army pointed out that in Iraq and Afghanistan, the Marines were engaged in prolonged land campaigns—the job of the Army—and America did not need two armies. As so often in the past, the long knives were out.

As America moves into the second decade of the twenty-first century, there will be other attempts to diminish or lessen the role and missions of the Marine Corps. Whether or not those efforts succeed will depend on two things: first, whether a Marine officer steps forward to take over where the Krulaks left off, and second, whether the Marine Corps continues, in Brute Krulak's words, to meet "the high—almost spiritual—standards" of the American people.

## ACKNOWLEDGMENTS AND COMMENTS

First among those to whom I owe thanks is Paul K. Graham, a genealogist par excellence. Next is another genealogist, Sharon Lass Field, in Cheyenne, Wyoming, who also did splendid work.

Researcher Kristin Wohlleben has the intuitive gift of knowing how to broaden and deepen a search while staying on point. She saved me a full year of research. Dr. MariaChristina Mairena found valuable materials at the National Archives and Library of Congress.

Jon Hoffman, one of the Marine Corps's most prominent historians, took time to read the manuscript and offer invaluable comments. Dr. Fred Allison of the Marine Corps History Center provided helpful direction. Retired Marine Corps colonels John Keenan and Walt Ford, editors of the *Marine Corps Gazette* and *Leatherneck*, respectively, read the manuscript and offered corrections that only salty editors would catch.

In Hawaii, Chuck Little at Camp Smith provided crucial historical details, and Glen Butler at Kaneohe Bay, who is writing a book about HMX-1, guided me through Brute Krulak's early involvement with helicopters. Colonel Gerry Glavy and Major Doug Ogden gave me the tour of HMX-1 and the presidential helicopter, a tour granted to few people who do not hold "Yankee White Access." Larry Taylor provided an exegesis of Marine Corps records. Jeff Roberts of the *Denver Post* was of much help. Dr. Jennifer Bryan, of the Nimitz Library at the U.S. Naval Academy, and Ellen Guillemette, of the Command Museum at the Marine Corps Recruit Depot in San Diego, found and explained arcane data. Norm Hatch, who did most of the production work on *Bombs over Tokyo*, remains deeply committed to that important documentary. In New Orleans, Jerry Strahan, the biographer of Andrew Jackson Higgins, was generous in the extreme with his time. G. I. Wilson, a retired colonel of Marines, showed me the way. And J. B. Coram, my brother and a great Marine, told me how this book should end.

## Acknowledgments and Comments

I owe a particular debt to Chuck Krulak, whose patience during the past three years has been exemplary.

My deepest gratitude goes to my wife, Jeannine Addams. I could not have done what I have done without her.

RESEARCH uncovered a dimension of the U.S. Army that was neither planned nor expected. My father spent thirty-three years in the Army, and I know that the Army I found is not the Army in which he served, but rather the "Big Army," or the institutional Army.

Few things have been written about as much as the wars in which Victor "Brute" Krulak participated: World War II, the Korean War, and the Vietnam War. To read every report, article, or book on those topics would be impossible. Thus military historians may find their favorite sources absent here. My goal was not to retell the stories of these American wars, but to tell the parts of those stories relevant to the life of General Krulak.

Some aspects of Brute Krulak's early years are disturbing. I elected to take an explanatory stance toward those years. Some will say I should have replaced the frail reed of sympathy with the righteous sword of judgment. But my sins as a young man were scarlet, and they were many. I do not consider those green actions the defining moments of my life, and if am to be measured, let it be by the deeds of my later years. Here I afforded Brute Krulak what I would ask for myself.

Finally, a word about the United States Marine Corps. Marines are proud warriors and acutely aware of their heritage of valor and their unique ethos. To them, the world is divided into Marines and non-Marines. More than once I was asked, "How can you write about the Marine Corps when you were not a Marine?"

This book is my answer.

Robert Coram
Moonpie Studio
Harris Neck, Georgia
2010

# Partial Bibliography

Abrams, Jeanne E. *Jewish Women Pioneering the Frontier Trail*. New York: New York University Press, 2006.

Alexander, Joseph H. "Bloody Tarawa." *Naval History*, November/December 1993.

———. *The Final Campaign: Marines in the Victory on Okinawa*. Washington, DC: U.S. Marine Corps, History and Museums Division, 1996.

———. "The U.S. Marines in World War I." *Leatherneck*, November 2008.

———. *Utmost Savagery: The Three Days of Tarawa*. Annapolis, MD: Naval Institute Press, 1995.

Asprey, Robert B. *At Belleau Wood*. Denton: University of North Texas Press, 1996.

Axelrod, Alan. *Miracle at Belleau Wood: The Birth of the Modern U.S. Marine Corps*. Guilford, CT: Lyons Press, 2007.

Baldwin, Neil. *Henry Ford and the Jews: The Mass Production of Hate*. New York: Public Affairs, 2001.

Ballendorf, Dirk A., and Merrill L. Bartlett. *Pete Ellis: An Amphibious Warfare Prophet, 1880–1923*. Annapolis, MD: Naval Institute Press, 1997.

Ballentine, David A. *Gunbird Driver: A Marine Huey Pilot's War in Vietnam*. Annapolis, MD: Naval Institute Press, 2008.

Beauchamp, Bill R. "The Challenge of the Post–World War II Era: The Marine Corps, 1945–1957." War in the Modern Era Seminar, Marine Corps Command and Staff College, Quantico, VA, 1989.

Bergerud, Eric. *Touched with Fire: The Land War in the South Pacific*. New York: Penguin, 1996.

Browning, Robert M., Jr. "Semper Paratus: Douglas Munro." *Naval History*, Winter 1992.

"The Brute & Co." *Time*, November 22, 1943.

Camp, Dick. *Leatherneck Legends: Conversations with the Marine Corps' Old Breed*. St. Paul: Zenith Press, 2006.

# Partial Bibliography

Capron, Walter C. "An Amphibious Role for the Coast Guard." *Naval History*, Winter 1989.

Catlin, A. W. *With the Help of God and a Few Marines*. Nashville: Battery Press, 2004.

Chang, Iris. *The Rape of Nanking*. New York: Penguin, 1998.

Chapin, John C. *Fire Brigade: U.S. Marines in the Pusan Perimeter*. Washington, DC: U.S. Marine Corps, History and Museums Division, 2000.

————. *Top of the Ladder: Marine Operations in the Northern Solomons*. Washington, DC: U.S. Marine Corps, History and Museums Division, 1997.

Chenoweth, H. Avery. *Semper Fi: The Definitive Illustrated History of the U.S. Marines*. New York: Main Street, 2005.

Chiles, James R. *The God Machine: From Boomerangs to Black Hawks—The Story of the Helicopter*. New York: Bantam, 2007.

Chin, G. B. "China's Leader and Her Military Situation in Pre-War Days." *U.S. Naval Institute Proceedings*, October 1944.

Christ, James F. *Mission Raise Hell: The U.S. Marines on Choiseul, October–November 1943*. Annapolis, MD: Naval Institute Press, 2006.

Clark, Eugene Franklin. *The Secrets of Inchon: The Untold Story of the Most Daring Covert Mission of the Korean War*. New York: Berkley, 2002.

Clark, George B. *Treading Softly: U.S. Marines in China, 1819–1949*. Westport, CT: Praeger, 2001.

Clay, James P. "Pearl River Log: A Different Navy, A Different World." *U.S. Naval Institute Proceedings*, September 1970.

Clifford, Kenneth J. *Progress and Purpose: A Developmental History of the United States Marine Corps, 1900–1970*. Washington, DC: U.S. Marine Corps, History and Museums Division, 1973.

Coffin, C. E. Jr. "Effects of Aerial Bombardment in China." *U.S. Naval Institute Proceedings*, September 1938.

Colbourn, Colin. "Caught in the Crossfire: Marines in North China, 1945–49." *Leatherneck*, April 2008.

Cooper, Norman V. *A Fighting General: The Biography of General Holland M. "Howlin' Mad" Smith*. Quantico, VA: Marine Corps Association, 1987.

Corson, William R. *The Betrayal*. New York: Ace, 1968.

Costello, John. *The Pacific War, 1941–1945*. New York: Quill, 1982.

Croizat, Victor J. *Across the Reef: The Amphibious Tracked Vehicle at War*. London: Arms and Armour Press, 1989.

Culp, Ronald K. *The First Black United States Marines: The Men of Montford Point, 1942–1946*. Jefferson, NC: McFarland, 2007.

Davidson, Phillip B. *Vietnam at War: The History, 1946–1975*. New York: Oxford University Press, 1988.

Donovan, Robert J. *PT 109: John F. Kennedy in WWII*. New York: McGraw-Hill, 1961.

Dyer, Edward C. Oral History. Interviewed by Benis M. Frank. U.S. Marine Corps, History and Museums Division, Washington, DC, 1973.

Estes, Kenneth W. "Into the Breach: The 1st Provisional Marine Brigade Fights in the Pusan Perimeter, August–September 1950." Unpublished manuscript, 2008.

Evans, William R. *Soochow and the 4th Marines*. Rogue River, OR: Atwood, 1987.

Finney, Charles G. *The Old China Hands*. Westport, CT: Greenwood Press, 1959.

Fitzgerald, Frances. *Fire in the Lake: The Vietnamese and the Americans in Vietnam*. New York: Vintage, 1973.

Forester, C. S. *Rifleman Dodd*. Quantico, VA: Marine Corps Association, 1996.

Frank, Richard B. "The Amphibious Revolution." *U.S. Naval Institute Proceedings*, August 2005.

———. "'…Nailed the Colors to the Mast.'" *Naval History*, Winter 1992.

Franken, Daniel J. "Strike One, Task One." *Naval History*, Fall 1992.

Fussell, Paul. *The Great War and Modern Memory*. London: Oxford University Press, 1975.

Galula, David. *Counterinsurgency Warfare: Theory and Practice*. Westport, CT: Praeger Security International, 1964.

Gibbons, Floyd. *And They Thought We Wouldn't Fight*. New York: George H. Doran, 1918.

Gillum, Donald E. "Gallipoli: Its Influence on Amphibious Doctrine." *Marine Corps Gazette*, November 1967.

Griffin, W. E. B. *Semper Fi*. New York: Penguin, 1986.

Halberstam, David. *The Best and the Brightest*. New York: Ballantine, 1993.

Hanson, Victor Davis. *Carnage and Culture: Landmark Battles in the Rise of Western Power*. New York: Anchor, 2001.

———. *Ripples of Battle: How Wars of the Past Still Determine How We Fight, How We Live, and How We Think*. New York: Doubleday, 2003.

Harbord, James G. *Leaves from a War Diary*. New York: Dodd, Mead, 1925.

Hastings, Max. *Retribution: The Battle for Japan, 1944–45*. New York: Alfred A. Knopf, 2008.

Haythornthwaite, Philip J. *Gallipoli, 1915: Frontal Assault on Turkey*. New York: Osprey, 1991.

Hearn, Chester G. *The Illustrated Directory of the United States Marine Corps*. St. Paul: MBI, 2003.

Heinl, Robert Debs, Jr. "The Cat with More Than Nine Lives." *U.S. Naval Institute Proceedings*, June 1954.

———. Oral History. Interviewed by Benis M. Frank. U.S. Marine Corps, History and Museums Division, Washington, DC, 1976.

———. *Soldiers of the Sea: The United States Marine Corps, 1775–1962*. Baltimore: Nautical & Aviation, 1991.

———. *Victory at High Tide: The Inchon-Seoul Campaign*. Charleston, SC: Nautical & Aviation, 1979.

Hemingway, Al. *Our War Was Different: Marine Combined Action Platoons in Vietnam*. Annapolis, MD: Naval Institute Press, 1994.

Henderson, Charles W. *Marshalling the Faithful: The Marines' First Year in Vietnam*. New York: Berkley, 1993.

Herr, Michael. *Dispatches*. New York: Avon, 1978.

Higgins, Marguerite. *Our Vietnam Nightmare*. New York: Harper & Row, 1965.

Hoffman, Jon T. *Chesty: The Story of Lieutenant General Lewis B. Puller, USMC*. New York: Random House, 2002.

# Partial Bibliography

————. *From Makin to Bougainville: Marine Raiders in the Pacific War*. Washington, DC: U.S. Marine Corps, History and Museums Division, 1995.

————. *Once a Legend: "Red Mike" Edson of the Marine Raiders*. Novato, CA: Presidio Press, 2000.

————. "Red Mike Fights On." *Naval History*, November/December 1993.

Holwitt, Joel Ira. "The Judaic Experience at the U.S. Naval Academy." Honors thesis, U.S. Naval Academy, 2002.

Homsher, David C. "Securing the Flanks at Belleau Wood." *Marine Corps Gazette*, June 1997.

Hoy, Richard Harold. "Victor H. Krulak: A Marine's Biography." Master's thesis, San Diego State University, 1974.

Hubbard, Elbert. *A Message to Garcia*. White Plains NY: Peter Pauper Press, 1977.

Hubler, Richard G. "Mission: To Raise Hell." *Marine Corps Gazette*, March 1944.

Isely, Jeter A., and Philip A. Crowl. *The U.S. Marines and Amphibious War: Its Theory and Its Practice in the Pacific*. Princeton, NJ: Princeton University Press, 1951.

Jersey, Stanley Coleman. *Hell's Islands: The Untold Story of Guadalcanal*. College Station: Texas A&M University Press, 2008.

Kehoe, James P. "The Impact of the Press on Modern Warfare." Article, Marine Corps Educational Center, Quantico, VA, 1967.

Keiser, Gordon W. *The U.S. Marine Corps and Defense Unification, 1944–47*. Baltimore: Nautical & Aviation, 1996.

Keresey, Dick. *PT 105*. Annapolis, MD: Naval Institute Press, 1996.

King, Kendall. "LSTs: Marvelous at Fifty." *Naval History*, Winter 1992.

Knox, Dudley W. "The Disturbing Outlook in the Orient." *U.S. Naval Institute Proceedings*, June 1938.

Krulak, Charles. Oral History. Interviewed by David B. Crist. U.S. Marine Corps, History and Museums Division, Washington, DC, 2003.

Krulak, Victor H. "Fighting the Abstract War." *Marine Corps Gazette*, January 1963.

————. *First to Fight: An Inside View of the U.S. Marine Corps*. Annapolis, MD: Naval Institute Press, 1984.

————. "The Inchon Operation: It Couldn't Happen—but Did." *Shipmate*, September 1958.

————. *Organization for National Security: A Study*. Washington, DC: U.S. Strategic Institute, 1983.

————. Personal Papers. Marine Corps Recruit Depot, Command Museum, San Diego.

————. "Second Parachute Battalion (Reinforced) War Diary from October 27 to November 4, 1943. Operations on Choiseul, British Solomon Islands." Unpublished manuscript, 1943.

————. "Tidewater Warrior." Unpublished manuscript, n.d.

Lacouture, John. "Disaster at Savo Island." *Naval History*, Fall 1992.

Larrabee, Eric. *Commander in Chief: Franklin Delano Roosevelt, His Lieutenants, and Their War*. New York: Touchstone, 1987.

Leckie, Robert. *Okinawa: The Last Battle of World War II*. New York: Penguin, 1995.

————. *Strong Men Armed: The United States Marines vs. Japan*. New York: Da Capo Press, 1997.

# Partial Bibliography

Lee, J. A. "Between Wars in the Far East." *U.S. Naval Institute Proceedings*, January 1939.

Legers, Lawrence J., Jr. "Unification of the Armed Forces." Ph.D. diss., Harvard University, 1950.

Lorelli, John A. *To Foreign Shores: U.S. Amphibious Operations in World War II*. Annapolis, HD: Naval Institute Press, 1995.

Lundstrom, John B. "Frank Jack Fletcher Got a Bum Rap." *Naval History*, Fall 1992.

Macdonald, Peter. *Giap*. London: Fourth Estate, 1993.

MacGregor, Morris J., Jr. *Integration of the Armed Forces, 1940–1965*. Washington, DC: U.S. Army, Center of Military History, 1985.

Manchester, William. *American Caesar: Douglas MacArthur, 1880–1964*. New York: Dell, 1979.

———. *Goodbye, Darkness: A Memoir of the Pacific War*. New York: Little, Brown, 1980.

Marutollo, Frank. "A Good Bowl of 'Chowder' Saved the Marine Corps Following WWII." *Marine Corps Gazette*, December 1978.

———. "Preserving the Marine Corps as a Separate Service." *Marine Corps Gazette*, June 1988.

McClellan, Edwin N. "The Battle of Belleau Wood." *Marine Corps Gazette*, December 1920.

———. "Capture of Hill 142, Battle of Belleau Wood, and Capture of Bouresches." *Marine Corps Gazette*, September 1920.

———. "The Fourth Brigade of Marines in the Training Areas and the Operations in the Verdun Sector." *Marine Corps Gazette*, March 1920.

———. "The United States Marines in the World War." Monograph, U.S. Marine Corps, Historical Branch, Washington, DC, 1920.

McClelland, J. Mac. "Flashbacks." *Flying*, March 2008.

McCutcheon, Keith B. "Equitatus Caeli." *Marine Corps Gazette*, February 1954.

McGee, William L. *The Solomons Campaigns, 1942–1943: From Guadalcanal to Bougainville*. Santa Barbara, CA: BMC, 2002.

McKean, William Baggarley. *Ribbon Creek*. New York: Dial Press, 1958.

McMaster, H. R. *Dereliction of Duty: Lyndon Johnson, Robert McNamara, the Joint Chiefs of Staff, and the Lies That Led to Vietnam*. New York: HarperPerennial, 1998.

McMillan, George. *The Old Breed: A History of the First Marine Division in World War II*. Nashville: Battery Press, 1949.

Melson, Charles D. *Up The Slot: Marines in the Central Solomons*. Washington, DC: U.S. Marine Corps, History and Museums Division, 1993.

Metcalf, C. H. "The Marines in China." *Marine Corps Gazette*, September 1938.

Michel, Henri. Translated by Douglas Parmee. *The Second World War*. Vol. 1. New York: Praeger, 1975.

Millett, Allan R. *In Many a Strife: General Gerald C. Thomas and the U.S. Marine Corps, 1917–1956*. Annapolis, MD: Naval Institute Press, 1993.

———. *Semper Fidelis: The History of the United States Marine Corps*. New York: Free Press, 1980.

# Partial Bibliography

Montross, Lynn. *Cavalry of the Sky: The Story of U.S. Marine Combat Helicopters*. New York: Harper & Brothers, 1954.

———. "Flying Windmills in Korea." *Marine Corps Gazette*, September 1953.

Moran, Jim, and Gordon L. Rottman. *Peleliu, 1944: The Forgotten Corner of Hell*. Oxford: Osprey, 2002.

Moyar, Mark. *Phoenix and the Birds of Prey: Counterinsurgency and Counterterrorism in Vietnam*. Lincoln: University of Nebraska Press, 2007.

———. *Triumph Forsaken: The Vietnam War, 1954–1965*. New York: Cambridge University Press, 2006.

Mueller, J. N. "The Goettge Patrol." *Naval History*, Winter 1992.

Nagl, John A. *Learning to Eat Soup with a Knife: Counterinsurgency Lessons from Malaya and Vietnam*. Chicago: University of Chicago Press, 2002.

Nahorniak, Michael. "Foozling Tanga: The Failed British Amphibious Operation in German East Africa." *Marine Corps Gazette*, October 2002.

Nalty, Bernard C. *Statemate: U.S. Marines from Bunker Hill to the Hook*. Washington, DC: U.S Marines Corps, History and Museums Division, 2001.

Nelson, Andrew G., and Norman G. Mosher. "Proposed: A Counterinsurgency Task Force." *U.S. Naval Institute Proceedings*, June 1966.

Nelson, Craig. *The First Heroes: The Extraordinary Story of the Doolittle Raid—America's First World War II Victory*. New York: Penguin, 2002.

Nickerson, Hoffman. *The Turning Point of the Revolution, or Burgoyne in America*. Vols. 1 and 2. Port Washington, NY: Kennikat Press, 1928.

Noble, Dennis L. *The Eagle and the Dragon: The United States Military in China, 1901–1937*. New York: Greenwood Press, 1990.

O'Donnell, James P. "The Corps' Struggle for Survival." *Marine Corps Gazette*, August 2000.

Okumiya, Masatake. "The Lessons of an Undeclared War." *U.S. Naval Institute Proceedings*, December 1972.

Perry, Hamilton Darby. *The Panay Incident: Prelude to Pearl Harbor*. Toronto: Macmillan, 1969.

———. "Rehearsal for World War II." *American Heritage*, April 1967, available at http://www.americanheritage.com.

Perry, Mark. *Partners in Command: George Marshall and Dwight Eisenhower in War and Peace*. New York: Penguin, 2007.

Probst, Rodney R. "The Marine Helicopter and the Korean War," U.S. Marine Corps, Command and Staff College, 1989, available at http://www.globalsecurity.org.

Prouty, L. Fletcher. *The Secret Team: The CIA and Its Allies in Control of the United States and the World*. Costa Mesa, CA: Institute for Historical Review, 1973.

Rawlins, Eugene W. *Marines and Helicopters, 1946–1962*. Washington, DC: U.S. Marine Corps, History and Museums Division, 1976.

Reynolds, Nicholas E. *A Skillful Show of Strength: U.S. Marines in the Caribbean, 1991–1996*. Washington, DC: U.S. Marine Corps, History and Museums Division, 2003.

Ricks, Thomas E. *Making the Corps*. New York: Touchstone, 1998.

Robinette, Hillary M. "Practical Counter-Insurgency Training." *U.S. Naval Institute Proceedings*, July 1964.

# Partial Bibliography

Ross, Bill D. *Peleliu: Tragic Triumph—The Untold Story of the Pacific War's Forgotten Battle*. New York: Random House, 1991.

Rottman, Gordon L. *U.S. Marine Corps Pacific Theater of Operations, 1943–44*. Oxford: Osprey, 2004.

———. *U.S. Marine Corps Pacific Theater of Operations, 1944–45*. Oxford: Osprey, 2004.

Royster, Charles. *A Revolutionary People at War: The Continental Army and American Character, 1775–1783*. Chapel Hill: University of North Carolina Press, 1979.

Russ, Martin. *Breakout: The Chosin Reservoir Campaign, Korea, 1950*. New York: Penguin, 1999.

Russell, John H. "A Plea for a Mission and Doctrine." *Marine Corps Gazette*, June 1916.

Sachar, Abram Leon. *A History of the Jews*. New York: Alfred A. Knopf, 1965.

Sarantakes, Nicholas Evan. *Keystone: The American Occupation of Okinawa and U.S.-Japanese Relations*. College Station: Texas A&M University Press, 2000.

———, ed. *Seven Stars: The Okinawa Battle Diaries of Simon Bolivar Buckner, Jr., and Joseph Stilwell*. College Station: Texas A&M University Press, 2004.

Schell, Jonathan. *The Real War*. New York: Pantheon, 1987.

Schlesinger, Arthur M., Jr. *A Thousand Days: John F. Kennedy in the White House*. New York: Houghton Mifflin, 1965.

Schneller, Robert J., Jr. *Breaking the Color Barrier: The U.S. Naval Academy's First Black Midshipmen and the Struggle for Racial Equality*. New York: New York University Press, 2005.

Seese, Robert J. "Alligator by Roebling." *Naval History*, Spring 1990.

Sheehan, Neil. *A Bright Shining Lie: John Paul Vann and America in Vietnam*. New York: Vintage, 1989.

Shepherd, Lemuel C., Jr. "Chosin Reservoir to Hungnam." *Marine Corps Gazette*, February 1951.

———. Oral History. Interviewed by E. H. Simmons. U.S. Marine Corps, History and Museums Division, Washington, DC, 1967.

Shi-Fu Wang. "Naval Strategy in the Sino-Japanese War." *U.S. Naval Institute Proceedings*, July 1941.

Shultz, Richard H., Jr. *The Secret War Against Hanoi: The Untold Story of Spies, Saboteurs, and Covert Warriors in North Vietnam*. New York: Perennial, 2000.

Simmons, Edwin H. *Frozen Chosin: U.S. Marines at the Changjin Reservoir*. Washington, DC: U.S. Marine Corps, History and Museums Division, 2002.

———. "The Marines: Survival and Accommodation." Paper, George C. Marshall Foundation Conference, Lexington, VA, 1977.

———. *Over the Seawall: U.S. Marines at Inchon*. Washington, DC: U.S. Marine Corps, History and Museums Division, 2000.

———. *The United States Marines: A History*. Annapolis, MD: Naval Institute Press, 2003.

Simmons, Edwin H., and Joseph H. Alexander. *Through the Wheat: The U.S. Marines in World War I*. Annapolis, MD: Naval Institute Press, 2008.

Sledge, E. B. *With the Old Breed: At Peleliu and Okinawa*. New York: Oxford University Press, 1981.

# Partial Bibliography

*Small-Unit Leader's Guide to Counterinsurgency*. Quantico, VA: Marine Corps Combat Development Command, 2006.

Smith, Holland M., and Percy Finch. *Coral and Brass*. New York: Ace, 1948.

Smith, Oliver P. Oral History. Interviewed by Benis M. Frank. U.S. Marine Corps, History and Museums Division, Washington, DC, 1973.

Sorley, Lewis. *A Better War: The Unexamined Victories and Final Tragedy of America's Last Years in Vietnam*. San Diego: Harcourt, 2000.

———. "Reassessing ARVN." Lecture, Vietnam Center, Texas Tech University, Lubbock, March 17, 2006.

———. *Thunderbolt: From the Battle of the Bulge to Vietnam and Beyond—General Creighton Abrams and the Army of His Times*. Washington, DC: Brassey's, 1998.

Strahan, Jerry E. *Andrew Jackson Higgins and the Boats That Won World War II*. Baton Rouge: Louisana State University Press, 1994.

Sturkey, Marion F. *Warrior Culture of the U.S. Marines*. Plum Branch, SC: Heritage Press International, 2002.

Suskind, Richard. *The Battle of Belleau Wood: The Marines Stand Fast*. New York: Macmillan, 1969.

———. *Do You Want to Live Forever!* New York: Bantam, 1964.

Sweetman, Jack. *The U.S. Naval Academy: An Illustrated History*. Annapolis, MD: Naval Institute Press, 1979.

Thomason, John W., Jr. *Fix Bayonets!* New York: Charles Scribner's Sons, 1927.

Thompson, Edgar K. "An Ancient Amphibious Assault." *U.S. Naval Institute Proceedings*, January 1947.

Tolley, Kemp. *Yangtze Patrol: The U.S. Navy in China*. Annapolis, MD: Naval Institute Press, 1971.

Tuchman, Barbara W. *The Guns of August*. New York: Ballantine, 1962.

———. *The March of Folly: From Troy to Vietnam*. New York: Ballantine, 1984.

———. *Stilwell and the American Experience in China, 1911–45*. New York: Grove Press, 1970.

Twining, Merrill B. *No Bended Knee: The Battle for Guadalcanal*. New York: Ballantine, 1996.

———. Oral History. Interviewed by Benis M. Frank. U.S. Marine Corps, History and Museums Division, Washington, DC, 1975.

Uchill, Ida Libert. *Pioneers, Peddlers & Tsadikim: The Story of Jews in Colorado*. Boulder: University Press of Colorado, 2000.

Uris, Leon. *Battle Cry*. New York: Bantam, 1954.

*The U.S. Army–Marine Corps Counterinsurgency Field Manual*. Chicago: University of Chicago Press, 2007.

Valentine, Douglas. *The Phoenix Program*. Lincoln, NE: iUniverse.com, 2000.

Wakeman, Frederic, Jr. *The Shanghai Badlands: Wartime Terrorism and Urban Crime, 1937–1941*. Cambridge: Cambridge University Press, 1996.

Waller, L. W. T., Jr. "Machine Guns of the Fourth Brigade." *Marine Corps Gazette*, March 1920.

West, Bing. *The Village*. New York: Pocket, 2003.

Westmoreland, William C. *A Soldier Reports*. New York: Dell, 1980.

# Partial Bibliography

White, W. L. *They Were Expendable: An American Torpedo Boat Squadron in the U.S. Retreat from the Philippines*. Annapolis, MD: Naval Institute Press, 1942.

Wirkus, Faustin, and Taney Dudley. *The White King of La Gonave*. Garden City, NY: Doubleday, Doran, 1931.

Wood, David Bowne. *A Sense of Values: American Marines in an Uncertain World*. Kansas City, MO: Andrews McMeel, 1994.

Wouk, Herman. *War and Remembrance*. New York: Little, Brown, 1978.

Woulfe, James B. *Into the Crucible: Making Marines for the 21st Century*. Novato, CA: Presidio Press, 1998.

Wright, Derrick. *Tarawa, 1943: The Turning of the Tide*. New York: Osprey, 2000.

Yingling, Paul. "General Failure." *Armed Forces Journal*, May 2007.

Zabecki, David T., ed. *Chief of Staff: The Principal Officers Behind History's Great Commanders*. Vol. 2. Annapolis, MD: Naval Institute Press, 2008.

# Index

# Index

# Index

# Index

# Index

# Index

# Index

# Index

# Index

## About the Author

Robert Coram is the author of seven novels and five nonfiction books, including *American Patriot: The Life and Wars of Colonel Bud Day* and *Boyd: The Fighter Pilot Who Changed the Art of War.* He lives in Atlanta.